Religion In Contemporary Thought

Religion In Contemporary Thought

George F. McLean, O.M.I.

alba house
DIVISION OF THE SOCIETY OF ST. PAUL
STATEN ISLAND, N. Y. 10314

Library of Congress Cataloging in Publication Data

McLean, George F
  Religion in contemporary thought.

  Includes bibliographical references.
  1. Religion—Philosophy—Addresses, essays, lectures.
2. Death of God theology—Addresses, essays, lectures.
I. Title.
BL51.M236   200'.1   72-6837
ISBN 0-8189-0256-6

Designed, printed and bound in the U.S.A. by the
Fathers and Brothers of the Society of St. Paul as
part of their communications apostolate.

THAT LIFE IS followed by death, that "the paths of glory lead but to the grave," has been a constant note throughout the history of heroic literature. Religious literature has been equally marked by the opposite truth: that death leads to new life, whether this death be symbolic in the baptismal rite or real upon a cross. In either case, death not only precedes the new life but, as the seed of that life, continually determines its characteristics.

Nowhere in contemporary culture is this relationship between death and life more striking than in the recent history of the religious fact itself. The concentration upon the secular, which began in the Renaissance and evolved through modern times, seems to have reached a certain natural culmination in the renewed affirmation of the death of God. Being subject to the inherent ambiguity of all death, the death of God facilitated the unilateral emphasis upon the affirmation of human meaning while this meaning, in turn, suggested transcendent dimensions of value. In a word, the death of God in secular culture has led to a new position of the problem of God and opened a search for new experiences of religious meaning. It is the purpose of this volume to survey the bases, manner, and initial direction of this new search for God. A companion volume, *Traces of God in a Secular Culture*, looks into the detailed work already under way in this search by the use of analytic, person-centered, and process techniques.

The present volume investigates this dialectic of death and life in the question of God and religious meaning. Part I searches for the roots of the modern attention to man as the key to understanding the ambiguous relation of recent thought to the problem of meaning. Part II analyzes the various ways in which this has secularized culture by seeing this affirmation of man as implying a denial of God. Part III attempts to essay that strange combination of elation and despair which marks man's new appreciation of himself and his world and which lays the foundations of a new search for religious meaning.

In order that this search might get to the roots of the crisis of modern thought itself, Part I reviews the origins of that thought in order to discover its native religious tensions and its inherent human possibilities. In "The Humanist Critique of Religion," W. Richard Comstock reviews the Renaissance criticism of the classical Christian position on human autonomy as real but conditioned. Precisely as a "rebirth," the Renaissance consisted in a discovery of the full independence of man and resulted in a new articulation of his world. Whether it be in the area of science or geopolitics, the new focus was both dramatically proclaimed and brilliantly executed. More than an idea, it became a veritable way of life to which subsequent thought must speak under pain of being simply unintelligible. At this point, more than at any other, it is possible to sound the significance of modern concentration upon man's independence, and Dr. Comstock undertakes to analyze its direct relation to the modern problem of God.

Being too proud to be arrogant, the Renaissance mind was too convinced of the dignity of man to abandon man to himself. It initiated instead a process of philosophical investigation which increasingly honed the capabilities of the human mind against the hard and asperate problem of the relation of God and man. The culmination of this work may have been achieved in the philosophical system of G. W. F. Hegel who attempted to mediate all—knowledge and feeling, man and world, finite and Infinite—in his one idealistic dialectic. His work has been a landmark for the philosophy of God and the article of Kenneth L. Schmitz shows how it constitutes not only a definitive achievement, but a new point of departure. By this as by most tests Hegel proves to be outstanding; Nietzsche, Kierkegaard, and Marx all measure their own work in large part by its contrast to the work of Hegel. The very success of Hegel's project had made it clear that attempts by the modern speculative intellect to achieve a knowledge of God were trapped in an insoluble dilemma between issuing in an empty concept and creating a God who left no place for man.

Given the Renaissance insistence upon man's absolute independence there was little question about the direction to be taken by those who would dissent from this verdict. Nietzsche and others charted the particular concerns which would mark the mind of man to the present day. On the one hand, Nietzsche's conjunction of the principle of inequality with humanism led to his notion of the Superman and to a fundamental collision with the Christian outlook of universal charity. On the other hand, Marx's concentration upon the complete equality and sufficiency of man in the actual exercise of his life led not only to a speculative forebearance on the religious question but an aggressive atheism. As part of the same reaction against the universal systematization of Hegel's dialectic, Kierkegaard set out to identify faith as the ultimate exercise of human freedom. Because man meets the divine in and through his existential crisis, this meeting is of the most penetrating significance for man's life in this world. These issues are studied in the articles by Wilfred Desan and Louis Dupré.

Part II, "Humanism and the Problem of Atheism," follows as a logical outgrowth of this discovery of man. As this discovery had been linked to a rejection of God a century ago, the recent renewal of the proclamation of the death of God should not have caused such great amazement. Hence, the fact that it did have such broad and deep impact, when coupled with the continuing orientation of religious thought toward the secular, shows that the negation of God was an idea whose time had truly arrived. It is the intent of Part II to search out the way in which a series of developments in psychology, and sociology converged with those in philosophy and religion to produce this proclamation of the elimination of God from contemporary culture.

Daniel Callahan in his study, "God and Psychological Man," investigates the psychological dimension of man's new awareness of himself, thereby uncovering some of the steps in the development of the position that man, his life, and his society must be understood simply in terms of himself. Callahan's review of the writings of Philip Rieff, Norman O. Brown, and Herbert Marcuse on this subject elucidates the way in which this affirmation of man led to a negation of God and religion in any previous sense of these terms.

This concurs with the Marxist social approach as developed in the article of Howard L. Parsons, "Atheism and Man": in order to be fully man one must do away with God and see all within the perspective of a continuing process without definitive fulfillment. From a Marxist point of view atheism is above all a strong humanism, naturalism, and secularism, conceived not so much against God as against any oppression of man. In this situation the Marxist can share a considerable community of interest with the theist, while his materialist dialectic requires that, in the final analysis, he reject the notion of God in order adequately to carry out his own conception of humanism.

This rejection of the divine is not only the result of Marxist dialectical materialism. Others find it implied in the character of the dialectic itself. Religion is not only an opium which delays progress; the negation of the notion of the divine understood as transcendent, as described by Thomas J. J. Altizer's "Catholic Theology and History," is a necessary step in the overall historical development of man. The autonomy of man is accomplished not despite or within this negation, but by means of it. Hence, the negation is one step in an all-embracing historical process, which itself includes what is authentic in the religious notion of God. This atheism remains, nonetheless, Christian.

Even this retention of a divine in terms of an historical process is questioned as an adequate recognition of the full extent of the problem. Carrying the Protestant principle further than Dr. Altizer, the article of Manfred Hoffmann, "The Protestant Tradition and the Death of God," would negate even his final resolution of God, man, and world in a higher synthesis. For him the negation of God must be complete and not allow for its re-creation in another form at the conclusion of the process, as is done in the thought of Teilhard de Chardin. This makes the process of secularization one of radical discontinuity with the divine in any form. Salvation loses any relation to hope or to Jesus, and consists simply in one's "not trying to be more than he is—man."

Having arrived at so pervasive a negation of God, one could no longer say of this position, as had been said of earlier protestations of atheism, that it was a theism despite itself. On the contrary, it would now seem that the affirmation of man had been carried out in internally consistent terms predicated upon a rejection of God. It might be said that just as classical theism had rejected any meaning of man alongside of God as destructive of its notion of divinity, so the contemporary thought rejected any meaning of God alongside of man as destructive of its notion of the independence of man. Consequently, D. A. Drennen in his article, "Alternatives to Atheism," does not believe that it would be correct to look toward a future internal development of contemporary atheism toward a theistic position.

This, however, does not foreclose the religious question. Death is not life; but it has been known to contain the seeds of new life. Though atheism would seem to have developed an internally consistent position, it has been able, not to eliminate the concerns of the theist, but only to do without them in working toward its own goals. What is more, atheism has never been able to identify itself outside of some relation to theism and its concerns. Above all, the recent evolution of atheism has not been nihilistic but humanistic, being derived from a positive concern for the meaning of man. As a result, atheism and theism find themselves with a certain community of interest in the meaning of human life and the evolution of work upon the issue has opened new forms of awareness of religious meaning.

Initial ground for a positive response to this question appears in the life style and interests of the "new" culture. It is the work of Part III, "Humanism and the Problem of Theism", to survey some of the indications that the new concern with human meaning is not adequately stated in any restrictive sense of man, but instead positively implies some factors of transcendence.

This work is initiated in the article of Michael Novak, "The Beauty of Earth," which develops the ways in which the contemporary mind can find within nature an unlimited meaning. Working extensively with the analysis of Camus, he identifies the importance of this incarnation of the sources of religious meaning, not only for the life of religion, but for the meaning of man within his contemporary technological culture. From having thus related God and nature there results still another question: can this understanding of God in nature avoid the twin dangers of naturalizing and thus losing the divine, on the one hand, and of becoming a 'pantheism', on the other?

By studying this question, the article of Gabriel Vahanian, "The Death of God in Contemporary Culture," makes some valuable contributions to the development of an effective and balanced view. Analyzing a number of Christian religious approaches, he shows that the so called "death-of-God" theologies were not isolated phenomena, but integral implications of the negation of divine transcendence by a surprising number of biblical and dialectical religious positions. There is need then to identify not only the presence of God in nature but his transcendence, lest immance be left without transcendence and result in the loss of any notion of God whatever, that is, in what he refers to as a post-Christian paganism. How this transcendence might be realized in such a way that it enhances rather than negates the significance of the secular becomes the new form of the religious problematic.

The article of Richard L. Rubenstein, "After the Death of God," is a further step in this direction. He develops a way in which the divine can be seen as present to all while being distinct from everything that is realized upon it. In this perspective the ancient notion of one God above all others is notably transformed, while still making its essential contribution of protecting the whole process of reasoning from devolving into a simple naturalism and/or secularism. This said, however, there still remains the question of how man's mind proceeds, not only from, but through his involvement in the secular to an awareness of God as both present and transcendent.

A first and universal step in this process is taken in "The Religious Meaning of Secularity" by Louis Dupré who shows the importance of avoiding all reductionism. This is reinforced by clarifying the fact that even negative theology itself is not intelligible without a positive acknowledgement of transcendence which sets the goals for detailed work upon the religious issues, whether in terms of process, personalist, or language philosophies.

For this work one can turn to *Traces of God in a Secular Culture* where these types of investigations are carried forward.

There, Part I develops the insights of pragmatic and process philosophies concerning the religious meaning of the secular. Part II, reflecting particularly upon the recent development of insight concerning the person, examines its significance for the development of a reasoning process which would be rational in character and yet fully founded upon the concrete and personal experience of the factors of contingency, relativity, temporality, and autonomy which have been so central to the recent critique of theism. Finally, a section on linguistic analysis studies the contributions of this work to re-examining and clarifying both the philosophy and theology of God.

The project is as large as life itself, but it has always been the contention of the religious man that religion, which draws life from death, is basically concerned with possessing life, and that more abundantly.

THE EDITOR WISHES to acknowledge his special appreciation to the many distinguished scholars who have contributed to this work. Acknowledgment is made also to the following: to Robert Adolfs for permission to quote from Robert Adolfs, "Is God Dead," **The Meaning of the Death of God**, ed. B. Murchland (New York: Random House, 1967); to Beacon Press for permission to quote from Herbert Marcuse, **Eros and Civilization** (Boston: Beacon, 1962); to Charles Dessart for permission to quote from Antoine Vergote, **Psychologie Religieuse** Brussels: C. Dessart, 1966); to Harper and Row, Inc., for permission to quote from Philip Rieff, **The Triumph of the Therapeutic** (New York: Harper and Row, 1966); to Roger Hazelton for permission to quote from Roger Hazelton, "The Future of God," **The Meaning of the Death of God**, ed. B. Murchland (New York: Random House, 1967); to Humanities Press, Inc., and George Allen & Unwin Ltd. for permission to quote from: J. N. Findlay, **Hegel: A Reexamination** (New York: Humanities Press, 1964; London: Allen & Unwin, 1958), and G. Hegel, **The Phenomenology of Mind**, trans. J. B. Baillie (New York: Humanities Press, 1964; London: Allen & Unwin, 1949); to Alfred A. Knopf, Inc., for permission to quote from: Albert Camus, **The Myth of Sisyphus** (New York: Knopf, 1960) and **The Rebel** (New York: Knopf, 1956), and John Updike, **Pigeon Feathers and Other Stories** (New York: Knopf, 1962); to Liveright Publishing Corporation and Hogarth Press Ltd. for permission to quote from Sigmund Freud, **The Future of an Illusion** (New York: Liveright, 1964; London: Hogarth, 1961); to the Macmillan Company for permission to quote from Harvey Cox, **The Secular City** (New York: Macmillan, 1965); to W. W. Norton & Company and Hogarth Press Ltd. for permission to quote from Sigmund Freud, **Civilization and Its Discontents**, trans. James Strachey (New York: Norton, 1962; London: Hogarth, 1961), © 1961 by James Strachey; to Sheed & Ward for permission to quote from **Confessions of St. Augustine**, trans. F. J. Sheed (New York: London: Sheed & Ward 1943); to D. Van Nostrand Company for permission to quote from **Early Christianity**, ed. Roland H. Bainton (Princeton, N. J.: D. Van Nostrand, 1960), © 1960 by D. Van Nostrand Company; to Wesleyan University Press and Routledge & Kegan Paul Ltd. for permission to quote from Norman O. Brown, **Life Against Death** (Middletown, Conn.: Wesleyan University Press, 1959; London: Routledge & Kegan Paul, 1959); to The Westminster Press and William Collins Sons & Co. for permission to quote from Thomas J. J. Altizer, **The Gospel of Christian Atheism** (Philadelphia, Pa.: Westminster Press, 1966; London: William Collins Sons & Co., 1967), © 1966 by W. L. Jenkins; to George Allen & Unwin Ltd. for permission to quote from Friedrich Nietzsche, **The Philosophy of Nietzsche** (London: Allen & Unwin, 1937); to F. Aubier for permission to quote from Jean Wahl, **Etudes Kierkegaardiennes** (Paris: Aubler, 1959); to Cambridge University Press for permission to quote from C. S. Lewis, **The Discarded Image** (Cambridge, England: University Press, 1964); to Harper and Row, Inc. for permission to quote from: Ludwig Feuerbach, **The Essence of Christianity** (New York: Harper, 1957); Immanuel Kant, **Religion Within the Limits of Reason Alone** (New York: Harper, 1960), © 1960 Harper & Row, Inc.; to Herder & Herder, Inc. for permission to quote from Roger Garaudy, **From Anathema to Dialogue** (New York: Herder & Herder, 1961); to International Publishers and Lawrence and Wishart for permission to quote from Karl Marx, **The German Ideology** (New York: International Publishers, 1938; London: Lawrence and Wishart, 1938); to Librairie Armand Colin and World Publishing Company for permission to quote from Paul Vignaux, **Philosophy in the Middle Ages: An Introduction** (Paris: Librairie Armand Colin, 1959; Cleveland: World Publishing Company, 1959); to the Macmillan Company and G. Bell & Sons Ltd. for permission to quote from Herbert Butterfield, **The Origins of Modern Science** (New York: Macmillan, 1957; London: G. Bell & Sons Ltd., 1957), © G. Bell & Sons Ltd., 1957; to McGraw-Hill Book Company for permission to quote from Karl Marx, **Early Writings** (New York: McGraw-Hill, 1964); to Princeton University Press for permission to quote from: S. Kierkegaard, **Concluding Unscientific Postscript**, trans D. Swenson and W. Lowrie (Princeton, N. J.: Princeton University Press, 1944); S. Kierkegaard, **Either/Or**, trans. D. and L. Swenson (Princeton, N. J.: Princeton University Press, 1944); and S. Kierkegaard, **Fear and Trembling**, trans. W. Lowrie (Princeton, N. J.: Princeton University Press, 1944); to Random House, Inc. for permission to quote Immanuel Kant, **The Philosophy of Kant**, ed. Carl Friedrich (New York: Random House, 1949); to Charles Scribner's Sons for permission to quote from: George Santayana, **Reason in Science** (New York: Charles Scribner's Sons, 1906); and Etienne Gilson, **Spirit of Medieval Philosophy** (New York: Charles Scribner's Sons, 1940); London: Sheed & Ward, 1936); to the University of Chicago Press for permission to quote from **The Renaissance Philosophy of Man**, eds. Ernst Cassirer, Paul Oskar Kristeller, John H. Randall, Jr. (Chicago: University of Chicago Press, 1948); to Yale University Press for permission to quote from Ernst Cassirer, **The Individual and the Cosmos in Renaissance Philosophy** (New Haven, Conn.: Yale University Press, 1964).

Contents

Religion In Contemporary Thought

The Independence of Man
and Modern Humanism

The Humanist Critique of Religion

◇

W. Richard Comstock

Introduction

IN EVERY CULTURE in which it has appeared religion has been subjected to some kind of rational critique. Even in pre-literate societies, where religious forms dominate thought and behavior, the presence of the critic has been discovered.[1] It is not surprising, then that the historical transition from medieval civilization to the post-medieval culture of western modernity has been marked by a critical re-examination of the function and value of religion in human life.

From the standpoint of intellectual history, modernity is usually defined as the western cultural ethos that succeeded the decline of the medieval synthesis of politics, economics, ethics, and faith. The emergency and growth of this "modern mind" in European civilization is a fascinating phenomenon whose further development is still in process at the present time. However, in the fourteenth through eighteenth centuries it is possible to detect the basic elements of what Ernst Cassirer calls the "intellectual development through which modern philosophic thought gained its characteristic self-confidence and self-consciousness."[2] On this interpretation, basic characteristics of modern thought emerged in distinctive form in the Italian Renaissance of the fifteenth century and continued through the scientific revolution of the sixteenth and seventeenth centuries. The Enlightenment period that followed interpreted itself as the fruition of modern

[7]

approaches to the problems of human life and culture inaugurated in the preceding centuries.[3]

This complex and creative period of early modernity was involved necessarily in an important critique of religion in general, and of Christianity in particular. Where formerly Christian faith had served as the unifying center of the medieval synthesis of politics, ethics, and faith; now, with the distintegration of that synthesis, this same faith became a "problem" rather than an "answer" to the builders of the emerging cultural form of modernity. Even so, the "modern mind" was not necessarily inimical to religious faith. Instead, it experienced the need for a re-evaluation of religion congenial to the basic presuppositions of its new perspective. It is this re-examination of religious faith which shall be designated in the present essay as "the humanist critique of religion."

The phrase "humanist critique" is not meant to imply that the position outlined here is the basic stance of a specific movement or school. "Humanism" as a specific philosophical school that assumes institutional forms is a late phenomenon of the nineteenth and twentieth centuries. During the Renaissance, the preferred terms, "humanities" and "humanist," referred primarily to the efforts of scholars to devise "an educational and cultural program based on the study of the classical Greek and Latin authors".[4] In this essay, "humanist" refers not to these specific tenets and programs, but in a general way to the tendency of early modernity as a whole to give priority of emphasis to human autonomy, whether or not the particular terms "humanist" and "humanism" are used.

Furthermore, the phrase "humanist critique" does not presuppose that the period of early modernity from the Renaissance to the Enlightenment possessed a tight and completely resolved unity of direction. Even if such a unity existed, it clearly would be impossible to state and explore it in all its complexity in a short essay. Assuming that modernity possesses related but diverse tendencies, directions, and foci, the present essay seeks to distinguish but one important tendency which has special pertinence to the question of religion. Even on the subject of religion, it is not claimed here that this attitude is the only one evident within the period. I intend to distinguish one significant approach to religion among many that can be detected in the development of modern thought. "The humanist critique of religion" which I shall outline here is "an ideal type," which has probably not appeared in any single thinker of the period in the exact form here described. Nevertheless, I want to maintain that this "ideal type" represents one of the significant options concerning religion that is implicit in the presuppositions of the modern mind.

It is argued here that the basic stance of the "humanist critique of religion" should not be interpreted as essentially hostile to a religious attitude. Although leading thinkers of early modernity were in conflict with some tenets of the Christian religion, especially with the social power of its institutional forms, this conflict seldom led to total repudiation. For example, the leading members of the Italian Renaissance were not anti-religious or even anti-Christian. On the contrary; they tended to see themselves as exponents of a predominantly religious affirmation of human life, which, they hoped, would serve as the basis of a renewed Christian civilization.[5] Similarly, leading figures of the scientific revolution continued to espouse a more than nominal religious approach. Thus, referring to the Enlightenment, Ernst Cassirer writes: "All apparent opposition to religion which we meet in this age should not blind us to the fact that all intellectual problems are fused with religious problems and that the former find their constant and deepest inspiration in the latter."[6]

All appearances to the contrary, the humanist critique of religion has a basically conservative thrust. It seeks to protect certain values of the modern prospective it feels are threatened by some religious positions. Its primary posture is, therefore, defensive rather than offensive, seeking to maintain and safeguard crucial values from alien domination and destruction. Forms of religion are attacked militantly only when they seem to present incontrovertible threats to the preservation and cultivation of these values.

Furthermore, I want to show how the humanist critique tends to apprehend as religious threats to its own values the dualistic structures that are felt to inhibit the realization of humanist goals. Finally, I shall argue that the most significant attempts of the humanist critique to meet this threat to its own values while still maintaining a religious position involve the development of a still more radical dualism that, in para-doxical fashion, provides a possible solution to the problem generated in the first place by an unsatisfactory dualistic scheme.

THE BASIC VALUE: HUMAN AUTONOMY

What is the axiological center around which the defensive posture of the humanist critique takes shape? Ernst Cassirer asserts that the Renaissance was concerned with

> the transformation or renovation of religion. The Renaissance strove for a religion of affirmation of the world and of the intellect, a religion which conceded to both their specific value, and which found the real poof and seal of divinity not in the degradation and destruction of the world and the human intellect, but in their exaltation.[7]

We may further characterize this "specific value" of intellect and world, which early modernity accented, as a radical affirmation of the autonomy of man and of the natual world in which he lives.

Autonomy may be defined as the capacity of a phenomenon to act and maintain its distinctive integrity according to its own immanent potentialities without dependence on external forces. Autonomy is the essential integrity of the phenomenon in question, undistorted by powers alien to its own being. In the thought of an emerging modernity the growing emphasis on autonomy can be seen to assume a polar form: the autonomy of man and the autonomy of the natural cosmos are affirmed as correlative and reciprocal aspects of a single dynamic relationship. The acceptance of autonomous cognitive powers in man leads to the recognition of an autonomous world that is the epistemological object of these powers.

The autonomy of man is affirmed by a radical confidence in

the capacity of his cognitive powers of sense perception and reason to attain trustworthy knowledge of the world when allowed to operate without restraint according to their immanent potentialities. For example, Pomponazzi, a representative Renaissance thinker, insists that his faith can never force his reason to make assertions that are contrary to its own autonomous principles. He asserts: "A philosopher cannot do this, especially if he be a teacher, for in so teaching he would be teaching falsehood, he would be an unfaithful master, his deception could be easily detected and he would be acting contrary to the profession of philosophy."[8]

Later, Immanuel Kant's famous essay on the Enlightenment summarizes and brings to a focus the impetus of the modern mind toward such autonomy. He writes:

> Enlightenment is man's leaving his self-caused immaturity. Immaturity is the incapacity to use one's intelligence without the guidance of another. Such immaturity is self-caused if it is not caused by lack of intelligence, but by lack of determination and courage to use one's intelligence without being guided by another. *Sapere Aude!* Have the courage to use your own intelligence! is therefore the motto of the enlightenment.[9]

An autonomous natural world is the correlate of human autonomy. The world of nature assumes shape before autonomous man as a system of powers and forces that can be "understood through itself and investigated according to its own principles."[10] Independent man discovers within himself the power to understand an independent world that has its existence and intelligibility implicit in the integrity of its own specific being.

> "Nature" therefore does not so much signify a given group of objects as a certain "horizon" of knowledge, of the comprehension of reality. To nature belongs everything in the sphere of "natural light" *(lumen naturale)*, everything whose understanding and confirmation require *no* other aid than the natural forces of knowledge.[11]

This manifests an attitude of optimism and confidence concerning man's cognitive capacities. His sense perceptions and his reason are to be trusted as dependable vehicles through which genuine knowledge of the world is achieved.

One threat to such optimism has come from forms of philosophical scepticism. On the religious level the Christian doctrine of sin seems to undermine confidence in the humanist program of trusting and utilizing man's cognitive powers to their fullest. Thus both Renaissance and Enlightenment humanists often find themselves in debate with theologians who accuse them of having lost a proper understanding of the damaged state of man's being caused by sin. A notable example of this is the struggle between Erasmus and Luther.

Close attention to this point of tension, however, will reveal that the doctrine of sin does not require a view of man that formally contradicts stress on man's dignity and confidence in his natural powers. Although some statements of the doctrine of "original sin" do perilously approach the notion of a total corruption of man's very being, it cannot be said that such a position is actually affirmed by any major Christian theologian. Even those Christian thinkers most impressed with the effects of evil and sin never affirm an ontological corruption of human nature. Etienne Gilson points out that Thomas distinguishes between the original nature or essence of man and the accidental state of his present existence which has been damaged by the misuse of his will.[12] What Gilson says of Thomas is also true of the Church Fathers and (*pace* Gilson) of the Reformers as well. All of them hold that sin has wounded and distorted, but not essentially destroyed man's natural endowments.

The formal characteristics of reason, for example, must remain exempt from the damaging influence of sin; otherwise, theology itself would fall into incoherence. Even in a sinful state, the laws of identity, contradiction, and valid inference must remain efficacious. Otherwise, such a simple line of reasoning as "man needs God; therefore, he should seek God" might be invalid and the opposite judgment, "man should not seek God," might be true. On this point, major theologians in both the Catholic and

Protestant traditions are agreed. "As a consequence of being created, of coming immediately from God, man has an incorruptible nature, which remains intact even in the sinner."[13]

The real issue at stake in the tension between Christian sin and humanist dignity lies elsewhere. The rise of modernity represents a shift in fundamental viewpoint from man as passive responder to man as active creator. Renaissance thinkers stress man's freedom. In turn, this leads irresistibly to a sense of man's potentiality for creative acts that do not simply maintain an already existing situation but bring forth that which is qualitatively different from the past.

Paul Kristeller points out how the emergence of this sense of human freedom and creativity can be observed through a comparison of the somewhat similar discussions on human dignity offered by Ficino and Pico.[14] Ficino argues that the dignity of man resides in his privileged place in the hierarchy of being whereby his intellect participates in all of its forms. Since the human soul is directed both toward the intelligible and corporeal worlds, it participates in both the divine and the mundane.

> This (the soul) is the greatest of all miracles in nature. All other things beneath God are always one single being, but the soul is all things together. . . . Therefore, it may be rightly called the center of nature, the middle term of all things, the series of the world, the face of all, the bond and juncture of the universe.[15]

Pico accepts the same viewpoint but transforms it in an important way. Whereas to Ficino the dignity resides in the central character of the position occupied by man in the hierarchy of being, Pico stresses man's freedom and creativity to transcend hierarchical limits. Pico argues that as man is "a creature of indeterminate nature," from his central position in the "middle of the world," it is granted to him "to have whatever he chooses, to be whatever he wills."[16] He can turn either to the corporeal world and to the beasts, or to the intelligible world of divine value. According to Kristeller, Pico describes man as the only creature whose life is determined not by nature but by his free choice. Thus, man no longer occupies a fixed though distinguished place in the hierarchy of being; he exists outside this hierarchy as a kind of separate world.[17]

> Cassirer characterizes this emphasis on human freedom as a reversal of the relationship we are accustomed to accepting between *being* and *acting*. The old scholastic proposition *operari sequitur esse* is valid in the world of things. But it is the nature and peculiarity of the human world that in it the opposite is true. It is not being that prescribes once and for all the lasting direction which the mode of action will take; rather, the original direction of action determines and places being. The being of man follows from his doing: this doing is not only limited to the energy of his will but rather encompasses the whole of his creative powers.[18]

Here is a radical emphasis that anticipates the later motifs of Marxist and Sartrean thought: man makes himself.

Again, however, it must be insisted that there is no formal contradiction between this radical affirmation of human creativity and the doctrine of sin. Indeed, if sin is the misuse of freedom and creativity, it can be argued that the very notion of sin as something for which man is responsible is intelligible only within a view of man as active and free.

This point is important if the humanist stress on autonomy is not to be inevitably united with a naive and romantic view of man, devoid of sin, distortion, and tragedy. The humanist view is rather that the integrity and being of man involves and indeed is the full exercise of his reason, freedom, and creativity as the proper powers of his nature. Since man's being is his action, passivity or the refusal to realize what it is in man to do cannot heal any distortion of that being by sin. However salvation may be appropriated by man, it is man the actor—the thinker, knower and doer—who will thereby be made whole. Thus, the doctrine of sin as a counsel to passivity and a refusal through fear to act and think responsibly is rejected by the humanist critique. On the other hand, the doctrine of sin as the recognition of tragedy in existence and pervasive distortions in man's being is accepted by many humanists. The most notable example of this is Kant, who considers a radical emphasis on the autonomy of man to be the precondition rather than the antithesis of a recognition in man of "radical evil."[19]

LIMITED AND UNLIMITED AUTONOMY

The humanist stress on autonomy represents an attitude of confidence in man's natural powers of reason and freedom that can be expressed in a rule of procedure. On a level of extreme generality, we might say that this rule is the dictum that the cognitive powers of the integral man are to be exerted without external limits of any kind being placed upon their range of applicability within the independent world of nature.

Essentially, the autonomy of man is a dynamic rule for epistemological activity, not a static statement of simple essence. Thus, the crucial point is not that man has the capacity to reason, but the dictum that this capacity shall be allowed unrestrained development according to its own inherent structure and potentiality without regard to external limitations of any kind. In a correlative manner, the autonomy of nature refers to the rule that nature, whatever it may be, shall be understood in terms of the structures of its own integral constituent parts, not by reference to non-natural phenomena which inhibit rather than perfect the clarification of nature's particular mode of being.

The autonomy of modernity thus refers to the capacity of human powers to perform their functions according to potentialities inherent in the integrity of their own nature. Rational autonomy is the ability of reason to recognize the transparent intelligibility of a given concept, without assistance from any power external to the rational capacity itself. As Kant puts it, the need is "to institute a tribunal which will assure to reason its lawful claims, and dismiss all groundless pretensions, not by despotic decrees, but in accordance with its own eternal and unalterable laws."[20]

To this dual affirmation of the autonomy of man and of nature correspond both the methodological principle of continuity and the cosmological rule of homogeneity. The first is the rule that the extension of knowledge in any sphere is accomplished by tracing the implications of the data with which one begins along lines that, while leading to new data, maintain intelligible and continuous relations with the nature of the original data. The second rule is that the various parts and aspects of nature must be understood in terms of some kind of homogeneous relationship. Santayana, at a later period, states the principle with his customary clarity when he observes that

> a chief characteristic of science is that in supplementing given facts it supplements them by adding other facts belonging to the same sphere, and eventually discoverable by tracing the given object in its own plane through its continuous transformations. Science expands speculatively, by the aid of merely instrumental hypothesis, objects given in perception until they compose a congruous, self-supporting world, all parts of which might be observed consecutively.[21]

If, however, the humanist is concerned with the unrestrained exercise of his natural powers, does this rejection itself of limits have any limitations? The humanist affirmation of autonomy contains a degree of complexity that is not always apparent to a cursory glance. It combines polar contrasts in a way that, at best, generates the tension of coherent complexity, though a slight error in emphasis can lead rather to ambiguity, paradox, or contradiction. Thus, the humanist critique combines confidence with humanity, and the rejection with the acceptance of limits and, as will be seen in the conclusion, of dualisms.

Nevertheless, no logical contradiction is involved, because what is affirmed is not identical in meaning with what is denied. For example, it is important to distinguish internal from external limits. The humanist declares that man's powers have unlimited extension within their proper sphere of applicability. This very infinity in scope of action, however, presupposes the inherent finitude of the powers themselves in the sense that they are definite, specific, concrete, and determinate. Thus autonomy and human integrity are in one sense finite, though in another sense they have an infinite range of applicability; in the same way, a line has the finitude of definite specifications, even while being capable of infinite extension according to the rules of its own constitution.

The basic attitudinal stance behind the humanist affirmation discloses a similar complexity combining a radical exuberance with circumspect caution. On the one hand, the celebration of autonomy contains a radical accent both in its recognition of man's cognitive powers of sense apprehension and reasoning capacity and in its advocacy of a dictum that these capacities shall be allowed the full exercise of their dynamic potential without external restraint. On the other hand, this emphasis is not necessarily identical with the imperialistic claim that the autonomous object of human knowledge is coterminous with, and exhaustive of reality, although some humanist adherents and some of their opponents have made the identification. In point of fact, the stance more congenial to the basic thrust of the humanist affirmation is one in which confidence is sharply distinguished from *hubris* and positively combined with a kind of cosmic humility. According to this interpetation of the humanist perspective, man's dignity resides in the attentive recognition of his own proper powers and the maximum development of their inherent potential without identifying this maximum realization with that infinity of knowledge and power that is the prerogative of the integrity of God rather than of man.

Erwin Panofsky has pointed out the ambivalence in the Renaissance conception of the meaning of *humanitas*. On the one hand, it reflects a classical distinction between *humanitas* and *barbaritas*, which underlines the distinctive value of the human self when he maintains his particular form of rational being by which he is above the level of animals and barbarians. On the other hand, a medieval antithesis between *humanitas* and *divinitas* is also present in the Renaissance approach, by which being human implies an awareness of one's essential finitude.[22] The humanist perspective seeks, then, to maintain the integrity of the human self in the face both of that which is below and of that which is above. It stresses man's dignity and power by holding him to be more than the animal world of sensitive irrational souls; at the same time, it rejects *hubris* and vain aspirations to transcend the area of man's proper being. As Montaigne observes: "The finest lives are to my mind those that put themselves alongside the common and human model, with order but without miracle, without extravangance."[23] Human integrity is recognized as human, there by distinguishing rather than identifying its distinctive mode of being and that of the divine.

If this is the main thrust of the humanist celebration of human dignity, it may well be wondered why and how, at this time, there should emerge the necessity for a new critique of religion and Christian faith. As already noted, the difference between this humanist affirmation and the preceding medieval anthropology has sometimes been grossly exaggerated. It is not that the Renaissance affirms an autonomous humanism unsuspected or vigorously resisted by the medieval thinkers. On the contrary, in spite of an important shift in emphasis, Renaissance humanism is a development of a humanistic perspective already present in medieval thought as a continuation and reaffirmation of the classical humanism of Greece and Rome.[24]

Indeed, medieval scholasticism can be fairly interpreted as an impressive attempt to harmonize the deliveries of the autonomous powers of man with the deliveries of divine revelation. Defenders of medieval thought thus refer with some justice to its Christian humanism as an essential element of its basic structure. At its best, scholasticism is held to have succeeded in the impressive task of respecting the distinctive integrities of reason and revelation and then demonstrating their coherent interaction in a theology that is both rational and cognizant of the Mystery which transcends the autonomous realm of reason and nature.

The humanism of the Renaissance and of early modernity clearly has its historical roots in this medieval synthesis. Nevertheless, as Cassirer points out, the Renaissance is not a repetitious continuation without significant transmutation. If the form and categories of thought remain constant, the center of gravity shifts, thereby requiring a reworking and rethinking of the medieval scheme.[25] Religion and faith become a problem to early modernity because their harmonious relationship with human autonomy is disturbed by a shift in the center of emphasis. Synthesis then gives way to tension, and harmony disintegrates into conflict and struggle.

The nature of this shift in the center of gravity which disturbed the equilibrium and balance of the medieval position can most aptly be characterized as the transition from a dependent autonomy within a hierarchical universe to an independent autonomy within an infinite and homogeneous universe. Though both medieval thinker and modern humanist affirm the autonomy of man, the medieval understanding of a dependent autonomy comes finally to be apprehended as a threat to the full autonomy aspired to by modern man.

HIERARCHICAL AUTONOMY

The medieval thinker and his modern defender can justly claim that their basic position is a humanism in which the specific integrity of man and his reason are recognized and safeguarded. Indeed, scholasticism can be interpreted as the recognition of the specific differences between man and God, reason and revelation, nature and grace, and the radical effort to preserve the integrity of both while combining them in a single comprehensive position.

The basic method by which this goal is achieved is an appropriation of the hierarchical scheme from the Greeks and its transformation into a distinctive Christian world-view. In this scheme

we can discern the ascending orders or ranks of forms
from the forms of inorganic substances, through vegetative
forms, the irrational sensitive forms of animals, the rational
soul of man, to the infinite and pure Act, God.[26]

Between man and God are angelic beings defined as created beings of an immaterial or spiritual form, in contrast to human being as material or corporeal beings of a rational form.

God is at the apex or center of the hierarchical scheme of being. All created or finite beings move from a potential state to an actual state. God is the One Unique Being who does not participate in a finite transition from potentiality to actuality, but already is completely actual and able to bring to actualization the other finite beings of the world. It can also be said that, in contrast to all other beings whose essence does not necessarily include their existence, He is the one Being in whom essence and existence coincide.

It is clear that this scheme conveys the implicit axiological judgment that form and actuality are better than matter and potentiality. Thus, the scale of being increases in value as it more closely approximates the level of pure form and pure actuality eminently realized in God. The sacred-profane distinction also operates in this scheme. Thus, beings of the material realm and the sciences by which they are studied are characterized as mundane or profane, whereas beings of the immaterial realm and their corresponding science are considered holy: theology is designated by the scholastics as sacred doctrine.

Thusfar, it might seem that this hierarchical scheme is a useful device for preserving both a theological orientation and a recognition of the distinctive integrity of the natural order. It might be wondered why the humanist of early modernity found in this scheme any threat to his own concerns for surely, among the many levels of being of the hierarchy, an adequate place for human and natural autonomy has been designated.

Yet closer scrutiny reveals some difficulties. For example, the hierarchical scheme seems to imply a dependent rather than independent autonomy. Though the levels of being have their proper integrity, each must accept its subordinate role within a scheme of ascending dignities and powers. In this view, the integrity of a given level of knowledge or being presupposes for its own development its dependence on a higher level. Duns Scotus, for example, argues: ". . . there seems to be a controversy between philosophers and theologians. The philosophers posit in effect the perfection of nature and deny the perfection of the super- natural. But the theologians *know what is lacking in nature* and consequently the necessity for grace and supernatural per- fection."[27]

Vignaux points out that the classical philosophical humanism of the Greeks has been transformed by medieval thinkers into a theological humanism. He observes:

> logically, a man who defines himself as a nature integrated in the natural order of a harmonious world admits the suffi- ciency of this nature; such is the sense of the Aristotelian maxim that nature is not deficient in what is necessary. On the other hand, the believer recalls a passage in St. Augustine: "The object of our faith is such that we can neither be ignorant of it, nor know it through our own powers." By placing man in this paradoxical situation, the theologians say to the philoso- phers that they merely recognize the essential deficiency of nature.[28]

Thus Gilson observes that "of all the temptations that beset the creature the most dangerous, the most firmly to be resisted is the temptation to set up a claim to *independence*."[29] And again:

> The question is not whether the world is good or evil, but whether the world is sufficient to itself, and whether it suffices. The testimony, and, we may add, the secular experience of Christiandom is that nature itself is powerless to realize itself, or even fully to survive as nature, when it attempts to do this without the help of grace.[30]

Modernity may be characterized by a general abandonment of this position, which is now considered to generate the destruc- tion rather than the perfection of human autonomy. Dependent autonomy now seems an incoherent union of incompatible notions, like a square circle. Deliberately or unconsciously, important thinkers of the renaissance begin to cultivate the use of autonomous human powers which, in the exercise of their proper function, are independent of a higher realm different from their own. Thus a Renaissance thinker like Pomponazzi "leaves the transcendent world of ecclesiastical faith intact; but he does not conceal that he needs this world neither for ethics nor for the construction of science, i.e., psychology and the theory of knowledge. For Pomponazzi, these are based on their own autonomous foundations; they have become independent of theological forms."[31]

This independence can be viewed from two vantage points. On the one hand, independence excludes the need of non-natural assistance in order for reason to realize its own autonomous potential. It is not pride but natural confidence which leads man to affirm his inherent capacity to do that which is within his own prerogative. Secondly, independence means that the exercise of man's cognitive powers shall know no restraint in their application to their own realm of being.

On this point, the medieval hierarchy is curiously ambiguous before the goal of an independent autonomy. On the one hand, its emphasis on a hierarchical scale of being seems to protect the unity and homogeneity of the universe and to maintain a basic ontological continuity between all its parts. On the other hand, its pronounced dualism between heaven and earth, other world and this world, form and matter, infinite and finite being, actual God and potential man, sacred and profane realms tends to rend the the hierarchical scheme into two disparate parts. Scholastic thought can be interpreted as a herculean effort to maintain this dualism in such a way that the underlying unity of the hierarchy of being is not finally destroyed. The efforts to show the correlation and connections between reason and revelation, philosophy and theology, the human science and the divine science are all evidence of this struggle.

Despite these efforts, the dualisms reappear and rend sharply the continuity. The independent and integral autonomy of man is threatened by simultaneously insisting that the human realm is necessarily related to higher realms of being and placing ontological limitations on the capacity of man's natural powers to comprehend these superior levels of reality. Thus man is provided with contradictory dicta, being admonished to exercise his natural cognitive powers in order to recognize and understand realms of being which he is also told are beyond the scope of his knowledge.

The medieval scheme seems to have united a principle of continuity and a principle of separation in a way that does not maintain their respective integrities but, on the contrary does violence to both. The principle of continuity between the realms of being is disturbed and destroyed by the affirmation of radical dualism between the mundane and divine realms, while the purity of the separation between them is also dissipated by insistence on ontological continuity.

The dependent autonomy of the hierarchical scheme is thus discovered to be fraught with ambiguity and confusion. Its appearance of coherence and clarity is deceptive, for, while seeming to encourage the full use of autonomous human powers, it so conceives the context within which these powers are exercised that they are frustrated in the very process of realization. The most striking example of the way in which the hierarchical and dualistic medieval scheme clearly acts as an inhibition rather than a support to human autonomy can be detected in the efforts of modern science to devise a cosmology that is consonant with the methodological rules of humanist autonomy.

COSMOLOGICAL DUALISM

The hierarchical scheme of the medieval period is used to fashion both a metaphysical and cosmological system. On the metaphysical level, the hierarchy of being is a graduation of level of beings, from the most material to the pure spirituality of the Divine Act. On the cosmological level, the hierarchical principle serves as a means for describing levels of physical reality which comprise the visible cosmos of physics and astronomy. In an important manner, the emphasis upon continuity in both the metaphysical and the cosmological schemes is disturbed by a radical dualism.

This relation between continuity and discontinuity can be seen in the original Aristotelian system upon which the medieval system was founded. Aristotle describes a cosmos that is a single finite sphere centered on the earth and bounded by the sphere of the fixed stars. This cosmos, however, reveals an important point of division at the region of the moon: from the moon upward to the first heaven, in which the fixed stars are placed, there are rotating spheres which convey the planets and other heavenly bodies; below the moon there is the region of the earth.

The radical difference between these regions is mainly determined by the corruptible nature of the substance of the sublunary region and the incorruptible nature of the heavenly realm. The sublunary region is composed of the four elements: earth, air, fire, and water; it is subject to the four kinds of change: quantitative or growth, qualitative or alteration, coming into being and passing out of being or genesis and decay, and finally spatial movement. The heavenly region is composed of a fifth element or "quintessence" that is incorruptible and unchanging except for circular movement which is the most perfect kind of motion because it most closely approximates unchanging perfection.[32]

Medieval cosmology is a development of that of Aristotle. It usually presents a universe of seven planetary spheres containing, respectively, the moon, Mercury, Venus, the Sun, Mars, Jupiter, and Saturn. Beyond these seven is the sphere of the Fixed Stars, beyond which is the sphere of the *Primum Mobile* containing no heavenly bodies but conveying motion to all the rest. Finally, in some medieval schemes such as that of Dante, there is a "Tenth Heaven, or Empyrean, the true abode of God and of his Saints."[33]

The transition from this classical cosmology to the one prevailing in modernity makes a fascinating account.[34] The medieval autonomy gives the scientist full leave to exercise his reason and his sense perceptions within the sublunary realm, considered their proper area of application. But incorruptible substances in the heavenly regions beyond the moon imposed limits on the kind of investigation accepted without question in the sublunary region. The modern emergence of independent autonomy rejects such a dualism as a violation of the methodological principle of continuity. As the heavenly bodies of the stars and planets are objects of the same sensual vision as are the objects of earth, how can one maintain a radical dualism between the two kinds of objects? The breakdown of this cosmological dualism is generated, then, by a renewed sense of independent autonomy that accepts no limitations, to the deliveries of its sense perceptions and the application of its rational principles on their own level of intelligibility.

For example, Galileo's observations of "spots" on the sun leads to the conclusion that the "substance" of the heavens is corruptible like that of earth. Laws of physics applicable to changeable elements of earth are found to apply with equal force to elements of the heavens. As Butterfield puts it

> Copernicus had taken one course in treating the earth as virtually a celestial body in the Aristotelian sense—a perfect sphere governed by the laws which operated in the higher reaches of the skies. Galileo complemented this by taking now the opposite course—rather treating the heavenly bodies as terrestrial ones, regarding the planets as subject to the very laws which applied to balls sliding down inclined planes. There was something in all this which tended to the reduction of the whole universe to uniform physical laws, and it is clear that the world was coming to be more ready to admit such a view.[35]

It is now almost universally accepted that the affirmation of the independent autonomy of man and nature on the level of cosmology has been justified. What is not always recognized with sufficient clarity is the fact that the hierarchical dualism of the medieval period was a real and not merely an imagined threat to this independent autonomy. The hierarchical dualism, whether presented in cosmological or metaphysical form, imposed an improper limit on the independent autonomy of men that had to be resisted and broken if that autonomy was to assume its fully developed maturity.

Here, the improper limits on the principles of continuity and homogeneity can be distinguished. The first is the boundary between the sublunary and heavenly realms which we have considered. A second barrier is broken when the outer limit of the cosmos is itself transcended and the finite sphere becomes an "infinite universe."[36] The phrase "infinite universe" aroused hostility in theological circles[37] which found a certain impiety in the application to the mundane world of a characteristic usually reserved for Divinity. However, the assertion of a natural extension without limitation along the homogeneous lines of spatial dimensions is compatible with the judgment that the natural cosmos nevertheless exhibits a specific set of principles and laws which render it de-finite, and, in that sense, finite. We might say that independent autonomy in the modern conception of the cosmos is held to be infinite as regards limitations external to its own natural dimensions, but finite inasmuch as it has the internal or inherent limitations of its own specific integrity and set of characteristics.

The medieval version of the "limit" of a "finite universe" generated further confusion by bringing onto a single plane of discourse the finite world and the spiritual yet (cosmological (?)) heaven beyond it. According to Aristotle, because space is finite and circular, speaking about anything "beyond" the outer sphere of the Heavens loses all intelligible meaning. Aristotle argues: "Outside the heaven there is neither place nor void nor time. Hence, whatever is there is of such a kind as not to occupy space, nor does time affect it."[38] Nevertheless, perplexity caused by the phrase "outside the heaven" is accentuated by the medieval reference to the Empyrean Heaven "beyond" the nine spheres. Is the Empyrean Heaven a spatial place "beyond" the ninth sphere, in the same sense that the ninth is beyond the eighth, the eighth beyond the seventh, and so forth?

Modern defenders of the sophistication of medieval thought deny that such is the case. Dorothy Sayers writes:

Beyond all nine spheres lies the Tenth Heaven or Empyrean, the true abode of God and His Saints. It has neither position nor velocity nor movement nor duration: it is eternal and infinite, and to it all space-time measurements are wholly irrelevant and meaningless. The idea that "the Middle Ages" believed in—a localized, temporal and material Heaven—is entirely false; intelligent Christians no more believed such a thing than they do now.[39]

Surely, this defense of meaning for the phrase "beyond all nine spheres" in inadequate. Granted that 'beyond' can have many different uses, of which some are non-spatial, a confusion is generated here by first establishing a certain image to 'beyond' in relation to the nine spatial spheres. If a new sense is now introduced, the context makes the change in meaning unclear.

C. S. Lewis also makes a valiant defense of the freedom of the Heaven of God from spatial entanglements, but his very defense is a confession of confusion. He notes:

So when Dante passes that last frontier he is told, "We have got outside the largest corporeal thing *(del maggia corpo)* into that heaven which is pure light, intellectual light, full of love" (*Paradiso*, XXX, 38). In other words . . . at this frontier the whole spatial way of thinking breaks down. There can be, in the ordinary spatial sense, no "end" to a three-dimensional space. The end of space is the end of spatiality. The light beyond the material universe is intellectual light.[40]

Lewis' summary is no doubt a fair account of the medieval position, but it serves only to accentuate the ambiguous mixture of a mundane world of "the ordinary spatial sense" with a radically different realm of "intellectual light." If the former has no spatial continuity with the latter, then the juxtaposition of the two in cosmological discourse is an incoherent synthesis of disparate kinds of discourse. The destruction of this "limit" between finite universe and infinite heaven was clearly a boon to clarity in both cosmology and theology.

A third limit was also broken by the burgeoning autonomy of man when the notion of a metaphysical world of formal potencies able to cause physically in the natural world was finally dispelled. This point is more fiercely resisted than the others by some metaphysicians. While acknowledging an improper mixture of realms within the medieval cosmological scheme itself, they do not always recognize a confusion that can still remain between an autonomous physics and some kinds of meta-physics. However, the humanist drive toward autonomy, with its methodological principles of continuity and homogeneity tends to discover the same difficulty in hierarchical dualisms, whether they are stated in a cosmological or a metaphysical form. If one affirms a natural continuity between the sublunary world and the heavenly worlds, then the assertion of the radical dualism between their substances seems unacceptable; but the assertion of a metaphysical world above the physical world seems to perform the same operation and to be beset by the same difficulties.

We have already seen how the cosmological scheme moved ambiguously from a ninth heavenly sphere, that was still physical in some refined sense, to a tenth sphere of the Empyrean Heaven, which now had become completely metaphysical. Yet an analogous movement is performed by Gilson when he summarized the medieval perspective.

> The science of natural or "physical" beings we call physics. Beyond this science there is another—the science of beings which are beyond physical beings. Hence it is called the science of "meta-physics," or, as we say, metaphysics. What distinguishes this second group of beings from the first is that they are forms subsisting in themselves and free from all matter. Without matter, such beings are entirely in act; they are said to be pure acts. . . . Thus they can be called "meta-natural" quite as well as "metaphyiscal." Both amount to the same thing. Inversely, since they are above natural beings, these pure acts of Aristotle can be "superphysical" beings or "supernatural" beings. It makes no difference. So, for Aristotle, the boundary between the natural and the supernatural is

that which separates material from pure forms. Owing to the force of circumstances, it is this same boundary which separates the natural world from the divine world.[41]

Although metaphysics has many meanings, in this interpretation it is clear that metaphysics posits a dualism between a physical world of corporeal forms and a metaphysical world of incorporeal ones. This kind of metaphysics is unacceptable to a humanistic commitment to the principles of continuity and homogeneity. The problem is not in the distinctions themselves, but in the fact that, as Cassirer points out, they are conceived "in a purely substantival manner."[42] If nature and spirit, matter and form, body and soul are conceived as separate substances, worlds are posited in a contradictory manner as existing in a state of continuity, while at the same time there is an absolute dualism between them. As Cassirer points out, the humanist solution to this problem is accomplished "when 'body' and 'soul,' 'nature' and 'spirit' are no longer related substantively, as one thing to another, but rather *functionally*."[43]

The modern humanist is not opposed, per se, to metaphysical distinctions like form and matter, soul and body, potency and act, if they are understood functionally or dialectically as aspects of a single natural process, for in that case, the question is simply to decide which terms are most useful and illuminating in describing the continuous system of the natural universe. But a substantial metaphysics that divides the world into a supposedly autonomous physical world that can nevertheless be affected on the natural level by potencies and powers from a metaphysical world of immaterial forms must be resisted by the humanist critique. Autonomous reason operating in an autonomous natural world accepts the interaction of diverse powers within that world; it cannot accept the destruction of its own autonomy by "another world" that is both a dynamic part of the physical world and yet somehow radically separated from it.

The same hierarchical dualism in its three forms between sublunary and heavenly worlds, between finite universe and Empyrean Heaven, between physical and metaphysical world is considered a threat to the emerging autonomy of humanist man. In conclusion, it must be asked what positive relation between independent autonomy and religious faith may yet remain.

THE HUMANIST'S POSITIVE APPROACH TO RELIGION

This rapid sketch of the humanist critique of religion has emphasized its essentially defensive posture. I have argued that the humanist of early modernity is interested less in attacking religion than he is in protecting the independent autonomy of man. Nevertheless, I have tried to show how this defense involves a major tension with religious dualisms that seems to pose a threat to that autonomy. In conclusion, I wish now to point out that this tension is not only very real but exceedingly complex, and that is sometimes assumes a final shape different from that which first appears upon superficial glance.

We have already seen that a total opposition between an other-world faith, centered on the divine and a this-world humanism, centered on man, is too simplistic. As a matter of historical fact, the medieval hierarchical scheme provides a humanistic respect for the integrity and autonomy of man; conversely, the humanism of early modernity continues to respect the orientation of man toward the Divine. The humanist critique of religion that emerges in the early modern period is not fundamentally a frontal attack on religion and Christian faith, but an attempt to rethink the relation between human autonomy and faith and to correct what begins to appear as important defects in the medieval synthesis.

This sketch has emphasized the humanist goal of an independent autonomy that is structured by the two norms of methodological continuity for the cognitive principles employed, and of homogeneity for the elements of the objective system studied. In view of this it would appear that the assertion of methodological or ontological dualisms is the main threat to these humanist ideals and norms. We must now consider how some important qualifications and amplifications of this judgment are in order, if we are to specify adequately the central focus of the humanist critique.

In his masterful survey of Renaissance philosophy, Cassirer points out that this medieval scheme is one attempt to resolve the tension between the Platonic stress on dualism and separation and the Aristotelian stress on continuity and development.[44] According to Cassirer, Plato's vision of the world is characterized by a sharp division or separation *(chorismos)* between the sensible and the intelligible world. As the two worlds of the "visible" and the "invisible" do not lie on the same plane, they admit of no immediate comparison. Nevertheless, Aristotle's criticism of the Platonic doctrine is based on his objection to the radical separation of a realm of existence from a realm of ideal meaning and it searches for the point of participation *(methexis)* between them. Because, for Aristotle, reality is one, his thought emphasizes the essential continuities between distinctions like matter and form, becoming and being, sensible and supersensible. These distinctions can "only be understood as opposition if there is some means for going from the one pole to the other. Thus, for Aristotle, the concept of development becomes the basic category and the general principle for the explanation of the world."[45] Cassirer then argues that neo-Platonism mated the Platonic category of transcendence with the Aristotelian category of development to form the "bastard concept of 'emanation.' "[46] for Cassirer the "fundamental category of graduated mediation" derived from neo-Platonism through the pseudo-Dionysian writings. Defenders of scholastic thought are convinced that the main thrust of this position, as represented by a great thinker like Thomas, has achieved the proper balance and relation between "separation" and "continuity." The humanist critique of early modernity does not find this to be so for the reasons we have already considered and can now briefly review.

It is true that the medieval commitment to the hierarchical scheme of being allows for some attention to the humanist values of autonomy and continuity. If, in the medieval view, God is separated from man, it is also true that God and world have been placed in a system of ontological continuity through the hierarchical principle. However, it is this situation which turns out to be the source of the frustrating impasses that beset the humanistic spirit wishing to assert the independent autonomy of man. Indeed, these considerations lead to an unexpected conclusion, for it now appears that the problem which the medieval system raises for the modern humanist is its emphasis not on dualism, but on ontological continuity. It is not that too drastic a separation has been made between God and man; it is that the distinction is not drastic and radical enough.

By placing the Divine into too direct a continuity with the autonomous world of nature along the lines indicated both the integrity of the Divine is threatened and the full maturation of human autonomy is inhibited. From this there follows the need for the essentially defensive posture of the humanist critique. In view of this, one must now ask whether this critique has any alternative approach of its own to religion. I think that several possibilities are present in the modern mind, and one of them in particular represents the heart of the humanist ethos.

The various humanist options represent some of the alternatives which were rejected by the basic medieval position, but which again become viable when the medieval synthesis disintegrates. We have seen how a central concern of medieval thought is the establishment of the proper relation between the integrity of human reason and the deliveries of revelation. In Gilson's classic book on *Reason and Revelation in the Middle Ages,* three major solutions to this problem are distinguished.[47] First "the primacy of faith" is espoused by fideists who commit themselves to a theology of faith in revelation unaffected by the deliveries of reason. Second, the "primacy of reason" is asserted by rationalists who are concerned to develop the implications of human reason unaffected by the dictums of faith in any form. Finally, the focus of the main forms of scholastic thought, especially in the great Thomistic synthesis, seeks to establish "the harmony of reason and revelation." According to Thomas, the deliveries of reason, properly attained, will not contradict those of revelation. Reason will either support revelation or maintain a neutral silence about truths of faith which, while not contradicting reason, have transcended the area of rational competence and applicability.

Defenders of the harmony or synthesis approach consider it to have preserved the respective autonomies of fideists and rationalists without having to maintain an unnatural break between them. The breakdown of the medieval synthesis and the transition to modernity is interpreted by a medievalist like Gilson as the failure of modernity to appreciate the cogency of the Thomistic solution. From the perspective of modernity we may rather say that it was the failure of the previous attempt to "harmonize" faith and reason which made necessary a humanist critique of religion in which the alternatives rejected by medieval thinkers become viable options.

It is true that one strand of humanist thought can be interpreted as continuing the medieval synthesis. Thus, for example, the Platonic wing of the Italian Renaissance, while celebrating the autonomy of man, maintains this autonomy within a series of continous gradations from the mundane world to a sacred apex, from secular reason to mystical ecstasy. The Aristotelian wing, however, represents a more radical shift to the second of Gilson's options: a fully autonomous reason separated from theological influence.

This approach could lead to a kind of humanistic rationalism in which the autonomy of man and nature are held to be exhaustive of all meaningful discourse. A different form of rationalism is maintained, however, when the autonomy of reason is combined with some continued reference to the deliveries of faith without maintaining the harmony of the Thomistic synthesis. Pomponazzi, for example, develops a relation between faith and reason that is often identified with a "double truth" position maintaining a "watertight separation" between revelation and reason.[48] The "double truth" approach has received many different interpretations. The most interesting and sophisticated would not admonish the thinker to hold truths of faith and truths of reason even though these might directly contradict each other, but might maintain that truths of faith and of reason cannot contradict each other because, even when using the same words, their meanings refer to realms that between themselves have no onto-logical continuity. Hence, to follow Cassirer's typology, the Platonic *chrismos* supersedes both the Aristotelian *methexis* and the Plotinian emanation.

This point suggests further attention to Gilson's first option of fideism. The theology of the Reformation, clearly influenced by the Humanists and yet suspicious that reason threatens the integrity of revelation, can be interpreted as a replacement of the disintegrated medieval synthesis by fideism. On this view, the theologian, protecting the integrity of revelation, and the philoso-pher, protecting the integrity of reason, concur in their desire to maintain a radical separation between the two realms.

For example, the attacks of Luther on "reason" and "philoso-phy" are grossly misunderstood if they are interpreted as a rampant irrationalism, oblivious to humanist values. Luther is not attacking the proper use of reason in its own sphere. On the contrary, he is fully agreed with the humanist emphasis that reason should be allowed unlimited use within the human domain. Luther's point is that knowledge of the divine cannot be attained through the use of human autonomy, but that, on the contrary a distinct spiritual organ, faith, is required. Thus, if a radical dual-ism between faith and reason is maintained, and the independent autonomy of both is respected, then a proper relationship between the two can be achieved. For example, Luther writes:

> In temporal affairs and those which have to do with men, the rational man is self-sufficient *(da ist der mensch vornünftig genug)*: here he needs no other light than reason's. Therefore, God does not teach us in the Scriptures how to build houses, make clothing, marry, wage war, navigate, and the like. For here the light of nature is sufficient. But in godly affairs, that is, in those which have to do with God, where man must do what is acceptable with God and be saved thereby—*here,* however, nature is absolutely stone-blind, so that it cannot even catch a glimpse *(eyn harbreytt anzeygen)* of what those

things are. It is presumptuous enough to bluster and plunge into them, like a blind horse; but all its conclusions are utterly false, as surely as God lives.[49]

In such a way a radical separation of faith and reason is fashioned, so that the proper integrity of each can be respected in its own terms.

The manner of maintaining this "separation" can take many forms, only one of which is a dogmatic theology contrasting revelation and reason. Some of the most significant "makers of the modern mind" have worked out impressive philosophical positions in which human autonomy and divine reality are related in such a way that the radical separation between them is not protected.

As examples, let us briefly consider the achievements of Cusanus as a representative of the most sophisticated and profound Renaissance thought and those of Kant as the the most brilliant spokesman of the Enlightenment.

Cassirer points out that the work of Cusanus can be interpreted as a rejection of the neo-Platonic confusion of the categories of "separation" and "participation" and as an attempt to return to "genuine Platonic basic concepts" that maintain a proper understanding of these categories.[50] On the one hand, Cusanus develops a view of the cosmos that establishes the principles of continuity and homogeneity. According to Koyre, he does not quite reach the notion of an "infinite universe," but rather stresses its indeterminateness.[51] For our purposes, what is the important point is that, according to Cusanus, the cognitive powers of mathematical reason are "unlimited."

On the other hand, this acceptance of a radical human autonomy of unlimited extension does not prevent Cusanus from also accepting the presence of the Maximum or the Infinite as that which, like the Platonic Good, is "beyond being" and "separated" from the unlimited extension of the natural world. Cusanus stresses that the Infinite cannot be understood as simply the highest member along the line of natural continuity. "On the contrary, it must be understood as the complete anti-thesis to every possible comparison, to every merely quantitative-gradual procedure. The Maximum is not a quantitative, but a qualitative concept."[52] Nevertheless, Cassirer argues: "with the same decisiveness and acuteness that he applied to the ideal of 'separation,' Cusanus now worked out the idea of 'participation.' Far from excluding each other, separation and participation (*chorismos* and *methexis*) can only be thought of through and in relation to each other."[53]

The difficulty in such a position is the establishment of the intelligibility of any reference to an "Infinite" radically separated from the autonomous realm of nature. We cannot here pursue Cusanus' brilliant exploration of this problem, which seems to involve at least three factors: mathematical considerations of the relation of infinity to the unlimited extension of an homogeneous numerical series; a mystic sense of individuality and its participation in the totality of the Divine; and a Christology in which Christ is "the genuine *natura media* that embraces the finite and the infinite in one."[54]

For our purposes, it is sufficient to note the formal structure of Cusanus' thought, which establishes a radical dualism. This is not within the realm of human autonomy, which is rather allowed unlimited extension on its own plane. Instead, the dualism is between this unlimited autonomy and the integrity of the Divine, which rather than violating or limiting human autonomy, "participates" in it. Cassirer summarizes the position as follows:

Now we have a negative theology with a positive theory of experience. Neither contradicts the other; rather, each represents one and the same theory of knowledge seen from two aspects. The one truth, ungraspable in its absolute being, can present itself to us only in the realm of otherness; on the other hand, there is no otherness for us that does not in some way point to the unity and participate in it. We must renounce any attempt at identifying the two, any thought of resolving the dualism or of letting the one realm overlap into the other. But it is just this renunciation that gives our knowledge its relative right and its relative truth. In Kantian language, it shows that our knowledge, to be sure, is bounded by insurmountable limits placed upon it. Even in otherness, knowledge can and should extend in all directions. By denying any overlapping of the two realms and by teaching us to see the One *in* the other, and the other *in* the One, the separation itself guarantees the possibility of true participation of the sensible in the ideal.[55]

While differing in many ways from the thought of Cusanus, Kant's position is another significant example. Kant is probably the most brilliant and radical defender of human autonomy in the modern world, and for that reason can be considered as the paradigmatic representative of the humanistic critique we have here considered. However, the dualistic strains found in his distinctions between phenomena and noumena and between theoretical and practical reason have seemed to many to represent a vacillation and confusion in his otherwise rigorous and consistent commitment to autonomy. However, although there may be important details where Kant's position is unsatisfactory, his basic correlation of humanist autonomy with religious belief is consistent with his own principles and a brilliant application of the new approach we are here considering. According to his method, Divine Reality is understood not as a part of the natural world but as that which intersects with that world without violating its integrity, just as a horizontal plane may intersect with a vertical one without disturbing its autonomy.

The famous essay on "Religion within the Limits of Reason Alone" is an excellent example of this method in action. Very often the title is interpreted as the expression of a reductionist intent to contain religion within the limits of reason. According to this view, Kant is attempting to describe the religion of reason that has been determined by the independent autonomy of reason alone. The careful reading of the essay will disclose that Kant's intent is exactly the opposite. Thus, in the essay, Kant suprisingly accepts a valid use of the category of religious mystery which has no place within the categories of reason. It is a counsel to incoherence to assert that a certain belief is both rational and yet mysterious in the sense of irrational at the same time and in the same sense. However, reason can itself understand the situation of a phenomenon that, while understood on its own autonomous principles, also reveals a dimension that is opaque to the scrutiny of reason. Kant finds such a phenomenon in moral experience and the exercise of freedom. He observes:

> Thus freedom, an attribute of which man becomes aware through the determinability of his will by the unconditional moral law, is no mystery, because the knowledge of it can be *shared* with everyone; but the ground, inscrutable to us, of this attribute is a mystery because this ground is *not given* us as an object of knowledge. Yet it is this very freedom which, when applied to the final object of practical reason (the realization of the idea of the moral end), alone leads us inevitably to holy mysteries.[56]

The details of this argument cannot be considered here, nor do I contend that Kant is entirely successful in achieving his goal of correlating a radical autonomy with a recognition of that which transcends the limits of that autonomy. It is sufficient to note that Kant's purpose is to show how moral experience has an autonomy which renders it completely independent of religious or theological tenets, but which nevertheless, points to that which transcends the autonomy without violating it in any way.

These examples of Cusanus and Kant, as two outstanding representatives of the thought of early modernity, disclose the possibility of a religious approach in which the independent autonomy of man is consonant with a radical recognition of divine transcendence. Indeed, we may now amplify our original thesis by remarking that the defensive posture of the humanist critique of religion is two-fold. It seeks to defend both the autonomy of man from dualistic threats and the integrity of the Divine. It does this by severing those improper connections between discourse about the Divine and discourse about the mundane that succeed only in reducing the former to the latter. Protecting the autonomy of man is an important aspect of protecting the divinity of God.

Of course, serious problems remain. The basic one is that of establishing the point of contact or participation between the realm of human autonomy and discourse about the Divine. Otherwise, an ontological humanism affirming that the limits of this autonomy are the limits of reality seems an inevitable consequence of the modern approach. If the elucidation of this point of contact is necessary for a viable religious approach, the hierarchical method, emphasizing some sort of continuity between human and divine realms even while asserting their separation, may still be useful. Thus, James Collins has recently provided a brilliant study of modern humanist philosophy in which he suggests that philosophies of human autonomy can yet be correlated with the metaphysical approach to God. According to him, "these two philosophical disciplines respond to distinct intentional aims of the inquiring mind, whose guiding purpose is not to displace the one by the other, but to insure the evidential soundness of each and also to to work out their integrating relationship."[57]

Such an approach, if substantiated, would represent a modern version of Thomas' achievement in the medieval period. Indeed, as we have seen, the Thomist can feel with some justice that his tradition has already considered the possibilities of an autonomous fideism and an autonomous rationalism, and rejected them in favor of the attempt to harmonize the two. However, we have seen the serious difficulties this attempt presented to the emerging modern mind, and the reasons for seeking to devise alternative approaches.

Indeed, all positions we have considered must deal with the same fundamental problems: having established a drastic *chorismos* between human autonomy and divinity, how can a point of contact allowing for *methexis* be established. The danger of the hierarchical dualism between human autonomy and divine mystery is incoherence, resulting from an improper mixture of disparate parts; the danger of a radical dualism is unintelligibility, as reference to that which has absolutely transcended the realm of human reason thereby becomes meaningless. The continued perplexity of modern man discloses that a fully satisfactory solution has not yet appeared. What does seem clear is that whatever form philosophy of religion and theology presently assume, it will be a mode that does not find the autonomy of man a threat to its own concerns. On the contrary, it will welcome the maturing of human powers and the unlimited exercise of all that it is in man to think and do.

◊

1. Paul Radin, **Primitive Man as Philosopher** (New York: Dover, 1957), **passim.**

2. Ernst Cassirer, **The Philosophy of the Enlightenment** (Boston: Beacon, 1955), p. vi.

3. **Ibid.** Cf. Myron Gilmore, **The World of Humanism, 1453-1517** (New York: Harper Torchbooks, 1962), p. 268.

4. Ernst Cassirer, Paul Oskar Kristeller, and John Randall, Jr., **The Renaissance Philosophy of Man** (Chicago: Phoenix Books, 1948), p. 3. Hereafter, **Renaissance Philosophy.**

5. Gilmore, **The World of Humanism,** Chap. VIII; Crane Brinton, **The Shaping of Modern Thought** (Englewood Cliffs, N. J.: Prentice-Hall, 1963), Chap. I; Ronald Gregor Smith, "Post-Renaissance Man," in **Conflicting Images of Man,** ed. William Nichols (New York: Seabury, 1961), pp. 35-36.

6. Cassirer, **The Philosophy of the Enlightenment,** p. 136. See Peter Gay, **The Enlightenment: An Interpretation** (New York: Alfred A. Knopf, 1966), esp. Chap. II for examples of hostility of Enlightenment to Christianity.

7. Cassirer, **The Philosophy of the Enlightenment,** p. 137.

8. **Renaissance Philosophy,** p. 275.

9. Immanuel Kant, **The Philosophy of Kant,** ed. Carl Friedrich (New York: Modern Library, 1949), p. 132.

10. Ernst Cassirer, **The Individual and the Cosmos in Renaissance Philosophy** (New York: Harper Torchbooks, 1964), p. 145. Hereafter designated as **Cosmos.**

11. Cassirer, **Philosophy of the Enlightenment,** p. 39.

12. Etienne Gilson, **The Spirit of Medieval Philosophy** (New York: Charles Scribner's Sons, 1940), esp. Chap. VI. B. A. Garrish, **Grace and Reason: A Study in the Theology of Luther** (Oxford: Clarendon Press, 1967), for approach of reformers to sin.

13. Paul Vignaux, **Philosophy in the Middle Ages: An Introduction** (New York: Meridian, 1959), p. 212.

14. **Renaissance Philosophy,** secs. III and IV.

15. Paul Oskar Kristeller, **Renaissance Thought** (New York: Harper & Bros., 1961), p. 129.

16. **Renaissance Philosophy**, p. 225.

17. **Ibid.**

18. **Cosmos**, p. 84.

19. Immanuel Kant, **Religion within the Limits of Reason Alone**, trans. T. M. Greene and H. H. Hudson (New York: Harper Torchbooks, 1960), **passim.**

20. Immanuel Kant, **Critique of Pure Reason**, trans. Norman Kemp Smith (London: Macmillan, 1958), p. 9.

21. George Santayana, **Reason in Science** (New York: Charles Scribner's Sons, 1906), pp. 14-15.

22. Erwin Panofsky, **Meaning in the Visual Arts** (New York: Doubleday Anchor Books, 1955), pp. 1-7.

23. H. J. Blackman, **The Human Tradition** (London: Routledge and Kegan Paul, Ltd., 1953), p. 22.

24. Vignaux, **Philosophy in the Middle Ages: An Introduction**, p. 15.

25. **Cosmos**, p. 81.

26. **Ibid.** Cf. Frederick Copleston, **A History of Philosophy**, Vol. II, **Augustine to Scotus** (London: Burns, Oates and Washbourne, Ltd., 1950), p. 329.

27. Vignaux, **Philosophy in the Middle Ages: An Introduction**, p. 89.

28. **Ibid.**, pp. 89-90.

29. Gilson, **Spirit of Medieval Philosophy**, p. 129.

30. **Ibid.**, p. 127.

31. **Cosmos**, p. 81.

32. D. J. Allan, **The Philosophy of Aristotle** (London: Oxford Univ. Press, 1957), p. 57. Cf. pp. 35-36.

33. Dorothy Sayers, trans., **The Divine Comedy, I, Hell** (Middlesex: Penguin Books, 1959), p. 294. Cf. A. C. Crombie, **Medieval and Early Modern Science** (New York: Doubleday Anchor Books, 1959), I, p. 81.

34. Crombie, **Medieval and Early Modern Science**; Herbert Butterfield. **The Origins of Modern Science** (New York: Macmillan, 1960).

35. Butterfield, **The Origins of Modern Science**, p. 67.

36. Alexandre Koyre, **From the Closed World to the Infinite Universe** (New York: Harper Torchbooks, 1958).

37. **Ibid.**, p. 8.

38. C. S. Lewis, **The Discarded Image** (Cambridge: University Press, 1964), pp. 96-7.

39. Sayers, **The Divine Comedy**, I, p. 294.

40. Lewis, **The Discarded Image**, p. 97.

41. Etienne Gilson, **The Christian Philosophy of St. Thomas Aquinas** (New York: Random House, 1956), p. 166.

42. **Cosmos**, p. 141; cf. pp. 136-8.

43. Ibid., p. 142.

44. Ibid., pp. 116-20.

45. Ibid., p. 17.

46. Ibid., p. 18.

47. Etienne Gilson, **Reason and Revelation in the Middle Ages** (New York: Charles Scribner's Sons, 1952), **passim**.

48. Ibid., pp. 58 ff; **Renaissance Philosophy**, sec. V.

49. Gerrish, **Grace and Reason**, p. 12.

50. **Cosmos**, p. 20.

51. Koyre, **From the Closed World to the Infinite Universe**, p. 8.

52. **Cosmos**, p. 20.

53. Ibid., p. 22.

54. Ibid., p. 39.

55. Ibid., pp. 23-4.

56. Kant, **Religion within the Limits of Reason Alone**, p. 129.

57. James Collins, **The Emergence of the Philosophy of Religion** (New Haven: Yale Univ. Press, 1967), p. 449.

Hegel's Philosophy of Religion

◇

Kenneth L. Schmitz

AMONG THOSE WHO have read him, as well as among those who have not, Hegel has inspired both intense enthusiasm and intense suspicion. If we are to believe an early English enthusiast, Professor J. H. Stirling, the launching of the study of Hegel in English over a century ago caused something of a commotion. Most Anglo-Saxon philosophers have resisted the heady flights of Hegelian speculation, and have shrugged off his claims as rather curious ones. In this, the notorious difficulty of his language has been a significant factor. Even Stirling complained that he had to make a "most anxious and painful" attempt to soften for the reader "the uncouth unintelligibleness of that extraordinary new German"—and of this even Germans complain. Stirling concluded sadly:

> The melancholy fact remains, however, that all these *Beings*—Being-for-itself, Being-for-another, Being-for-one, Being-for-a, etc.—are hopeless; like a child that first reads, one has been obliged to syllabify.[1]

Nevertheless, some of Stirling's students did contract virulent forms of Hegelian speculation. What attracted Stirling and others is indicated in his description of how he first came to know of Hegel:

> [When] supping with two students of German before [he]

was in German as deep as they . . . [he heard] this Hegel talked
of with awe. . . . It was understood that he had not only completed philosophy, but, above all, reconciled to philosophy
Christianity itself. That struck![2]

Within Hegel's thought philosophy and Christianity confront one
another in a delicate and subtle relation, and no interpretation
of Hegel is satisfactory if it backs off from a decision concerning
that relation. The aim of the present essay is more modest; it
seeks only to sketch the role of the philosophy of religion in
that relation.

Even here not all things can be done once, nor—impressions
of Hegel to the contrary—can all things be said at once. I will
restrict myself to several leading concepts in order to trace
Hegel's philosophy of religion in very general lines. The important questions about the early Hegel and the development of his
philosophy of religion will not be taken up and, for the most
part, I will confine myself to themes of his mature teaching as they
have come to us in his *Lectures on the Philosophy of Religion.*
Because these Berlin lectures were not published by Hegel in his
lifetime, they pose some difficult textual problems.[3] Nevertheless,
the concerns of the following pages are general enough to avoid
the embarrassments of the still not completely satisfactory condition of the German text.

As the several themes to be presented touch upon some
leading ideas in post-Hegelian discussions on the nature of
religion, the essay will have three parts. The first will say something of how Hegel sees the philosophical enterprises within which
he assigns an important role to the philosophy of religion. The
second will present Hegel's discussion of religion by means of
three themes. The third and concluding part, will make sugges-
tions for an evaluation of his enterprise. He will not submit to verification in the present sense of that word, but neither does he
expect us to submit passively to whatever he says. Hegel, too,
argues for his positions. The problems then, is to devise tests,
both empirical and reflective, which render his expressed thought
responsive to the demands of philosophical enquiry.

HEGEL'S CONCEPTION OF
THE PHILOSOPHIC ENTERPRISE

To discover how Hegel sees the enterprise of philosophy one must turn to that most notorious, obscure, and central Hegelian conception: Spirit. Its meaning may be seen in barest outline through two other conceptions: human consciousness and Reason.

Human consciousness has a history which Hegel records in his first great work the *Phenomenology of Spirit,* and in each of his other works. One of the most important moments in the history of human consciousness occurred during the century of Hegel's birth. The importance of the eighteenth century Enlightenment for Hegel's thought cannot be exaggerated. Again and again he insisted that it enabled human consciousness to gain a new confidence and insight into its own nature, purposes, and power. It raised more clearly than ever before an indispensable battle-cry: Everything meaningful must be measured by the standards of reason!

Hegel understands this demand to imply two distinct claims: (1) that there is nothing which is not already in relation to consciousness: in his own words, that there is nothing which is not for-consciousness; and (2) that the primary nature of everything is this very relation to consciousness: in his words, that the essential being of everything is to be for-consciousness. The second claim is stronger than the first, and both are arguable; but what is especially noteworthy is that Hegel thinks these claims are true—once the *full* nature of consciousness is recovered.

For all its insights, the Enlightenment held within its demand the serious flaw of considering knowledge to be a wholly finite, limited activity producing a finite, restricted, and conditioned result. The Enlightenment was proud of its famous clear and distinct ideas, its careful definitions, its specified conclusions, which it held to be the noblest products of human thought.

In the generation preceding Hegel's, however, Kant had already begun to recover the more ample appreciation of consciousness which medieval thinkers had sensed but not properly understood. Kant's great step was to draw the distinction between things as they appear under specified conditions and that which does not appear but lies beyond human knowledge. He called the latter the absolutely unconditioned. For Kant, this unconditioned remained negative and unknowable; human knowledge was uncompromisingly conditioned and finite.

Nevertheless, Kant's distinction between conditioned and unconditioned restored a sense of the unconditioned, for in drawing the distinction consciousness embraces both sides of the distinction. Indeed, in the distinction Hegel sees the underlying dynamic thrust which discovers its own limits, and in that discovery already finds itself ahead of and beyond these limits.

In this discovery, consciousness finds that it has no limits; it finds instead its "own unconditioned actuality."[4] Consciousness does not halt at the present limits of its actual understanding, but leaps ahead to affirm its oneness with all possible meaning. Hegel writes

> We are men and have reason; what is human, or above all, what is rational vibrates within us, both in our feelings, mind and heart, and in our subjective nature generally.[5]

Hegel's strategy, then, is to keep from setting premature limits to what is rational and meaningful. More precisely, it is his position that there are no limits. By its nature meaning is not exhausted by our subjective feelings and understandings, but drives towards even larger spheres of objective realization.[6]

Just this overreaching of all conditions is ingredient in consciousness which is simply not confined to the finite dimension. It is neither a ship which fights to keep out the waters of a limitless ocean, nor a cabin confined to its own small piece of ground in a measureless desert. Finite and infinite do not lie apart from one another like inert spaces. Both finite and infinite are sustained in and by the dynamic thrust of consciousness, and held together in a tension in which they penetrate one another;[7] both share the same essential nature; both are for consciousness; and both are polarities within an all-encompassing whole, that is, within the very structure of meaning and truth as such.

Hegel's writings illustrate the history of the interpenetration of finite and infinite in the human spirit. In his view Parmenides properly began philosophy by the very act of explicitly acknowledging the All and grounding his thought solely in it.[8] In so doing limits were overpassed and a fullness was anticipated, and consciousness sought fullness. This inherent expectation of completeness led Hegel to call a mere spatial or temporal repetition of the same a suprious infinite. The true infinite is a totality that is complete and that exhausts all the essential possibilities of meaning. Far from being an endless repetition of the same, the true infinite contains the maximum of diversity and articulates the most varied possibilities of meaning. In sum, the essential nature of consciousness is to be both finite and infinite; it is both conditioned and unconditioned.

Consciousness, then, is the expectation of a totality of meaning and truth. What is more, however, consciousness is also the only means of fulfilling that expectation. Fulfillment comes neither from heaven nor from earth, for if the earth trembles or heaven thunders, consciousness must still decide upon their meaning. It is precisely as Reason that consciousness sets out to fulfill its deepest expectations.

Hegel did not think that the search for a totality of meaning and truth began with him. The Greeks and Latins were famous for the powers of analysis by which they uncovered the differences among things *(logos, ratio)*, but they also recognized a power which apprehends things in their original wholeness *(nous, intellectus)*. In more recent times, Kant also distinguished two faculties of consciousness. The first was the Understanding *(der Verstand)* or faculty of analysis by which differences are noticed and preserved. The second was the faculty of Reason *(die Vernunft)* or the original and underived expectation by consciousness that its knowledge can become a systematic totality. Such a totality is more than a mere collection of unrelated pieces of information, for the different parts of knowledge are seen to form a necessarily interrelated whole. Kant also remarked that it was the purpose of philosophy to fulfill this expectation of consciousness for an integrated totality of meaning and truth.

He added that nothing less than a universal and cosmic idea *(conceptus cosmicus, Weltbegriff)*:

> has always formed the real basis of the term 'philosophy.'
> . . . On this view, philosophy is the science of the relation
> of all knowledge to the essential ends of human reason.[9]

For Hegel, too, the understanding is the analytic power which establishes distinctions and preserves differences. The highest principle for the understanding is the principle of identity which affirms the sameness of each thing with itself: A is A, I am I (not you), a rose is a rose is a rose . . . an island is an island. Hegel did not, as it is sometimes loosely said, deny the principle of identity and contradiction. He carefully accepted the principle of simple identity, but went beyond it.

It is the task of Reason in the form of philosophy, then, to relate the individual and partial to the totality within which it exists. In so doing philosophy allows one to see the enlarged meaning of the individual and the partial as they function within the totality of all that is. Everything will be seen to be related to everything else in an interdependent structured totality. It will be necessary of course, to redefine the individual in terms of its relations within the totality, for Reason recognizes what the faculty of analysis cannot: that beyond the identity of an individual with itself (A is A) there is a legitimate and fundamental sense in which the individual's identity is contributory to and constituted by all else. Because Reason recognizes in what sense A is not A, only through Reason as the search for totality can the full meaning of the individual and partial be established and articulated.

To recapitulate this first part: There are two modes of totality. The first is the totality of structure, in which human consciousness is seen to be both conditioned and unconditioned, finite and infinite. The second is the totality of expectation, in which Reason searches out the inner connections in knowledge in order to form a systematic totality of meaning and truth. In the dynamic of Hegel's philosophy that consciousness as an implicit and undeveloped totality (the first mode) sets out through

Reason to trace and establish its own fulfillment (the second mode). In that adventure, Spirit finds its own more complete identity by a process in which it tests itself, hides from itself, and passes over into forms seemingly alien to it: first into nature and organic life, then into sensual forms of consciousness, until at the last it comes to recognize itself in all that appears foreign to it. Finally, it comes to its own fullest self-comprehension, which at the same time is a comprehension of all that is. As the faculty of totality moved by the objective of cosmos unity (Weltbegriff), Reason runs through all negation and difference and exploits all possibilities of opposition, alienation, and harmony, until at last it sees itself as identical with the systematic and structured totality of meaning, truth, and reality.

It is a notoriously ambitious enterprise and one which we are free to reject, but if we do, Hegel will accuse us of leaving the many destitute of the one. Of course, we may think them better so left, though in reply he might charge us with holding either a merely formal and empty idea of the total unity of meaning, or an ill-digested conglomerate of interesting bits of knowledge, or both. He would point out that these empty schemes and ununified. aggregates are the products of the faculty of analysis and that it is the enterprise of speculative thought to seek to comprehand through the faculty of totality the systematic and meaningful unity of all that is.

RELIGIOUS CONSCIOUSNESS

Having broken through the Kantian restriction of knowledge to the finite and recovered the sense of the unconditioned, Hegel must set forth the positive role of the unconditioned and show that it is no longer simply unknowable. It is at this point in the Hegelian enterprise that religion plays an absolutely decisive role by providing the key to the positive power of the infinite in the development of the totality which is consciousness. The aim of speculative thought is to reconcile finite and infinite and all other differences in a completed unity. In its many forms religion is an anticipation of that reconciliation. In its myths and dogmas, its sacrifices and sacraments, and its cults and rites, human consciousness opens out upon the whole of existence. In so doing, speculative thought transgresses the boundaries of life, gathering up both life and death, both time and eternity, and both self and other into one complete whole. Religion is the existential traffic between finite and infinite, and anticipates that final reconciliation which can be fulfilled only by Reason in the philosophical form of speculative thought. Within the Hegelian enterprise, then, the philosophy of religion must interpret the history and nature of the traffic between finite and infinite, and assign the various religions their part in developing that traffic.

Hegel recognizes this crucial role, for in the opening pages of the Berlin lectures he places religion at the very centre of the human spirit.[10] All the essential moments of spirit are to be found in religious consciousness in which the absolute is acknowledged and the finite is overcome and reconciled to the infinite. Indeed, only a completely developed religious consciousness anticipates the truth of speculative thought at its fullest, just as speculative religious consciousness comes even earlier to see that man and God are not absolutely different.[11] Indeed, the myth seems to be a proper vehicle of religious meaning just because it involves man and god *(coincidentia oppositorum)* and thus has the form of reconciliation. For Hegel, though sacrifice, prayer and cult also transgress the separation of finite and infinite by establishing concourse with the divine, it is the special task of the philosophy of religion to show the original unity, the separation, and the reconciliation of finite and infinite, conditioned and unconditioned. In this general presentation we will suggest this process with three moments of religious consciousness: religious feeling, religious representation, and religious cult.[12]

The Drive Inward: Religious Feeling

It is readily agreed today that religion includes a factor of interiority, subjectivity, and intimate feeling. According to Hegel religious consciousness thrusts towards a deeper sense of inwardness; in religion the infinite penetrates the sphere of subjectivity, of the "heart and mind."[13] However, for Hegel such a feeling is never purely subjective. In its minimal form it is neither subjective nor objective, though potentially it is both. Minimally it is an immediate unity of consciousness in which, in living *in* my pain, *in* my joy, *in* my fear, *in* my awe, I am just that particular sensuous vibration.[14] This immediate unity of feeling foreshadows the final and developed unity, though only in the most imperfect manner. Because the ultimate unity is one of reconciliation, it presupposes the breaking of the original and and almost fetal unity.

Moreover, according to Hegel, this initial feeling is not sufficiently inward, but lies like shallow water on the surface of conscious life. Not surprisingly, its superficiality is attended by purely external relationships with the divine, one of which is magic. Most scholars today would disagree with Hegel's location of magic at the threshold of religious consciousness as "the absolutely primary form of religion."[15] Even Malinowski,[16] however, would surely agree with Hegel's description of the essential features of magic as lacking a sense of inwardness, laying hands upon the sacred powers, and even cursing them when they are ineffective. Above all magic presupposes a superficial confidence in the harmony of man and the sacred powers, either forgetting or being unaware of man's separability from the sacred. Hence, for the development of a sense of inwardness one must look away from magic and towards ethics.

Hegel finds a quickened cultivation of interiority in the thousand years preceding the Christian era. During that period the major civilizations underwent a radical redefinition of the relation between man and the sacred, incorporating a new ethical consciousness within religion. For Hegel this redefinition was paramount because it released new possibilities of inwardness. He details the progressive freeing of religious consciousness for an inward relation to the divine. His obvious preference for Christianity in these speculations may ultimately offend many adherents of the Hindu, Buddhist, and other religions. Nevertheless, his failure to appreciate the unique riches of these religions should not argue against his chief point, namely, that taken together these religions upgraded religious consciousness insofar as they recognized within themselves the ethical imperative. As the sacred manifested itself less in natural and more in personal terms, the means of communication with it became less purely ritualistic and demanded an interior ethical concern.

It is notorious that Hegel seems to all but neglect the prophetic tradition in his discussion of the religion of Israel. This defect is caused by his desire to emphasize the transcendence of the Lord and of Israel's supposedly passive submission before the Mighty One. Nevertheless, he sees in the religion of Israel the recognition that man is the sphere of God's action: making spirit manifest in the world requires man's right action. Because by its nature religion aims at all the possibilities of Reason, it demands not simply action but righteous action. In the Greek religion man was asked to accept the infinite as Fate, but in Israel he is asked to accept it as law. In Israel, then, "morality thus characterizes itself as holiness."[17]

Today anticipations of this ethical concern are recognized in the Egyptian *Book of the Dead*. Hegel remarked that in the later Egyptian religion the God Osiris suffered death while man gained immortality.[18] What interests Hegel here is that this exchange brought God and man closer together. We know, too, that the sense of inwardness is found in the Babylonian penitential psalms, the Vedic polytheism, and in a more pronounced way in Zoroaster. Hegel, however, reserves for Christianity the highest and most intense form of inwardness. This is most deeply felt, he says, in the Protestant-Lutheran profound sense of sinfulness in which the individual stands over against the God of Justification, conscious of his total inner depravity.[19]

The Drive Outward and Upward: Religious Representation

The deepening of inwardness and of alienation from the sacred is accompanied by an opposite movement of human consciousness. This movement is outward and upward from finite subjectivity toward ever larger spheres of otherness; it is the

movement of religious consciousness out into the world and beyond it. Hegel sees this begin with perceptual consciousness in
which I do not simply live in my fear, awe, or joy, but also stand
before or over against the object which is fearful, awesome, and
joyful. The other appears "at a distance"; it is not my own, but
is outside myself and objective.[20]

The process of objectification finds its special religious form
in the religious representation *(die Vorstellung)*. This representation may be associated with myth, statue, dance, or other
symbol.[21] Though it is sensuous, it is not merely particular for in
the religious representation the sensuous image is "lifted to the
form of universality."[22] In this way a fundamental meaning is
held fast before the mind. Thus, in the representation of the Fall
it is the separation of man from God that is transparent, and a
host of particular sensuous details simply do not signify any
important meaning. Moreover, even the central idea is left unanalyzed; its elements—God, man, woman, tempter, exile, and
punishment—remain independent of one another and without
necessary relations.[23] It is the task of speculative thought to
exhibit the relationships as necessary ones within a systematic
unity.

Hegel especially emphasizes that the product of such an
effort to objectify reveals within itself the "essential moral
[and religious] forces which have been at work" in the struggle
for objective realization.[24] Religious belief, then, is the entry of
consciousness into the representation and living out of the
spiritual forces it exhibits.

The movement of religious objectification is drawn out by
the factor of transcendence within religious experience. Hegel
notices that in the early stages of religious consciousness, just
as there is no deep sense of inwardness, there is no developed
sense of transcendence. Neither God nor man have yet come
out of the general harmony with the natural world. Here again
one observes the familiar Hegelian pattern of interpretation at
the beginning of which there is an inherent and undeveloped
totality which only implicitly contains immanent and transcendent factors.

Against Hegel one might appeal to later studies which indicate that the transcendent sky-gods, which are remote, largely ineffectual, and generally benevolent, may be as ancient as any sacred powers.[25] It has been suggested that only in a later period were they crowded into the background as man began to take up more complex relationships with his immediate environs and turned for help to forms of the sacred that were closer to hand. At that point the cultivation of the fields and flocks would have made immanent and particular sacred powers more important.[26] Nevertheless, within his discussion of early religion Hegel has room for transcendent elements which are vague, impersonal cosmic forces, largely ineffectual and abstracted from the concrete world of men and things. For him, transcendence is implicit in religion from the beginning; he considers it part of the structure of religious consciousness itself. The "dread of the supersensuous," he writes, "expressed itself in the earliest times."[27]

Nevertheless, the focusing of the sense of transcendence is considered to have occurred especially in the religion of Israel, where he finds "a general feeling of fear produced by the idea of a Power above me." It is not a "particular fear of any particular thing";[28] indeed, it is deliverance from the fear of anything sensuous. Nor is it so much a feeling of dependence upon some ultimate Fate, as it is a surrender to an absolute self and to His will and righteousness. In Israel, and again in Islam, religious representation falters and religious consciousness passes over into pure imageless thought about God.

Here human consciousness reaches the farthest and loneliest outpost in the recognition of transcendence and otherness. The beginnings of the objectification of the infinite, which were foreshadowed in religious feelings, have now reached far to find the sacred. What first appeared in natural forms and powers and then in human forms, now has gone beyond them in Israel to recognize the total otherness of God from both nature and humanity. Nature becomes depressed to the status of a creature, and man is called to surrender to the will of God. Such a religious fear of God rises in man "when the natural element trembles, [and when] he raises himself above it, . . . renounces it, . . . [and taking] higher ground for himself, . . . passes over to thought."[29] Beyond the possibility of sensuous religious representation, pure imageless religious thought thinks God as the all-powerful and righteous subjectivity; man reaches out in religious fear and faith for that righteousness in order to shape his own spiritual being.

The study of religion in our own century has given emphasis to the feature of transcendence. Rudolf Otto, for example,[30] has argued that religion is primarily neither pious feeling, nor moral duty, nor intellectual dogma. It is an existential encounter in which man is directed outwards in radical fashion towards a distinctive "object." Religious experience is an extraordinary response to a more than ordinary reality which Otto called the Holy and the Numinous. It announces itself to man as a commanding alien presence, an absolute reality and overpowering majesty, a plenitude of power. It is experienced not as something produced by human agents, but as something outside man which commands his attention and calls for his service in a unique and urgent way.

Eliade[31] and others have stressed also the inherent dualism of religious experience exhibited in the distinction of sacred and profane. For theologians such as Karl Barth this dualism is the badge of the authenticity of religion: God is not man.[32] In this dualism of religious representation Hegel does not see the authenticity of religion, but the need of overcoming it. Such a dualism is inherent in the limits of religious representation, resulting from its tie to the sensuous and to the faculty of analysis and difference. Religious representation can depict the coming together of God and man, but it cannot demonstrate their essential oneness of being. The Church councils speak of the divine and the human in the person of Christ, but it is only speculative thought that can show the necessity which the finite and the infinite have for each other. Philosophical Reason can show what each contributes to the other as a moment in the same essential nature and dynamic process.

Though religious representation is limited to an unresolved

dualism, it can further the interpenetration of finite and infinite, human and divine, for it proportions the transcendent sacred to the dimensions of human consciousness and enlarges human consciousness in the experience of the divine. The Greeks, for example, could represent the divine only in the most appropriate and beautiful way they knew, as ideal human beings. Their anthropomorphism was an advance in the self-discovery of spirit, for the Greeks were conscious that both they and the gods shared intelligence and will as the proper marks of a spiritual being. The penetration of finite and infinite is enacted even more clearly in the incarnation, the crucifixion, and the founding of the Church in the unity of the Holy Spirit.[33]

Mediation, Interpenetration and Reconciliation: Religious Cult

Hegel calls man that "being who sets himself in opposition to his immediate nature . . . and reaches a state of separation."[34] Religion in its more developed forms represents this separation as sin, and its rites and sacrifices are intended to help annul this breach between human and divine. Religion demands of a man that he abandon the attitude of an observer and become an actor. Concrete religion requires finite actuality, and cult is the inter-action of God and particular men. In his discussion of cult Hegel plays down such sensuous elements as the sacraments because they are essentially limited and external. Indeed, cult does not bring about a general reconciliation but presupposes it. The function of cult is to bring the individual knowingly into partici-pation in that reconciliation.[35] In place of the sensuous elements, then, Hegel stresses the community of worshippers and locates in the community the full expression of the interaction of divine and human. Like present-day anthropologists he recognizes the functional role of religion within society. However, its primary social significance does not lie in special ends, such as burying the dead, securing the crops, or gaining victories, but in the community's recognition of what constitutes the ultimate relation between man and God. In religion man seeks the sensuous experi-ence of the ultimate meaning of power.

We cannot follow him here as he traces the development of power which is the category by which the finite represents the infinite.[36] Much of what he says accords well with present discussion of *mana* and other religious forms of power. He describes how sacred power recovers more and more of its true nature, that is, of the power which is proper to free consciousness. The fullest cult occurs, he concludes, when God freely gives his grace and when worshippers freely take it in faith. Worship is "the process by which the subject posits [himself] as identical with [his] essential being."[37] Man and God become one; all is in all.

Still, even cult fails to overcome the dualism inherent in religious representation and in religious consciousness as such.[38] This is more obvious in the archaic religions. The dancer receives the god as he puts on the mask, but it remains a mask to be laid down at the end of the dance. Worshippers speak of the presence and absence of the god among them. To be sure, Christians become one in the Holy Spirit as the peak of religious reconciliation. In Protestant Lutheran Christianity, moreover, members of the invisible Church live in a visible secular state with fellow citizens under freely accepted laws. The alienation between finite and infinite, man and god, secular and sacred is thereby cancelled out and overcome.

Nevertheless the reconciliation remains contingent. Only speculative thought can demonstrate that all that has manifested itself is necessary to the fulfillment of the possibilities of the life of Spirit. Philosophy is required in order to transform the contingent reconciliation of all into a necessary unity.

In sum: to the subjective emphasis or interiority, **Hegel** would reply: Yes, but religion is also objectivity; to the anthropological emphasis on social function, Hegel would reply: Yes, but religion primarily serves a transcendent end; and to the phenomenological emphasis on alien transcendence, Hegel would reply: Yes, but religion must pass from its inherent dualism into a reconciliation of thought that is provided by the offices of philosophy and marked by the necessity of thought *(Denken)*.

HEGEL'S PHILOSOPHY OF RELIGION TODAY

It may be useful to distinguish two levels in Hegel's Philosophy of Religion: one is a typology of religion which aims at description, the other is a strategy of religion which aims at interpretation. However, as Hegel seldom steps outside his interpretive role, his typology of particular religions must for the most part be reconstructed.

A typology can be expected to give an accurate description of each religion. Here one must distinguish first between inaccuracies in details and more important errors, though this distinction already introduces interpretive factors. One must also determine, concerning the nature of an inaccuracy, whether it contradicts the typology which later scholarship has more accurately established for a certain religion, whether it is only an omission, or whether it has been included but given too little or too much emphasis?

For such a critical evaluation detailed studies are required. However, I think that today Hegel's typology of religion would find itself open to at least two charges. First, the present increased sense of cultural relativity and the plurality of religions brings into relief his failure to appreciate the degree of inwardness present in such religions as those of Israel, Islam, and Catholic Christianity. Of course, it can be argued that this is a fault of emphasis rather than one of outright contradiction. Second, he draws the line between the essential and inessential in many religions at a different point than would the religious consciousness of the believers. Thus, for example, he gives indifferent values to many particulars which to the believer are of the utmost importance. Though he often recognizes this disparity he deliberately discounts the emotional tone of some religions in favour of their "reasonable" kernel. It would be unfair simply to charge him with allegorizing the sensuous, but it must be admitted that he bears down very hard upon one single element in the sensuous representation. This element he calls the universal significance of the representation. Thus, for example, his Prometheus is placid and progressive compared say, to that of Nietzsche,[39] early dread of the supersensuous is written off as crude,[40] and Medieval veneration of the host is called sheer external objectivism.[14] To the believer, however, these are the very presence of the god.

In Hegel's defence it should be noted that he cautions against attributing states of mind to alien men. We can, he says, no longer live out their experience. Indeed, we can no longer experience the classical Greek dramas as having religious import; we can only understand them to have had it once. Nevertheless, between Hegel's universal element and the religious experience of the believer, at least as described in some typologies, there remains a disturbing non-equivalence.

Turning to Hegel's strategy, we should remember that it is easily misunderstood. It is not a sterile triad of thesis, antithesis, and synthesis. Nor does it depend upon what he calls "unphilosophical platitudes which suggest an idea of contradiction that is entirely valueless."[42] Nor does Hegel rest his case upon a definition of consciousness which serves as a premise for deduction. Instead, the "one idea" which he sees consciousness bringing to everything it investigates, is the idea of completeness.[43]

His strategy is that of uniting all that is felt and thought with all that is. Of course, the mere intention to seek completeness does not give any objective status to his subjective purpose. But Hegel is convinced that, although such a purpose can be seen to arise in human consciousness, it is already found at work in the world. Unlike a separated Cartesian mind, the Hegelian Spirit is not choosy; it claims for itself everything that is in any way meaningful, whether matter, nature, or life. Thus, it is able to recognize its own purposes in the pre-conscious activity, between consciousness and world, which carries human consciousness out into the real world. Once there, it meets a pattern of development which confirms its deepest aspirations. Emil Fackenheim insists that the primary imperative of Hegelian philosophy is *to stay with the world*[44]

The Hegelian method is built up out of the world. It studies a certain religion by searching out in that religion the Gestalt of all elements which are involved in the relation of finite and infinite. This is the typology. It must then show how they are related to one another, and how they realize all the rational possibilities of these elements. In so doing, the strategy consists not simply in relating the elements one to another, but in showing why they must be so related.

Hegel's strategy, however, seeks more than coherence; it also seeks the objectivity of religion. For Hegel, objectivity is not that which is immediately given; nor is it a unanimity of theoretical opinion. Objectivity, for Hegel, results from the process of objectification, and the key to that process is to be found in the necessity of opposition. He defines man as that which sets itself in opposition to its immediate nature.[45] Subjectivity is "the force or energy which is able to endure this contradiction, and to dissolve it within itself.[46] Only consciousness can affirm itself (A is A), deny itself (A is not A), and recover itself (A is both A and not-A).

If one asks: Why must there be opposition, Hegel answers that opposition brings out what is implicit and untested, and exposes and tests it. The Hegelian consciousness is not simply a knowing power; it is spiritual life itself. Its dynamic is desire, and its power is properly will. Now, because the adequate test of will is counter-will, the essential force of opposition is counter-will. Objectification is a process in which force-in-the-form-of-subjectivity encounters force-in-the-form-of-another-subjectivity.

If one asks further: Why must opposition be self-opposition, there lies at the basis of the Hegelian speculative thought the insistence that there is no genuine opposition except self-opposition. I venture to suggest how Hegel came to that view. I do not think that he got it from the merely formal and empty logical possibility of saying A is not-A: nor from the metaphysical possibility of saying Being is Non-being. He got it from his profoundly tragic sense of life. He came to see the demand for self-opposition in the drama of alienation and reconciliation played out in religious consciousness, and especially in Protestant Christianity.

The theme seems to play itself out in his thought in this **way**: If God and creature were from the beginning radically other (i. e., if dualism or pluralism were the initial state), they would be absolutely separate, and there could be no process of separation. Nor could there be one of reconciliation, for this presupposes an original unity. Though Hegel finds a pale reflection of the process in the abstract dogma of the Trinity, the truest paradigm of separation and reconciliation is the painful separation expressed in the concrete by the need for sacrifice, by the Fall of man and by the saving death of God. This is a separation accompanied by infinite sorrow, and the maximum possibility of separation comes about through consciousness in the form of alienation and counter-will, that is, through sin. The final reconciliation of Easter Sunday transforms yet preserves the pain of Good Friday.

The law of consciousness and reality, then, is the law of the opposition of the same with itself. Aristotle had thought that only like can join with like. Hegel thinks that only like can oppose like, and that only the same can deny, prove, and receive back itself. The paradigm of concrete self-separation and self-reconciliation lies at the root of the Hegelian Spirit and its philosophy of religion.

◊

1. J. H. Stirling, **The Secret of Hegel** (rev. ed.; Edinburgh: Oliver and Boyd, 1898), p. xvii.

2. **Ibid.,** p. xviii.

3. See the four critical discussions by the editor, Georg Lasson, in his edition. G. W. F. Hegel, **Vorlesungen über die Philosophie der Religion** (Hamburg: F. Meiner, [1925] 1966), 2 Bde (Hereafter **VPR**). Also A. Chappelle, **Hegel et la religion** (Paris: Editions Universitaires, 1964), Vol. I, appendix II.

4. J. Collins, **History of Modern European Philosophy** (1st ed.; Milwaukee: Bruce, 1954), p. 309. For an excellent study by the same author, see **The Emergence of the Philosophy of Religion** (New Haven, Connecticut: Yale University Press, 1965), which includes a perceptive section on Hegel. Mention might also be made of a general consideration of several recent

German and French books on Hegel's Philosophy of Religion, by H. Kimmerle, "Zu Hegels Religionsphilosophie," **Philosophische Rundschau, XV** (Jan., 1968), 111-35.

5. **Lectures on the History of Philosophy,** trans. E. S. Haldane and Frances H. Simson (New York: Humanities Press, 1955), I, 68.

6. Cf. J. N. Findlay, **Hegel: A Re-examination** (New York: Collier, 1962), p. 42.

7. Cf. E. Fackenheim, **The Religious Dimension in Hegel's Thought** (Bloomington: Indiana University Press, 1968), p. 94. This challenging and controversial book is the most important work on Hegel's treatment of religion to appear in English.

8. Cf. **Lectures on the History of Philosophy,** I, 254.

9. **Kritik der reinen Vernunft,** A839 B867, trans. N. K. Smith (New York: Macmillan, 1950), pp. 657-58.

10. **VPR,** I.1, 1. Cf. G. W. F. Hegel, **Lectures on the Philosophy of Religion, trans.** E. B. Speirs and J. Burdon Sanderson (1895) (New York: Humanities Press, 1968), I, 1-2. (Hereafter **LPR**). (This translation is from the unreliable Marheineke second edition which appeared in 1840 and should not be used independently of **VPR**).

11. **VPR,** I.1, 44. Cf. **LPR,** I, 33. On **coincidentia oppositorum** see **VPR,** I.1, 111; **LPR,** I, 146.

12. This is a considerable simplification. Hegel actually distinguishes **das Gefühl, die Vorstellung,** and **das Denken** (**VPR,** I.1, 68), and introduces distinctions within and between these. He further introduces **der Kultus** as a concretion through action (**VPR, I.1,** 69). Moreover there is no simple equivalence of feeling with inwardness, representation with outwardness and cult with reconciliation. Interiority, objectification, and reconciliation are manifest in many ways. Indeed, Hegel carries on a polemic against subjective religion in his treatment of **das Gefühl.** See Findlay, **op. cit.,** pp. 347-48. Finally, this brief essay cannot suggest the dialectic tension in each moment and stage of development. Still the general structure which follows does present a sweeping view which integrates a great mass of historical phenomena in the Hegelian manner.

13. Hegel, **Lectures on the History of Philosophy,** I, 70-73.

14. Cf. **VPR,** I.1, 99. Also **LPR,** I, 126-27.

15. **VPR,** I.2, 78; **LPR,** I, 290.

16. Bronislaw Malinowski, **Magic, Science and Religion** (Garden City: Doubleday and Company, Inc., 1954), p. 88 ff.

17. **VPR,** II.1, 57; **LPR,** II, 171. For textual basis see **VPR,** II.1, 250.

18. **VPR,** I.2, 213-20. Cf. **LPR,** II, 99 ff.

19. Hegel, **The Philosophy of History,** trans. J. Sibree (New York: Dover Publishers, 1956), p. 412 ff.

20. **VPR,** I.2, 98-99. Cf. **LPR,** I, 126-27. Of course, this structure of representation has subjective factors.

21. **VPR,** I.1, 67.

22. **VPR,** I.1, 114-15; **LPR,** I, 142 ff.

23. Cf. **VPR,** I.1, 117. Also **LPR,** I, 147-48.

24. **VPR,** I.1, 112; **LPR,** I, 147.

25. For example, E. O. James, **Prehistoric Religion** (New York: Barnes and Noble Inc., 1957).

26. G. R. Levy, **Religious Conceptions of the Stone Age** (New York: Harper and Row, 1963).

27. **VPR,** I.1, 261; **LPR,** I, 223.

28. **LPR,** II, 207; **VPR,** II.3, 94.

29. **LPR,** I, 2̄90; **VPR,** I.2, 65.

30. R. Otto, **The Idea of the Holy,** trans. J. W. Harvey (London: Oxford University Press, 1950).

31. Mircea Eliade, **The Sacred and the Profane** (New York: Harper and Brothers, 1961).

32. Of course, Hegel firmly insists that "there cannot be a Divine Spirit and a human which are absolutely different" [**LPR,** I, 33; **VPR,** I.1, 43]. But he also avoids the trap into which Barth feared the neo-Hegelians had stumbled. Religion, Hegel says, "is not a discovery of man but a work of divine operation and creation in him." [**Ibid.,** VPR, I.1, 44].

33. Cf. **VPR,** II.3, 144-46; **LPR,** II, 254-55.

34. **VPR,** II.4, 114; **LPR,** III, 47. This separation may be implicit in less developed forms of religion. See **VPR,** I. 1, 265; **LPR,** I, 231.

35. **VPR,** I.1, 227; **LPR,** I, 210-11.

36. But see such passages as **VPR,** I.2, 150, 187 ff., especially 204, 225; II.3, 15, 65, 107 and elsewhere; or **LPR,** II, 12, 68 ff., 91 ff., 112-13, 133, 182, 220 and elsewhere.

37. **LPR,** I, 70; cf. **VPR,** I.1, 67 and 69.

38. See Fackenheim, **op cit.,** 189 n.

39. **VPR,** II.3, 131-32; **LPR,** II, 236-37.

40. **VPR,** I.1, 261; **LPR,** I, 223.

41. **VPR,** II.4, 210; cf. **LPR,** III, 133.

42. **VPR,** II.4, 184; **LPR,** III, 111.

43. Hegel, **Lectures on the Philosophy of History,** Introduction.

44. **Op. cit.,** 238

45. **VPR,** II.4, 114-15; **LPR,** III, 46-47.

46. **VPR,** I.2, 203; **LPR,** II, 86-87.

Friedrich Nietzsche and the Notion of God

◇

Wilfrid Desan

THE GROWTH OF A MIND

The Student

WITH PRACTICAL certainty it can be said that up to the age of seventeen or so Nietzsche, the son of a Lutheran minister and a devoutly religious mother, was a believing Lutheran. His father died in 1849 when young Friedrich was barely five years old. The son was a brilliant student and in 1858 was offered a scholarship by the very select gymnasium of Pforta. The young scholar, being only fourteen years old, left his family with great reluctance. Nevertheless, this departure set him free from the many women who surrounded him—his mother, his aunt, his sister—and placed him in more rugged surroundings.

At the gymnasium his study and private readings covered the great classics of ancient and modern times. He read Holderlin. Rousseau and Victor Hugo. Goethe fascinated him, and it may well be that Faust was already paving the way to the future idea of the Superman. Nietzsche's unlimited admiration for the Greeks, destined to last forever, dated from this period. He met for the first time the heroes of Shakespeare. "Our times no longer know men of that force," he wrote to the female household he had left behind.

In his theological studies Nietzsche, like many young men of his times, came more and more under the influence of the new

Biblical exegesis, such as that found in Strauss' *Das Leben Jesu*[1] (1835). According to Strauss, Christianity found its origins in the mythologization of the historical Christ. Jesus was real enough, but the expectation of the Messiah in the heart of a segment of the Jewish population endowed him with a role which was not his; he "became" the Messiah and Son of God. Strauss was merely placing in a biblical context one of the most fundamental ideas of Hegel's *Phenomenology of Mind;*[2] that is, that the structure of human consciousness is marked by a fundamental split between the finite and the infinite. Hegel maintained that the Jews of the Old Testament suffered from this dichotomy more than the Greeks. For centuries the Jew projected this awareness of the infinite *inside* himself into the concept of an Infinite Deity *outside* himself. It was only natural that at a certain moment in history this yearning for the absent God would become embodied in a concrete individual, who was both God and man, Jesus Christ, the God-man.

Yet this incarnation, which resulted in the Christianity that for centuries was the cult of the Western world, had in turn become obsolete. Reason had replaced it and become the new absolute: man finds in his own consciousness the ultimate explanation of the universe. His own reason not only explains, but also contains absolute knowledge. In the depth of his thought man is himself a God. He has become self-sufficient.

Under the influence of Hegel, in 1841 Feuerbach wrote his famous *The Essence of Christianity*.[3] This was in fact nothing but a more concrete application of Hegel's analysis of the unhappy consciousness to the Christian religion. According to Feuerbach, man is his own God: *Homo homini Deus*. This formulation in itself betrays his concern with religion, albeit in a negative way. Indeed, the younger Feuerbach still showed some interest in what may be called spiritual values, as opposed to the exclusive acceptance of political and economic realities. Later, however, he became thoroughly materialistic in his convictions.

Coming after Feuerbach, Marx dropped all reliance upon the spiritual dimension. He bothered to be an atheist only because the myth of the deity was considered to be an obstacle to the rehabilitation of the poor and an impediment to complete happiness by stressing the joy of the beyond and diverting attention from the suffering here on earth. Man was to be made free from all alienations. Religion concerned Marx only as one of these alienations, even though not necessarily the most important.

It was this atmosphere of scepticism and atheism that engulfed Friedrich Nietzsche in his student years. By the time he had finished his doctoral studies at the University of Leipzig, he had abandoned all formal belief in God. Nietzsche's masters were now and for years would be the Greek playwrights, Schopenhauer and Wagner. He would ultimately break off with both Schopenhauer and Wagner, but his soul and mind would be marked forever by their presence.

In *The World as Will and Idea*[4] (1818) Schopenhauer attempts to show that it is the Will that is the thing-in-itself, the inner content, the essence of the world, while life and the visible world are only a dim mirror of the Will. Individual perfection consists in the suppression of this Will within oneself through detachment and ascetical emptiness. Each individual must realize that he is only a moment in the fleeting stream of the universal Will. Nietzsche absorbed much of this vision of Schopenhauer, although in later years he took a more optimistic view of the deeper process called Will and glorified its embodiment within the individual man. With all its differences, Schopenhauer's World as Will was a definite milestone along the road to Nietzsche's Will to Power.

The Professor's Crystalization

In February, 1869, Nietzsche was appointed Professor of Classics at the University of Basel, and a few months later first met the man who was destined to have an immense influence upon him. On May 15, 1869, he was invited by Wagner to his country home on the Island of Tribschen, in the neighborhood of Luzern. Of this visit he wrote: "I have met a human being who better than anyone has revealed to me Schopenhauer's definition of the genius and who is totally penetrated by a wonderful interior vision."[5] Under the force of an inspiration that was at once grandiose and pagan, Wagner created giants for his operas who were heroes of self-renunciation and of death. Nietzsche admired the great composer as the creator of these supermen. However, Wagner, under the influence of his wife, Cosima, returned in his later life to a more Christian view. At this point, Nietzsche made a complete and painful break with his best friend.

During the Franco-German War of 1870, Nietzsche interrupted his teaching to become a nurse in the German Army. War did not deflect him from his train of thought, although the idea of God and religion did tempt him for a moment as a solution to the problem of suffering. He rejected energetically: Either we die from that religion or that religion dies on us. I believe in the old germanic word: All gods must die. *(Entweder sterben wir an dieser Religion oder die Religion an us. Ich glaube an das urgermanische Wort: alle Gotter mussen sterben.)*[6] What matters is to have the courage to live without God, like the Greeks, who faced their destiny without faltering or flinching. The Greeks had no theodicies, nor did they need one. Their gods had not created the world and were therefore not responsible for it or for any of the problems of life. They were merely a diversion, a mythology created by artists and esthetes to cover tragedy with a mask of beauty and thereby make it bearable.

For all their qualities, the Greeks were not incapable of corruption. The original concept of tragedy as exemplified in Eschylus included both Dionysian and Appolonian elements—the power of instinct and the clarity and precision of knowledge. This balance gradually was lost, chiefly under the influence of Socrates, whose rationalism worked toward an increase of the Appollonian element or complete intelligibility. It would be the privilege of the Germans, chiefly through the contribution of Wagner, to restore the Dionysian-Appolonian balance and thereby to reconstruct the ideal form of artistic achievement. These ideas were worked out by Nietzsche in a brochure appearing in 1871 under the title *The Birth of Tragedy*.[7]

The Positivist and the Philosopher

From 1873 until approximately 1880, Nietzsche's thought followed a trend of thought which has been called positivistic. He became the philosopher with the hammer, destructive and nihilistic at every point, admitting nothing but the findings of the natural sciences. In a crude and passionate way he rejected as obsolete values he had formerly accepted, such as those of art and the sentiments. His anti-religious attitude became more virulent. Both Schopenhauer and Wagner were considered too Christian and too metaphysical, for Nietzsche found nothing in metaphysics but a glorification of the spiritual and the religious. His growing antagonism toward Wagner, whom he considered to be decadent, dates from this period. It was also at this time that Nietzsche began to envolve the concept of the Superman, who he believed would some day surpass the average man, the "sick animal" of his day. This second phase of Nietzsche's evolution, beginning with the publication in 1875 of *Thoughts Out of Season*[9] and ending with *The Dawn Of Day*[8] in 1881, might best be summed up as a period of intellectualistic positivism.

Nietzsche's third and final phase deserves more detailed attention, for it is here that he appears at his greatest. This period, which starts with the publication of *The Gay Science*, (Joyful Wisdom)[10] in 1882 and ends with the author's insanity in 1888, was his most fertile and most profoundly original. It was the time of his works: *So Spake Zarathustra*[11] (1883-85), *Beyond Good and Evil*[12] (1886), *The Genealogy of Morals*[13] (1887), and *The Will to Power*,[14] which came out only after his death (1910-1911).

THE DEATH OF GOD

The Self and the Death of God

Concerning the genesis of the ideas contained in Zarathustra, Nietzsche made the following comment in his *Ecce Homo:*

"I would like to tell you the history of my Zarathustra. Its fundamental conception, the idea of *Eternal Recurrence*, the highest formula of affirmation that can ever be attained, belongs to August, 1881. I made a hasty note of it on a sheet of paper, with the postscript 'Six thousand feet beyond man and time.' That day I was walking through the woods beside Lake Silvaplana; I halted not far from Surlei, beside a huge, towering, pyramidal rock. It was there that the idea came to me."[15]

The idea was not so new as Nietzsche believed; it was a familiar theme to Brahmanism, Buddhism, and certain Greek philosophers, such as Heraclitus. Nietzsche was to make it peculiarly his own, however, for the question of "eternal return" is closely related to his atheistic position. The "eternal return" in his view is the return of the Self no less than the return of anything else. This emphasis upon the Self becomes the cornerstone of his philosophy. Man as center of a universe eliminates God as maker: the "eternal return" of the Self cancels the necessity of divine intervention, which at a certain moment in time through the act of creation sets the world going.

This was not yet the full *Zarathustra*. More ideas would emerge during Nietzsche's solitary walks along the Italian Rivieria.

"In the afternoon, whenever my health permitted, I would walk around the whole bay from Santa Margherita to beyond Portofino. This spot and the country around it is the more firmly enshrined in my affections because it was so dearly loved by the Emperor Frederick III. In the fall of 1886 I happened to be there again when he was revisiting this small forgotten world of happiness for the last time. It was on these two roads that all *Zarathustra* and particularly Zarathustra himself as a type, came to me—perhaps I should rather say—invaded me."[16]

Zarathustra is the atheist par excellence. Although at times the presentation is rhetorical and even confused, the message comes through clearly: God is dead. "When Zarathustra was alone, however, he said to his heart: Could it be possible! This old saint in the forest hath not yet heard of it, that God is dead.[17] The "death of God" has become the fame of Nietzsche. Although many influences have affected Western man in his belief or unbelief in God, Nietzsche has certainly been one of the supreme prophets of atheism. His "God is dead" formula constitutes the most succinct expression of a new spirit, the summation of much that is found in modern writing.

As we have seen, the famous quotation occurs in a dialogue of Zarathustra with the Saint. The Saint is an old man living in the forest, away from reality and from the happenings in the modern world. His happiness consists in praising God, but it is based upon ignorance. He is unaware that the men of his times have abandoned all belief in the deity and are no longer concerned with the praise of what does not exist. Although the Saint is no doubt innocent and even attracts Nietzsche's sympathy, he is nonetheless ignorant and like other men must be awakened by Zarathustra to that which is.

Furthermore, the message must be transmitted clearly: it is mankind who is responsible for the death of God, not God who on his own has disappeared from the horizon. The latter would imply that there once had been a God who at present for some strange reason is no longer. This is not what Nietzsche would have us understand. The phrase "God is dead" simply means that the faith in God which was very alive in the past no longer exists. What existed in the past was only faith; its object was always mythical. There is no God now and there never was a God. The killing of God, then, is merely a metaphorical murder; the men of modern times have actually done no more than turn their backs to a myth.

It was not Nietzsche's intent, however, to leave unoccupied the void left in the minds of men by God's departure. In a conversation with Mrs. Overbeck, the wife of his best and, as it will appear later in his life, perhaps his only lasting friend, Nietzsche said:

"There was one thought from which you must never separate yourself and which you carry unconsciously in you; as you are and as I always find you, even in this moment, one sublime thought dominates your life: it is the idea of God. As far as my own position is concerned, I have given it up; I want to create a thought which replaces it, I shall not and I can not go back on my steps."[18]

Man As the Replacement of God

Although he may have acted erroneously, Nietzsche did not act lightly. He was intensely aware of the tremendous importance of his revelation. The death of God was the message, but what a message it was! Already in *The Gay Science* he has alluded to the immense impact of the loss of God:

"I seek God! I seek God! As many of those who do not believe in God were standing around just then, he provoked much laughter. 'Why, did he get lost?' said one. 'Did he lose his way like a child?' said another. 'Or is he hiding?' 'Is he afraid of us?' 'Has he gone on a voyage? or emigrated?' Thus they yelled and laughed. The madman jumped into their midst and pierced them with his glances. 'Whither is God?' he cried. 'I shall tell you. We have killed him—you and I. All of us are his murders. But how have we done this? How were we able to drink up the sea? What did we do when we unchained this earth from its sun? Whither is it moving now? Whither are we moving now? Away from all suns? Are we not plunging continually? Backward, sideward, forward, in all directions? Is there any up or down left? Are we not straying as through an infinite nothing? Do we not feel the breath of empty space? . . . How shall we the murderers of all murderers comfort ourselves?' "[19]

The death of God is not looked upon with unmixed joy. Man should be aware of the sense of loss which the death of God implies, since the absence of God means the absence of any absolute of immortality, of religion and of the supernatural. "I conjure you, my brethren, remain true to the earth, and believe not those who speak unto you of super-earthly hopes! Poisoners are they, whether they know it or not."[20] As we shall see, the supernatural was done with as was the teaching of Christ himself; religion in any form was excluded. Man must be turned to the visible reality; it is on this earth and with the strength he draws from this earth that he must rebuild himself. This reconstruction of man will be the God of the future. "Lo, I teach you the Superman! The Superman is the meaning of the earth. Let your will say: The Superman shall be the meaning of the earth!"[21]

This concept and its multiple implications are now in need of careful examination. Because as we stated above, the replacement of God was man, it appears now that we can be more specific: the replacement of God is the Superman.

SUPERMAN

Inequality

If the god of the future is the Superman, it should be said from the start that the complete understanding of this term has never been made totally clear, even by Nietzsche himself. However, a step toward a fuller grasp of the concept is made with the recognition that the principle of inequality is inseparable from the Superman.

Our study will show that the conflict of Nietzsche with Christianity is not only concerned with the divine existence. It is also profoundly involved with the relation of man with his fellowmen. Nietzsche teaches an attitude toward others which may be called selective and preferential. Actually both trends are linked together for, in Nietzsche's own interpretation, it is precisely in the absence of God that equality must be rejected. This conclusion is not necessary, but it is the one Nietzsche himself favors.

The Sermon on the Mount is a central theme of Christian doctrine. "Blessed are the poor in spirit. Blessed are they that mourn. Blessed are they that suffer persecution for justice' sake, for theirs is the kingdom of heaven."[22] At first sight Christian Ethics appears to be an encomium of suffering. Whether this is always so or whether it has to be so is a question we shall not attempt to answer. In observing Christ himself in the Gospel, one cannot avoid the impression that he favors the suffering. This tendency is manifest in the choice of his parables—the parable of the prodigal son, of the lost sheep, of the Good Samaritan. It appears that love for our fellow men is, in its deepest essence, a love for the suffering. My fellow man is the one who suffers here and now—or so it seems. Why is this? Is this the true meaning of Christian Ethics or is it merely a misunderstood and pseudo-Christianity? The answer seems to be that all men are my fellow men and deserve my love, but that this is more true of the weak, the destitute, the outcasts. Christian charity is all comprehensive, but men must be reminded that is it unchristian to favor a ruthless competition and to curse the weak. Nietzsche does not share that view. He accepts the unequal distribution of talents, but then concludes that only the strong deserve one's attention. This inequality so highly favored by Nietzsche is observed in many of his writings, but most forcefully in three places.

The first of these reads as follows: "Do I advise you to neighbor-love? Rather do I advise you to neighborflight and to love the remotest."[23] The German text has neighborflight *(Nachstenflucht)* and love of the most remote *(Fernstenliebe)*. The meaning of this text seems to be that love should not go to what is near (or to my "neighbor") but to what is remote. However, the "remote" which my love should try to reach is not necessarily a person. Nietzsche's text clearly implies that my love may direct itself also to an idea—or as Nicolai Hartmann reads it—to a Platonic idea.[24] But whether this object of my love be a person, an idea, or better still an ideal, love of the nearest is not to be considered. This attitude draws from Nietzsche only scorn and contempt: "Your neighbor will be always like a poisonous fly."[25] "Love for one's neighbor is a virtue only of petty people."[26]

Our natural reaction to these statements is to raise the question why the remote should be more lovable. One might reverse the Christian trend by answering that the amount of love or preference which should be given to a certain person, object, or idea must be measured upon the amount of health or beauty or intellectual value present, and that this is present in the remote. In fact, Nietzsche's attitude is selective, and the distance is accidental. Love for the remote is merely a metaphor to stress the fact that love has to and should be preferential. Nietzsche is of the opinion that humanity is better served by favoring the strong over the weak. He wants to eliminate and to choose, to prefer and to repel; he wants an elite.

The Higher Man

The second point which deserves our attention covers more than one text; it is actually a whole theme spread over several texts. The theme promotes the idea of the preferential observed above and prepares for the main concept of the Superman. The theme is called *The Higher Man*. Research shows that the Higher Man is nowhere clearly defined. However, several vigorously written passages in *Zarathustra* and in *The Will to Power* show us his stature growing before our eyes.

First of all, it appears that mobility is that which places the Higher Man above the herd. "The tendency of the herd is immobility. It is directed upon conservation and has nothing creative."[27] The Higher Man, on the contrary, is the creator; his creative power is the hallmark of greatness. He has the talent and the courage to impose his world upon the world and to overthrow existing values. "You Higher Men, you long for the dangerous life."[28] More dramatically than ever, Nietzsche polishes his prose to describe the man of his dreams. "We the homeless from the outset *(wir Heimatlosen)*, we have absolutely no choice, we must be conquerors and explorers; with the hope that what we are missing, our descendants will perhaps inherit,—that we may leave them a home *(eine Heimat)*."[29] Ultimately the Higher Man must be the leader of the world. He has the power to resist resignation and other humble virtues preached by Christ.

The whole argument comes close to Marx's rejection of religion as opium, except that Marxism is a gospel for the masses, whereas the message of Zarathustra is a gospel for the masters of tomorrow, the higher men. With the death of God equality is gone, and the prohibition against growing to the utmost is no longer there. One need not live for one's neighbor, one can live for one self. It is evident that we are approaching the definition of the superman here. Indeed, at times the distinction between Superman and Higher Man disappears.

The Higher Man, Nietzsche claims elsewhere, is an "addition." This does not mean that he is a sum total, but rather that he is the result of the multiple experiences lived by himself and by others, now condensed into one person called The Higher Man. He is complex; there is no simple way to define him. In the *Nachlass* Nietzsche makes an attempt:

> "A splendid intellect is the result of several beautiful qualities, e.g., courage, energy, equity, seriousness in action—but it also contains a 'polutropeia,' a certain disarrangement, experience in paradoxes, (even) mischief, temerity, naughtiness, unruliness. In order that a splendid intellect be made, the ancestors of a person must have been in a prominent way both good and bad, spiritual and sensual."[30]

With all this, one may expect that the Higher Men will be few in number. It had been the dream of Greek philosophy to reduce the ultimate understanding of the world and of men to a few principles, imitating the Greek sculptors who were forever looking for a few specimens of perfect bodies. Similarly, the technique of producing higher men also has as its goal the making of only a few, but those few in every way perfect. Between those few and the lower strata there must be no bridge, only the wide abyss *(chasma magnum)*.

The Higher Man is both destiny and agony. In determining the values of a coming world, he is the one who gives meaning to the future. Nevertheless, and this is where the tragic enters, he is also under incessant menace. This menace is the mediocre man, who cannot tolerate anything above himself and incessantly tries to pull superior talent down to his own level. Hence the cry of help of the Higher Man, or as the German text has it, cry of distress *(Notschrei)*.[31]

Surprisingly enough, in other places, Nietzsche calls the Higher Man "cold, clear, farseeing and solitary," and excludes from the category martyrs, heroes, geniuses and fanatics, for their lack of coolheadedness. The Higher Man is cool, patient and slow. Obviously there is room for the diverse, yet in the *Nachlass* he writes: ". . . As a whole the destiny of the Higher Man in the present, the way in which they seem condemned to extermination, this comes to Zarathustra as a great cry of distress." This is not irony but sadness, although irony may be combined with it. The same wry humor may very well be present in Part IV of *Zarathustra*.

Ubermensch

Although we are discussing the concept of the Superman separately from that of the Higher Man, it cannot be denied that at times the terms overlap. In all other cases the Higher Man must be considered as a phase preliminary to the realization of the Superman. In *The Will to Power* Nietzsche makes the equation himself: "The Higher Man is the one who 'overcomes' man."[32] The meaning of this "overcoming" has often been misunderstood. Kaufmann has attempted to clarify the meaning of the Superman. First of all, he considers it a mistake to understand Superman as merely a biological sequel to the present-day man, even though a text in *Zarathustra* appears to favor this interpretation: "Man is a rope between animal and superman."[33] In the *Ecce Homo*, however, Nietzsche insists that a biological interpretation can only be made by "learned cattle."[34] According to Kaufmann, the *Ubermensch* is correctly understood as the one who "overcomes" himself and his mediocrity, his impulses and lower desires.[35] There is even an ascetical trend in this approach, however suprising this may seem, for the term *Ubermensch* designates the highest degree of perfection.[36] At times candidates for the title, such as Napoleon, Caesar, and Goethe, appear in Nietzsche's writings. However, in the final analysis there are as yet no *Ubermenschen*. "There has never yet been an *Ubermench*" *(Niemals noch hat es einen Ubermensch)*.[37]

If he is not yet here, the Superman is intensely hoped for and is expected in some future time. Though he is beyond the present, he is nonetheless not beyond the natural order; there is no supernatural domain. The *Ubermensch* is godless, for he is himself the god of tomorrow. "God died, now we want the Superman to live."[38] "There was a time that one said God, when looking over distant seas; at present I have taught you to say: *Ubermensch*."[39] We have already seen that the idea of the *Ubermensch* must be brought into relation with the death of God. When God is gone, man is free to develop himself into greatness.

It follows from the foregoing that this man-made-god becomes the creator of all values as well. Nietzsche has called himself the philosopher with the hammer. The same qualification fits the Superman, for he is also entitled to overthrow all existing values. "The Higher Man is both non-man and Superman" *(Der Hoheremansch ist der Unmensch und Ubermensch)*.[40] The same principle which guided man to grow above the animals will also be used to bring forth the Highest Man: power, shrewdness, patience, planning strength, the emotions of the warrior."[41] Immorality—in the traditional sense of the word—becomes a means because the *Ubermensch* can truly be said to be beyond good and evil. He is the new god, a result of neither incarnation nor sublimation; he is simply man "overcome."

THE WILL TO POWER

Atheism or Pantheism

Nietzsche rarely uses the term inequality but he frequently does use the word *Rangordnung*. *Rangordnung* can be translated by the word *precedence,* or perhaps by the word hierarchy. The egalitarian trend is for Nietzsche suicidal:

> "There is one strong movement: the levelling of men, the huge antsnests, etc.; there is another movement, my movement: it is the sharpening of all contrast, the widening of all gaps (and cliffs), the removal of all equality, and the creation of the all-powerful man. The former movement breeds the inferior man, my movement the *ubermensch.*"[42]

According to Nietzsche, the "rangordnung" is always there. Even when we are not aware of it, we act and think according to our rank.

Nietzsche's doctrine in inequality poses itself against two worlds, that of the Crucified and that of nineteenth century egalitarianism. Both are exorcized in one global condemnation, since, according to Nietzsche, Christ is the instigator of present day egalitarianism. In order to overcome this moral decline of the Western world, Nietzsche insists that we must return to the Greeks who had a clear grasp of the unequal. "We must overcome the Christian in us, become step for step more 'spacious,' supranational, European, supraEuropean, Mediterranean, finally Greek-overcome the Christian."[43]

In the last pages of *The Will to Power,* the opposition between Christ and Nietzsche is forcefully presented. Nietzsche identifies himself with Dionysus. This term, from the old Greek deity Dionysus, god of Instinct and force of Life and Passion, has already been mentioned as part of the famous Dionysian-Apollonian antithesis. According to Nietzsche, the core of all esthetic productivity lies in the synthesis of the Dionysian principle which represents the power of Life and the Apollonian principle which represents the elements of clarity and intelligibility. In *The Birth of Tragedy,* Nietzsche stressed the importance of both. In later years, however, Nietzsche gives more and more of his attention and admiration to the Dionysian, although he does not abandon the Apollonian element. At first Dionysus is merely the obscure, underlying element opposed to

Apollo. When man is ignored, Dionysus becomes the total dimension of a universe that is Power and Life, unrestrained, and boundless. The cosmos is Dionysus; it is as whole Will to Power.

Having reached this conclusion, we naturally wonder whether this concept of Will to Power could not be considered to be Nietzsche's deity as well. Before attempting to answer this question, we must state once more that for Nietzsche the notion of God in the traditional sense of the word as the supranatural entity, Creator of a world and Providence, is totally out of the question. If God is identical with the Will to Power, he can in no way be a transcendent, absolute Being. If deity it is, it must be viewed as an immanent force, which is both one and multiple; identical yet extremely diversified; harmonious yet full of contradictions; eternal yet moving in the cycles of "eternal return." Nietzsche has no intention of calling this force God, for he resents all theological implications. It is Will to Power and Force of Life. There is no dual world, one world of the temporal and another of the eternal; there is only one cosmos with its Power and Mobility of Life within.

Forgetting Nietzsche's own semantics for a moment and looking at his vision merely from the outside, the question arises whether the Christian tradition can claim an exclusivity in defining the deity itself as it does. Modern theology is thoroughly re-examining the traditional understanding of God, as can be seen from other articles published in this volume. It is not our task to consider these different answers. Yet in examining Nietzsche's standpoint of radical "atheism," the Christian who disagrees with Nietzsche should at times re-examine his own position.

The following question merits consideration. The Christian sees atheism as something negative, as the destruction of what is most dear to his heart. The elimination of God is considered to be a negation of his belief. By implication atheism is considered to be merely a negation, hence the privative "a" placed before the epithet "theist." However, the adequacy of this view is not so obvious, for what appears to me to be a negation is not so for the atheist himself. For him, in excluding the supernatural, the world which he accepts is something positively filled, a plenum. A-theism is viewed by the Christian as the view of a world without God. It must be conceded, however, that absence makes sense only when presence is expected. God is absent for me because I expect him to be there. The a-theist does not expect God to be there; hence the world itself is a self-sufficient Power. There is nothing else.

Nietzsche might be prepared to accept a world that with emphatic clarity is what it is all by itself, and conceals no hidden gods distinct and different in nature from the world. Modern terminology might still find room for a Nietzschean pantheism if it were prepared to accept the fact that the Will to Power, which pervades the cosmos and constitutes its force and mobility might be called divine. Such a name would probably not please Nietzsche but it would *de facto* not conflict with his own intentions. I believe this to be as close as one can come to reconciling Nietzsche with any concept of the deity.

In making this final assessment of Nietzsche, it is necessary to place oneself back into his period and to confront the choices which were his: orthodox theism or militant atheism, a transcendent God or no God at all. Let us not forget that Nietzsche was a prophet, the ancestor to the "godless Christians" of our day. The agony of standing alone on a mountain top, seeing a vision that no one else saw, was profound and finally broke the seer. Thanks to such thinkers as Nietzsche himself, a modern Nietzsche does not have to choose between god and man. Given the landscape within which he walked, we can more sympathetically understand the struggles that were his. His vision was not always an easy one to see, his message not always simple to write. It was not without struggle that he left his legacy.

Christianity

If our argument remotely attempted to make Nietzsche a pantheist, it does not make him a Christian. Nietzsche wants to keep the opposition between Dionysus and Christ, and this opposition is violent. While Dionysus stands for the Force of Life, Christ is the weakling—innocent, no doubt, but a weakling nonetheless. In favoring the poor, the weak and the suffering, he symbolizes the condemnation of Life. The Crucified one, mentioned once more in the last publications of Nietzsche, is a curse on life, whereas Dionysus is Life in full force. It is in the name of Dionysus that Christ must be eliminated.

Nietzsche's extreme aphorisms, couched in beautiful prose, have an impact which cannot be ignored. At times, however, they do not withstand close scrutiny. Is Christ really the weaklink that is described?[44] Is he the grand equalizer that Nietzsche accuses him of being? Is Christianity a herd of the feebleminded? Must the talented necessarily crush the less able? The answers to these questions are obvious. Leaving aside the problem of whether Christ is god or man, one can not easily agree that he was either a weakling or an equalizer; his teachings favor sanctity and heroism, which are hardly virtues of the mediocre!

At this point one may well wonder whether Nietzsche's understanding of the Gospel is authentic, for example, whether the Gospel is a book where suffering is loved for its own sake. This paper makes no claim to biblical exegesis, but it is clear to any attentive reader that the teachings of Christ, rather than exalting suffering for their own sake, teach men to make the best use of pain and tribulation. The Gospel, furthermore does not state that all men are equal—that is post French Revolution semantics —but it does insist that for the Christian love must be all-comprehensive. To the question: who is my fellow man? the answer is: everyone, even the outcast, whether he be Samartian or gentile.

The root philosophy here is that God loves everyone and that a way of rendering this love to God is to practice it towards men. The rejected and the weak are not necessarily more lovable. Because of their weakness, however, they are under a greater handicap and thus need more protection than the strong. It is part of the Christian attitude, therefore, to care for the rejected, whether he be near or far away. In Christian ethics, the word "neighbor" has no spatial implication.

One may wonder whether Nietzsche's attitude toward Christianity requires direct refutation. His virulent anti-Christian prose may very well have a different origin. Lou Salome, who for a short while was Nietzsche's friend, wrote a book entitled *Friedrich Nietzsche im seinen Werken*[45] while Nietzsche was still alive but insane. There are longer works and more erudite commentators, yet with feminine perspicacity Lou Salome has seen the conflict in the heart and mind of her friend. She, too, observes that Nietzsche builds up a striking opposition between Dionysus and the Crucified, but in her interpretation this dichotomy has psychological roots. Nietzsche—and to an extent every man—carries within himself a double range of values, the theme of Dionysus and the spirit of the Gospel. Nietzsche's writings reflect that double set of vaules and the combat within. His most violent aphorisms were a revolt against a past of Christian piety which was never entirely subdued. He was both a lover of the Greeks and an admirer of Christ. Thus, Nietzsche's attack against Christianity without must be seen as an attempt to stifle it within.

Such, then, is in brief the view of Lou Salome. No comment on this interpretation seems necessary; it is an hypothesis, nothing more. Yet the following quote is worth mentioning:

"Everything that is profound," wrote Nietzsche in his best prose, "loves the mask: the profoundest things have a hatred even of figure and likeness. Should not the contrary only be the right disguise for the shame of a God to go about in? They are not the worst things of which one is most ashamed: there is not only deceit behind a mask—there is so much goodness in craft." Perhaps Nietzsche too has used "speech for silence" and has "desired and insisted that a mask of himself shall occupy his place in the hearts and minds of his friends."[46]

◇

1. David Friedrich Strauss, **Das Leben Jesu** (Leipzig: A. Kröner, 1924).
2. Georg W. Hegel, **Phenomenology of Mind** (New York: Macmillan, 1931).

3. Ludwig Feuerbach, **The Essence of Christianity** (New York: Harper, 1957).

4. Arthur Schopenhauer, **The World as Will and Idea** (London: K. Paul, Trench, Trubner & Co., 1896).

5. Friedrich Nietzsche, **Briefe, Werke** (Munich: Beck, 1933), II, 347.

6. Friedrich Nietzsche, **Werke** (Leipzig: Kröner, 1910), VII, 3, No. 1.

7. Friedrich Nietzsche, **The Birth of Tragedy** (Garden City, N.Y.: Doubleday, 1956).

8. Friedrich Nietzsche, **Thoughts Out of Season** in **The Complete Works,** ed. Oscar Levy (London: J. Foulis, 1909-1913), Vols. IV and V.

9. Friedrich Nietzsche, **The Dawn of Day** (London: T. F. Unwin, 1903).

10. Friedrich Nietzsche, **Joyful Wisdom** (New York: Ungar, 1960).

11. Friedrich Nietzsche, **So Spake Zarathustra** (Berlin: W. Keiper, 1943).

12. Friedrich Nietzsche, **Beyond Good and Evil** (New York: Vintage, 1966).

13. Friedrich Nietzsche, **The Genealology of Morals** (Garden City, N.Y.: Doubleday, 1956).

14. Friedrich Nietzsche, **The Will to Power** (New York: Random House, 1967).

15. Friedrich Nietzsche, **Ecce Homo** in **The Philosophy of Nietzsche,** trans. Thomas Common (New York: Modern Library, 1937), p. 892.

16. **Ibid.,** p. 894.

17. Friedrich Nietzsche, **Zarathustra,** Prologue in **The Philosophy of Nietzsche,** p. 6.

18. Quoted by J. C. Lannoy in his **De denker Friedrich Nietzsche** (Brugge-Brussel: De Kinkhoren, 1944).

19. Friedrich Nietzsche, **The Gay Science,** 125 The Madman, in **Nietzsche,** ed. and trans. Walter Kaufmann (New York: Viking, 1954), p. 95.

20. Friedrich Nietzsche, **Zarathustra,** Prologue, 3, in **The Philosophy of Nietzsche.**

21. **Ibid.**

22. Matthew, V. 3, 4, 10.

23. Nietzsche, **Zar.,** Part I, On Neighbor-Love.

24. N. Hartmann, **Ethics** (New York: Macmillan, 1932), II, 311.

25. Nietzsche, **Zar.,** Part I, On the Flies of the Market Place.

26. **Ibid.,** Part IV, On the Higher Man.

27. Friedrich Nietzsche, **Gesammelte Werke von Friedrich Nietzsche** (Munich: Musarion, 1920-1929), Vol. XVIII, p. 207.

28. Nietzsche, **Zar.,** Part IV, Science.

29. Nietzsche, **Gesammelte Werke von Friedrich Nietzsche,** Vol. XIV, p. 307. (my translation)

30. **Ibid.,** p. 238.

31. Nietzsche, **Zar.,** Part IV, 2.

32. Nietzsche, **Gesammelte Werke von Friedrich Nietzsche,** Vol. XVIII, p. 308.

33. Nietzsche, **Zar.,** Prologue, 3.

34. Nietzsche, **Ecce Homo,** III, 1, in **The Philosophy of Nietzsche.**

35. Walter Kaufmann, **Nietzsche** (Princeton: Princeton Univ. Press, 1950), p. 274.

36. Nietzsche, **Ecce Homo,** III, 1.

37. Nietzsche, **Gesammelte Werke von Friedrich Nietzsche,** Vol. XIII, p. 118.

38. Nietzsche, **Zar.,** Part IV, On the Higher Man.

39. **Ibid.,** Part II, Concerning the Happy Islands.

40. Nietzsche, **Gesammelte Werke von Friedrich Nietzsche,** Vol. XIX, p. 350. **Unmensch** means the one who is ruthlessly inhuman, unemotional and hard.

41. **Ibid.,** Vol. XIV, p. 189.

42. **Ibid.,** p. 108.

43. Nietzsche, **Gesammelte Werke von Friedrich Nietzsche,** Vol. XIX, **Der Wille zur Macht,** Part IV, No. 1051.

44. Friedrich Nietzsche, **The Antichrist,** 7 in **The Portable Nietzsche,** ed. W. Kaufmann (New York: Viking, 1954).

45. Lou Andreas-Salome, **Friedrich Nietzsche in seinen Werken** (Wien: C. Konegen, 1894).

46. Friedrich Nietzsche, **Beyond Good and Evil,** n. 40, in **The Philosophy of Nietzsche.**

Marxism and Religion[*]

◊

Louis Dupré

MARX'S NEGATIVE attitude toward religion was not based upon speculative arguments for the non-existence of God. His reason for rejecting religion was its incompatibility with his theory of action. For this reason the "scientific" speculative atheism advocated in the Soviet Union and stemming from Engels, Lenin and Stalin, basically conflicts with Marx's philosophy even though Marx is indirectly responsible for it.

MARX AND FEUERBACH: RELIGION AS ALIENATION

Marx had inherited a speculative atheism from Feuerbach, and was an atheist long before he developed his theory of action. As his own theories grew, however this atheism underwent such basic changes that the two can no longer be considered to be of the same kind. Feuerbach's atheism is rooted in a speculative theory of man. According to *The Essence of Christianity*,[1] religion expresses man's relation to his own nature, but not to his own nature recognized as such. Since all the predicates which man ascribes to God are purely human, Feuerbach argues, there is no reason why the subject of these predicates should not be human also. Thus, man is his own God and the God of religion is an extrapolation of man's own powers of striving, thinking, and feeling. Such an extrapolation is inevitable in the earliest stages of the development of consciousness. As long as man is unable

---

[87]

to conceive of human nature, as a reality far transcending its individual realizations, he projects his own infinite powers onto a transcendent being.

Later, unfortunately, when man should know that the human race is not restricted to the powers of single individuals, he nevertheless maintains this projective attitude. Feuerbach attributes man's strange refusal to reappropriate what is his own to an immature desire to share with the entire human species the humiliating restrictions of one's private existence.

> "Man identifies himself immediately with the species—a mistake which is immediately connected with the individual's love of ease, sloth, vanity and egoism. For a limitation which I know to be merely mine humiliates, shames and perturbs me. Hence to free myself from the feeling of shame, from this state of dissatisfaction, I convert the limits of my individuality into the limits of human nature in general."[2]

The notion of alienation in Hegel's philosophy describes the dialectical opposition between the thesis and the antithesis of the dialectical movement. Feuerbach now applies this to the operation by which man estranges part of his own powers and projects them into an external, infinite being. For Feuerbach God is the alienation of man, the self-estrangement preceding the reappropriation of the divine into the human.

The young Marx accepted Feuerbach's view of religion as an alienation of man and never changed his position on that issue. In the *Economic and Philosophical Manuscripts* of 1844 in which Marx develops his own philosophy, he writes: "If I *know* religion as *alienated* human self-consciousness what I know in it as religion is not my self-consciousness but my alienated self-consciousness confirmed in it. Thus my own self, and the self-consciousness which is its essence, is not confirmed in *religion* but in the *abolition* and *supersession* of religion."[3]

Feuerbach, however, had not explained satisfactorily the origin of this alienation. There must be more serious grounds for maintaining man's self-estrangement than sloth and vanity. In an early commentary on Hegel's *Philosophy of the State and of History*,[4] written under the direct influence of Feuerbach, Marx points to the social and economic conditions of modern life as the cause of man's alienation. In fact these conditions are man's true alienation; religion is only its expression. Man takes refuge in the phantasy world of the beyond because he is profoundly frustrated in his earthly existence. The main culprit in maintaining these frustrating conditions is not religion but the political structure which legalizes and protects the social *status quo*. It is, therefore, to the State more than to religion that Feuerbach's theory of alienation applies. "The *political constitution* was, until today, the *religious sphere*, the *cult* of people's life, the heaven of its universality, as opposed to the earthly existence of its reality."[5] Yet, neither State nor religion reveals the roots of alienation; these lie in the economic conditions of a society determined by private property.

Marx illustrates the extent to which religion is subordinated to man's socio-economic conditions in an early article on the Jewish question. His former friend, Bruno Bauer, had proposed the thesis that the Jewish problem could be solved instantly if the Jew would cease to claim religious privileges from the State. By so doing, he maintains the religious State in existence and prevents his own as well as other people's emancipation. The emancipation of man requires a secular State that recognizes neither Christianity nor Judaism. Marx agreed that the existence of religion always indicates an incomplete emancipation, but he denied that religion is the cause of the problem or, for that matter, that political rights are the solution. Bauer simply identified religion with alienation and political equality with emancipation, but political emancipation is by no means human emancipation.

In fact, political emancipation may very well coexist with a thriving religious life. "To be *politically* emancipated from religion is not to be finally and completely emancipated from religion, because political emancipation is not the final and absolute form of *human* emancipation."[6] The situation of the United States offers an interesting illustration of this point. The

American State is entirely separated from the Church and Americans should therefore, according to Bauer's theory, be fully emancipated. Yet, Marx points out, the United States is considered to be the religious country *par excellence*. Far from implying the suppression of religion, political emancipation grants man the right to worship according to the religion of one's choice. Even if the State would suppress religion, its own existence would remain a profane expression of an alienation which in time would irresistibly produce its religious form. Thus, instead of being a remedy against religious alienation, the secular State is the purest symptom of its presence. More than religion, the State keeps alive the inhuman conditions that separate man from his fellow man and thereby prevent mankind from realizing its full potential. If religion means deception, the State is more religious than the Church.

> "The members of the political State are religious because of the dualism between individual life and species-life, between the life of civil society and political life. They are religious in the sense that man treats political life, which is remote from his own individual existence, as if it were his true life: and in the sense that religion is here the spirit of civil society, and expresses the separation and withdrawal of man from man."[7]

RELIGION AS PROTEST

Religion, however, is not merely an expression of alienation; it is also a protest against it. In his "Introduction to a Critique of Hegel's *Philosophy of Right*," written around the same time, Marx uses the famous expression that religion is the opium of the people. Yet, he adds immediately: "The abolition of religion as the illusory happiness of men, is a demand for their real happiness. The call to abandon their illusions about their condition is *the call to abandon* a condition which requires illusions."[8] From this text the French Marxist Roger Garaudy concludes that only the reflective aspect or ideological content of religion is illusory, while its element of protest expresses a profound truth about the human condition. It would be a mistake to describe Marx's view of religion only in terms of alienation, for as an expression of human misery and a protest against it, religion rightly questions the structure of society. Religion is false only in its answers, but it is most true in the questions which it raises.

Garaudy's interpretation is entirely correct, but it neither provides a legitimate basis for the continuance of religion in the Marxist society, nor justifies its present existence. The religious way of questioning man's situation already implies a wrong answer; the right answer cannot be given as long as the protest remains religious. Thus, even as a form of social protest, religion can only slow down the advent of the communist society. The first step toward a solution must be to abandon this way of posing the problem which makes a solution impossible. However, the abandonment of religion is merely a pre-condition and not, as Marx's atheist friends believed, the solution itself. Communism is much more than atheism, even though atheism is a prelimininiary condition for it. "Communism begins where atheism begins, but atheism is at the outset still far from being *communism;* indeed it is still for the most part an abstraction."[9] As long as Marx does not take seriously that content of its cry, it is small comfort to religion that he considers it a true cry of distress. For Marx religion is a symptom of social disease, not an articulate symbol. To expect the symptom to provide a cure would be most unreasonable: instead the symptom will disappear with the disease. Marx's distaste for Feuerbach's atheism originates not in a more open attitude toward religion, but from his conviction that atheism alone is insufficient to cure the ills of the human situation. It attempts to cure the symptoms without eradicating the disease itself, namely, man's social-economic condition in capitalist society. Theism will never be compatible with a free society, yet atheism itself is not sufficient to produce such a society. That religion must be unmasked as a deception is self-evident to Marx; but the more important question is:

What causes man to deceive himself? Neither Feuerbach nor
any other atheist philosopher ever seriously attempted to answer
that question. If they had, "the critique of heaven would have
been transformed into a critique of earth, the critique of law,
the critique of theology into a critique of politics."[10]

COMMUNISM: RELIGION AND PRAXIS

In the Paris *Manuscripts*[11] of 1844 Marx attempts to determine the precise connection between atheism and communism.
He again states that a full reappropriation of what man has
alienated from himself cannot be achieved by a mere annulment
of God, but only by an annulment of the social structure of
private property which produces the need for God. Just as
private property and religion are complementary aspects of the
same alienation, communism and atheism are the two facets of
the same reappropriation.

> "Atheism as the annulment of God is the emergence of
> theoretical humanism, and communism as the annulment of
> private property is the vindication of real human life as
> man's property. The latter is also the emergence of practical
> humanism, for atheism is humanism mediated to itself by
> the annulment of religion, while communism is humanism
> mediated to itself by the annulment of private property.
> Atheism and communism are not flight or abstraction from,
> nor loss of, the objective world which men have created by
> the objectification of their faculties. They are not an im-
> poverished return to unnatural, primitive simplicity. They
> are rather the first real emergence, the genuine actualization
> of man's nature as something real."[12]

Although the reappropriation process has a theoretical aspect, it
ultimately consists in re-establishing the true relationship between man and nature. This relationship is an active one, a
praxis. For Marx, as for the existentialists, to be human is not

to be something but to do something. Work and material production, not leisure and contemplation, constitute man's fulfillment.

It is most incorrect to brand this productive view of man as materialism. In a few remarks jotted down in 1845 and later published by Engels as *Theses on Feuerbach*,[13] Marx clearly rejects materialism as a simplistic reduction of consciousness to nature.

"The chief defect of all materialism up to now (including Feuerbach's) is that the object, reality, that we apprehend through our senses, is understood only in the form of the *object* or *contemplation*; but not as sensuous human *activity*, as *practice*; not subjectively. Hence in opposition to materialism the *active* side was developed abstractly by idealism— which of course does not know real conscious activity as such."[14]

Only the *praxis* holds both poles of the human reality, nature and consciousness, as well as their relationship, simultaneously present. All interpretations of man or of nature which explain either consciousness or nature independently of the active relation to the other term are by that very fact false. In *The German Ideaology*[15] Marx rejects these purely theoretical constructions as "ideologies." Idealist systems in which consciousness is the only active element are obviously ideological, but materialism is equally ideological, for the consideration of nature independently of the human activity in which alone it reveals itself can only give birth to an abstract, mental construction. The only true philosophy is a theory of action, for the truth of man is in what he does, not in what he knows or claims to know independently of his active relation to nature. This is the meaning of Marx's famous dictum: "The philosophers have only *interpreted* the world differently; the point is to change it."[16]

As a speculative philosophy atheism is not based upon *praxis* and therefore pure ideology. It misses the practical origin of all ideas, its own as well as the idea of God. Its entire approach to truth is therefore wrong, even though it accidentally results in correct conclusions. Its mistake lies in the assumption that ideas are independent of the social conditions of action and, consequently, that they can be changed without changing the conditions which produced them.

The recent rediscovery of Marx's anti-materialist attitude and of his final rejections of speculative atheism has aroused new hope of reconciling religion with Marxist pragmatism. Unfortunately, this hope is unjustified. In order to open Marxism to religion it would not be sufficient to prove that Marx was neither a materialist nor a speculative atheist. The very same argument which disposes of speculative systems as atheism and materialism also disposes of religion. The only reliable foundation for theory is *praxis*. A theory that does not have its roots in man's active relation to nature and the social conditions necessitated by this relation lacks the only possible foundation of any theory and is therefore totally unjustified. This is obviously the case for religion, for in religion man claims to transcend nature altogether.

RELIGIOUS NEUTRALITY?

It might be asked, nevertheless, whether the absence of a foundation in *praxis* positively excludes religion? Could one not argue that a consistent Marxist pragmatism ought to adopt a neutral rather than a hostile attitude toward any private beliefs that do not positively counteract the progress of socialist humanism? As this is already the attitude of most socialist parties in Western Europe, why could it not be adopted by communist regimes as well? Individual communists like Roger Garaudy have argued that religion may have some practical justification due to the fact that, as with all ideologies, religion is a "project" and that all action requires some "projecting" in order to transcend the given and to anticipate a new reality.[17]

Interesting as this acceptance of a transcendent dimension

is, it cannot change the Marxist position on religion, for this transcendence must always remain *within* the immanence of human possibilities. Action compels us to project beyond the present, but does not allow us to project beyond the human. Garaudy himself seems to be aware of this, for he writes of the transcendence projected by communism:

"This new frontier of hominisation, making of every man a man, questioning and creative, will mark a new detachment from the earth. The detachment, this time, will be from all the alienations which have been crystallized for thousands of years and have become so thoroughly customary as to seem to us like a *given* nature, like earth itself. It will free the spiritual energies of each man and of all men with such force that it is absolutely impossible . . . to imagine their nature and their use. This future, open to the infinite, is the only transcendence which is known to us as atheists.[18]

This frank and unambiguous statement shows how much the communist has in common with the believer, but it also shows why they can never agree on the basic issue, even after the believer has shed his other-worldiness.

The communist transcendent cannot be God, for, as Garaudy writes, "it is impossible to conceive of a God who is always in process of making himself, in process of being born."[19] The communist transcendent is transcendent with respect to the present rather than the future of man. Any absolute transcendence is out of the question. This is why, from a Marxist point of view, religious belief must always conflict with a truly humanist attitude. Creationist dependence and full human autonomy are incompatible. In the *Manuscripts* Marx writes:

"A being does not regard himself as independent unless he is his own master, and he is only his own master when he owes his existence to himself. A man who lives by the favor of another considers himself a dependent being. But I live completely by another person's favor when I owe to him not only the continuance of my life but also its creation, when he is its source."[20]

The question of creation cannot even arise for Marx, because it conflicts with the *praxis*.

Does such a positive exclusion of an absolute transcendent constitute a return to speculative atheism, and hence to pure ideology? Not really, for the independence of man which Marx asserts is primarily an independence of acting. Atheism, as a denial of supernatural reality is merely a conclusion concerning the independence of man's being implied in his independence of acting. That is the only reason why Marx supports his practical humanism by some atheistic considerations. If it were not for the ontological implication of an autonomous *praxis*, Marx would not even bother to call himself an atheist, for atheism is speculative and negative, while the entire attitude of the communist is practical and positive.

> "Creation conflicts with the choice of autonomy: that is the core of Marx's argument. He does not undertake a metaphysical analysis of the real or a phenomenological description of dependent behavior. His considerations are not true proofs, they rather provide apologetic weapons to support a thesis accepted on a different ground: creation is not possible because it conflicts with the choice of autonomy; that is a postulate."[21]

For Marx the *praxis* is an absolute which admits no further questioning. "How did man and nature originate?" This speculative question is ultimately meaningless because it views as non-existent the very act from which all questions of existence must originate. Though Marx mentions spontaneous generation, this is merely an expression to shrug off the problem. No questions of being can be asked beyond the *praxis*.

Two conclusions follow from the preceding: (1) religious beliefs are totally incompatible with the philosophy of Marx; and (2) the atheism which was the original starting-point of

Marx's philosophy gradually lost its primary importance and was reduced to a mere implication of a theory of the *praxis*. What became primary was an absolute autonomy of the *praxis* which excludes any transcendent principle of acting as well as of being. It is this closed autonomy that gives Marx's philosophy its forceful simplicity. Marx pays a high price for this simplicity, for besides excluding an entire dimension of human experience in which man knows himself as a contingent being, this simplicity unduly restricts *praxis* to a material production process. Space does not permit me to do full justice here to a thesis which I have developed at length in a work on *The Philosophical Foundations of Marxism*.[22] However, even a superficial look shows that Marx's theory of superstructures has unjustifiably narrowed his interpretation of action. For Marx man is autonomous only in his material life process. All cultural values intrinsically and indissolubly depend upon this original process. It is the economic character of *praxis* which led communist theoreticians in the past to interpret Marx in a materialist way. Though this interpretation is unfair, texts such as the following on the origin of ideas show how much responsibility Marx himself bears for the misinterpretation.

"We set out from real, active men, and on the basis of their real life-process we demonstrate the development of the ideological reflexes and echoes of this life-process. The phantoms formed in the human brain are also, necessarily, sublimates of their material life-process, which is empirically verifiable and bound to material premises. Morality, religion, metaphysics, all the rest of ideology and their corresponding forms of consciousness, thus no longer retain the semblance of independence. They have no history, no development; but men developing the material production and their material intercourse alter, along with this their real existence, their thinking and the products of their thinking."[23]

All claims of independence are "ideological" mystifications and embellishments of social conditions that need idealization. Consciousness is determined by social-economic relations, and these relations are determined by forces of production.

Marx never denies the originality of consciousness. He says explicitly that man could no more establish social-economic relations without consciousness than he could be conscious without social-economic relations. The same mutual causality applies to the relation between nature and consciousness. Marx never reduces consciousness to a physiological or chemical process of nature. The production process which determines man's thinking presupposes an *active* relationship with nature in which consciousness has as much impact upon nature as does nature upon consciousness. Consciousness as such is not a product of nature; the moment it becomes consciousness it opposes itself to nature. Engels, who is usually held responsible for Marxism's later development toward materialism, goes even further. At one point he admits a *mutual* causality between the production process and the other processes of consciousness. "Political, juridical, philosophical, religious, literary, artistic, etc. development is based on economic development. But all these react upon one another and also upon the economic basis. It is not that the economic condition is the *cause* and *alone active*, while everything else only is a passive effect."[24]

If this line of thinking had been pursued, the situation of Marxism with respect to religion would have looked entirely different. In that case Marx would merely have asserted the interdependence of the various levels of consciousness as well as their dependence upon the economic production process. The thesis that all states of consciousness are conditioned by the attainment of a certain level of economic production is perfectly compatible with the acceptance of religious values. However, what Marx and Engels say is not merely a claim that all states of consciousness are conditioned, but that they are intrinsically determined by the economic production process. Even the above text, which is probably the most reconciliatory in the entire Marxist literature, concludes with the following sentence: "There is, rather, interaction on the basis of economic necessity, which *ultimately* always asserts itself."[25] This implies that the ultimate explanation of all ideal values is to be found in economic processes. Such an economic determinism leads to unsatisfactory results in all fields of culture. To religion it strikes the death blow, for it excludes the existence of any reality independent of the material production.

CONCLUSION

The economism of the concept of *praxis*, then, as well as its absolute autonomy are the ultimate reasons why Marxism is incompatible with religious belief. Whether they are also final as far as Communism is concerned depends on whether Communism must necessarily retain all the principles of Marx's philosophy. Several have been abandoned already. Marx's predictions about the demise of capitalism and the proletarization of the masses is one important example. Lenin's "adaptation" of Marxism to the Russian situation is another. In some parts of Eastern Europe it is considered poor taste to quote Marx on economic matters. Could not Marx's theory of the *praxis* be widened from a closed economism to an open humanism?

It is true that autonomy and economic determinism belong to the core of Marxism which cannot be changed without deviating from Marx's basic intuition. Yet, even Marx's authority should remain subordinate to the cause of socialist humanism which he brought to the world. As long as the authority of its prophet remains an obstacle to the further development of its content, Marxism cannot claim to have fully overcome the anti-humanist dogma of Stalinism. Communism in the past has constantly decried revisionism as a half-hearted return to bourgeois theory, but is it not time to incorporate into its theory the changes which are taking place in its own living *praxis?* Ultimately such an attitude would be more consistent with Marx's philosophy than the rigid preservation of a theory which is rapidly proving too narrow to interpret the fullness of human action.

◊

1. Ludwig Feuerbach, **The Essence of Christianity** (New York: Harper, 1957).

2. Ibid., p. 153.

3. Karl Marx, **Early Writings** (New York: McGraw-Hill, 1964), pp. 210-11.

4. Georg W. Hegel, **Philosophy Of The State and Of History,** ed. G. S./ Morris (Chicago: S. C. Griggs, 1882).

5. Karl Marx and Fredrich Engles, **Historisch- kirtische Gesamtausgabe Werke, Schriften, Briefe,** ed. D. Rjaznov (Moscow: Marx-Engles Institute, 1845-1935), I, 436. Hereafter referred to as MEGA.

6. Marx, **Early Writings,** p. 10.

7. Ibid., p. 20.

8. Ibid., p. 44.

9. Ibid., p. 156.

10. Ibid., p. 44

11. Karl Marx, **Manuscripts in Early Writings.**

12. Ibid., p. 213.

13. Karl Marx, **Theses on Feuerbach,** appendix to Frederick Engles, **Ludwig Feuerbach and the Outcome of Classical German Philosophy,** ed. C. P. Dutt (New York: International, 1941).

14. Ibid., Thesis I, p. 82.

15. Karl Marx, **The German Ideology** (London: Lawrence & Wishart, 1938).

16. Marx, **Theses on Feuerbach,** Thesis XI, p. 84.

17. Roger Garaudy, **From Anathema to Dialogue** (New York: Herder and Herder, 1961), p. 76.

18. Ibid., p. 94.

19. Ibid., p. 95.

20. Marx, **Manuscripts in Early Writings,** p. 165.

21. Georges Cottier, **L'atheisme du jeune Marx** (Paris: J. Vrin, 1959), p. 345.

22. Louis Dupré, **The Philosophical Foundations of Marxism** (New York: Harcourt, Brace & World, 1966).

23. Marx, **The German Ideology,** p. 14.

24. MEGA, II, 504.

25. Ibid.

Kierkegaard on Man's Encounter with the Transcendent[*]

◊

Louis Dupré

MAN'S RECENT awareness of his creative autonomy has caused more problems for the notion of God than did any previous idea. If freedom constitutes itself and all its values, it excludes any pre-established order of values that is to be merely ratified rather than invented. Sartre, Merleau-Ponty, and a host of minor philosophers conclude, therefore, that the autonomy of man excludes the existence of a transcendent Creator. Religious existentialists have tried to get around this problem by giving the concept of autonomy itself a religious interpretation. It was God who created man to be the undisputed ruler over this world. Although they admit that this is man's world, they add that man is God's vassal.

Whichever attitude one takes, the basic problem remains. If man can take care of himself and of his situation in the world, how is he ever confronted with the transcendent? If the transcendent never touches his experience, the very notion of God becomes meaningless. Kierkegaard clearly anticipates this problem.

Kierkegaard's solution is to show that all autonomous self-realization leads by its inevitable failure to a confrontation with the transcendent. For him the question of the transcendent arises because the immanent is both autonomous and dependent. His description of the first negative encounter between freedom and the transcendent announces the opposition between the

religious and the secular that since has been so strongly emphasized by contemporary radical theologians. Yet, in Kierkegaard
the contact with the transcendent does not remain negative;
it restores man to his secular task by lifting him to a new level
of existence.

THE RELIGIOUS IMPLICATIONS OF
THE ETHICAL CHOICE

In *Either/Or*,[1] Kierkegaard's first major work, the religious
is not posited as a distinct sphere of existence. The problem here
is merely how man realizes his freedom, not what he must do
when this freedom breaks down. Even here, however, the realization of the self takes place within a total *givenness*, from which
freedom takes its origin and which is to be included in the
ultimate, existential choice.

The second part of *Either/Or* shows how the "aesthetic" attitude tries to escape the limitation, and thus the constitution,
of the self by a constant rejection of any commitment. The
"aesthete" has no self: his entire existence consists in a variety
of experiences determined by outside conditions. The frustration
which springs from the refusal of the spirit to posit itself results
in a strange oppressive melancholy. It would lead to despair
were it not that real despair is already an existential choice.
Indeed, one does not fall into despair; one freely chooses it.
In choosing despair one chooses onseself, since the object of
despair is never a particular situation (such as the loss of one's
fortune or of a beloved being), but oneself in a particular
situation. He who refuses to commit himself will eventually be
confronted with the almost unavoidable choice of accepting
or not accepting himself in this frustrated situation. This choice
can be made by an active decision. If he makes it, he posits
an absolute in the drifting relativity of his existence and this
absolute is precisely what the self is.

Not any choice of the self, however, posits the self in an
absolute way. To choose oneself only within a particular setting

of external circumstances is to choose an empirical, relative self. In an absolute choice, on the contrary, a man chooses himself regardless of any circumstances. For that reason, a choice of the authentic self always implies a despair of the relative self, the self in its empirical determinations.

Such an absolute choice of the self makes man into an ethical being, for it alone creates the essential condition for an absolute distinction between good and evil. To posit the self is to posit an absolute good and thus to create an absolute norm for good and evil. "In the fact that I choose the good I make *eo ipso* the choice between good and evil. The original choice is constantly present in every subsequent choice."[2] It is true that, speculatively, the distinction between good and evil can be understood without any personal commitment. On this speculative level, however, the distinction remains relative, for pure thought has no absolute contradiction. Even if two forms of being contradict each other logically, speculative reason (in Hegel's sense) is always ready to mediate between them, and thus to reconcile them in a higher unity. Only in the actual exercise of freedom does the distinction become absolute, because lived freedom posits good and evil in the real order, which is the only one in which they exclude each other absolutely. "The good *is* for me the fact that I will it, and apart from my willing it, it has no existence. This is the expression for freedom. It is so also with evil, it *is* only when I will it."[3]

The existential choice is absolute only when its object is the self in its totality. The fact that such an absolute choice is an unqualified good does not imply that everything in the self can be indiscriminately accepted. Much that man must accept as part of himself is repellent and will in the very act of choosing reveal itself as evil. Yet, if his choice is to be that of a total, concrete self, rather than of a relative, empirical one, it must also include these shadowy aspects of the self. How then can an absolute choice both include and reject the darker elements of the self?

In response to this question, Kierkegaard states that to be absolute and authentic the choice must be a choice in repentance.

In repentance alone is man able to express at the same time both that evil is part of his nature, and therefore to be included in his choice, and that evil estranges him from his true nature. As the very possibility of evil shows that the self is not an independent and perfect self a choice of the authentic self must therefore contain a recognition of its imperfection. By the same token, the choice in repentance is an implicit assertion of the self's dependence, for in rejecting evil (in the very act of choosing it), man implicitly affirms the self's dependence upon a transcendent Creator. "Only when I choose myself as guilty do I choose myself absolutely, if any absolute choice of myself is to be made in such a way that it is not identical with creating myself."[4] For an absolute choice of the self, the affirmation of the self's dependence is just as necessary as the acceptance of its evil.

This argument is conclusive only if one assumes that the distinction between good and evil is not created but merely posited by the choice, and consequently that man's relation to a transcendent is part of his very being. But what justifies such an assumption? Furthermore, we do not yet know that the ethical attitude which centers around the autonomous choice of the self will not eventually enter into conflict with the acceptance of this transcendental dependence. *Repetition*[5] and *Fear and Trembling*[6] show, dialectically and phenomenologically, how, in its autonomous choice, the self experiences itself as dependent. They also manifest how the acceptance of this dependence leads the self into an entirely new sphere of existence.

THE FAILURE OF THE ETHICAL

The problem of *Repetition* is: can man still be free after having encountered a transcendent fate? The question is posed in the story of a young man who is in love with a girl and who, because of his overly reflective disposition, feels unable to commit himself to the reality of marriage. He is never present to his fiancée. Instead, he dwells with the image that he has built of her in memory and imagination. Kierkegaard here obviously elaborates upon a personal experience first described in his diary and later repeated in the beginning of *Either/Or*:

"There is nothing more dangerous to me than remembering. The moment I have remembered some life relationship, that moment it ceased to exist. People say that separation tends to revive love. Quite true, but it revives it in a purely poetic manner. The life that is lived wholly in memory is the most perfect conceivable, the satisfactions of memory are richer than any reality, and have a security that no reality possesses. A remembered life-relation has already passed into eternity, and has no more temporal interest."[7]

In fact, the entire story may be read as a question posed to Kierkegaard's former fiancée, Regine Olsen: Will I still be able to marry you despite a psychological attitude which seems to exclude marriage? Unwittingly, Regine gave her answer before Kierkegaard had finished asking the question. Shortly before publication Kierkegaard learned that Regine was engaged. At the last moment he decided to change the conclusion of his book.

The basic problem of *Repetition* remains clear. The failure of autonomous self-realization reveals the existence of a transcendent limitation. How can freedom maintain itself in a situation which it has not chosen and which seems to obstruct all future choice? Or, since freedom is the very essence of the self, how can the self recapture itself after its free realization has been halted by a higher force.[8]

Philosophy offers no answer, since it can understand only the past while freedom operates in the time to come. Philosophy understands succession only backward, that is, insofar as each moment is already immanently present in the preceding one. It is unable to cope with the transcendent leap forward of freedom. The Bible, on the contrary, states the problem very clearly. In the story of Job we perceive the forward impulse of freedom, checked by the intervention of a transcendent power. Job's trial symbolizes the essential difficulty of human freedom.

In his failures man experiences the basic contingency of the self. He feels that he is limited and that between himself and the full realization of his self stands a transcendent force. Freedom is brought to a sudden halt in its self-conquest by the appearance of an insurmountable obstacle. If freedom is to be more than an illusion, man must come to terms with this intrusion into his existence.

Two attitudes are possible. One is to resign his autonomous freedom, consider his sufferings a punishment, and renounce the finite for the infinite. This is the attitude commended by Job's friends who try to convince him that he suffers because of his sins. This explanation, however, subsumes the transcendent under immanent ethical categories. God becomes merely an unpredictable judge of human freedom, who in the name of his superior power takes the place of man's moral responsibility. Such an arbitrary intervention makes any responsible action impossible. Job refuses to accept an explanation so insulting to moral dignity. In spite of his resignation to the transcendent, he firmly upholds the autonomy of the self.

Job's greatness is "that the *passion of freedom* within him is not stifled or tranquilized by a false expression." He maintains that he is right even though the whole world seems to conspire to make him look guilty.

> Fate had played him a trick in letting him become guilty. If this is the way it stands, he can never more recapture himself. His nature has become split, and so the question is not about the repetition of something outward, but about the repetition of his freedom.[9]

Contrary to the attitude of his friends, Job takes the transcendent for what it is: an intrusion of the infinite which threatens man's finite existence. Job knows that man has to fight with the transcendent, as Jacob wrestled with Jahweh, if he is to maintain his freedom. He knows that the Enemy is not an avenging angel bent on punishing man's shortcomings, but rather the totally

Other, before whose transcendence all ethical striving is deficient, regardless of its immanent righteousness.

The immanent and the transcendent are essentially opposed and cannot be reduced to each other. Nietzsche's attempt to absorb the transcendent into a superhuman immanence is no more justified than the willingness of Job's friends to abandon the immanent to the transcendent. Man must simultaneously accept the transcendent in resignation and uphold the rights of the immanent. Job is fully resigned to the loss of his possessions and says: "The Lord gave, and the Lord hath taken away: as it has pleased the Lord so is it done: blessed be the name of the Lord."[10] Yet, at the same time, he talks back to God and claims his innocence. He may be wrong, but he is wrong only before God; on his own autonomous level he pleads not guilty.

Nevertheless, the story of Job is misleading if one expects, on the basis of the added epilogue, a restoration of his original self to its previous existence. The true repetition is not a simple resumption of the self, but an elevation to a higher level of consciousness. After having gone through the infinite resignation, man can never be the same. Job merely teaches that the eternal and the temporal are to be maintained simultaneously, but he does not teach how this is to be done. The time "redeemed" from eternity cannot be the same as man's original temporal order: eternity opens a new dimension in existence which makes a simple return to the past impossible. If the young man had understood this from the beginning, he would not have been concerned about the outcome of the temporal event.

> What is called reality would in a deeper sense be of no importance to him. He would have drained off religiously all the dreadful consequences contained in the occurrence. Though reality were to turn out differently it would not change him essentially.[11]

The repetition, then, is in fact not a repetition at all, but a transformation of the self to a higher level of existence in which the ethical stage of freedom is sublated in the triple sense of annulled, preserved, and elevated.

It is precisely this transformation which makes the repetition into a religious rather than an ethical movement. Only the movement of faith can accomplish the paradoxical task of giving up the temporal and, at the same time, preserving it on a higher level. In the story of Job this movement is never mentioned—nothing indicates that Job believed in the restoration of his possessions. Job is religious only in a negative way: he knows that the transcendent is above all immanent categories and that the immanent may never be abandoned to the transcendent, but he does not hope to have the immanent restored.

It was Abraham who made the positive movement of faith. When God demanded the sacrifice of his son Isaac, Abraham was resigned as was Job, but throughout his reignation he steadfastly continued to believe that God would bless all future generations in his seed. This faith restored his freedom to its full integrity. Such a faith was not present in Job, even though a later addition to the story tells us that all his possessions were restored. Faith alone solves the dialectical tension between the transcendent and the immanent, the eternal and the temporal. No autonomous ethical movement can reconquer the temporal once the eternal has interrupted its flow. The temporal can *be* restored only from within the eternal, and this is precisely what faith does. Jean Wahl accurately describes the movement in the following passage:

> The absolute had us, in the suspension of the ethical, violently separated from the real, had turned us against it; then it revealed itself in its infinite aspect, and first became a sanctuary in our flight from the real; this was the movement of infinite resignation; finally, in the movement of faith, it violently returns us to the real and allows us to reconquer and transform it. Man recaptures himself outside the temporal and restores the temporal to himself.[12]

Once man admits the eternal and resigns the temporal, he becomes unable to return to the temporal by an immanent ethical movement. The impulse now must come from the transcendent. Man's autonomous freedom can be restored only by the transcendent to which he has resigned it. Thus, in the religious attitude, the immanent movement of freedom ends in the paradox of faith. Resignation is the last autonomous movement of freedom; it would be its downfall and destruction were it not followed by the transcendent movement of faith. The very preservation of freedom's autonomy requires that it be completed by the theonomy of faith.

THE INTRINSIC LIMITATION OF FREEDOM: GUILT AND REPENTANCE

In the cases of Job and Abraham the confrontation with the transcendent occurs through an extrinsic failure: both of them were on trial. In most cases, however, the failure is purely intrinsic. It is through the shortcomings in his attempts to lead a moral life that the ordinary man becomes aware of his own insufficiency. Freedom also has its intrinsic limitation, and this is expressed in repentance. *Fear and Trembling* shows how the ethical order leads to its destruction by its own internal contradictions. For the sake of argument, Kierkegaard here adopts the view of his main adversary, Hegel, and defines the ethical as the individual will elevated to the universal level of reason. However, whereas for Hegel the individual freedom succeeds in realizing itself through the universal, for Kierkegaard this attempt results in failure and the individual is ultimately thrown back upon himself. All ethical striving ends in guilt, and guilt places the individual outside the universal sphere of ethics. "An ethics which disregards sin is a perfectly idle science; but if it asserts sin, it is *eo ipso* well beyond itself."[13]

Repentance then is no longer a moment of the ethical consciousness, as it still was in *Either/Or;* it is its destruction, or, as Jean Wahl puts it, it completes the ethical by destroying it.

"As soon as sin makes its appearance, ethics comes to grief precisely upon repentance, for repentance is the higher ethical expression, but precisely as such it is the deepest ethical self-contradiction."[14]

Repentance, however, marks not merely the end of the ethical stage, but also the transition to the next stage. It is an attempt to make peace with the universal by accepting one's rejection from the universal. In sin man deliberately places himself in a negative relation to the absolute; this choice cannot be undone. Repentance's return to the universal marks an entirely new beginning. Yet, it alone cannot restore freedom to its previous integrity. "By his own strength he can make the movement of repentance, but for that he uses up absolutely all his strength, and hence he cannot by his own strength return and grasp reality."[15] Repentance may be equated with the movement of infinite resignation, which also abandons the autonomous order of freedom without being able to return to it. In both cases man makes a cloister-like movement by withdrawing from the autonomous realization of the self, but he is unable to return to the world. "The man who has performed the cloister movement has only one movement more to make, that is, the movement of the absurd."[16]

This movement of the absurd enables man to return to the finite after he has forsaken it in the act of infinite resignation. "After having made the movements of infinity, it [faith] makes those of finiteness."[17] In faith the finite is regained in such a way that, rather than being lost, it receives the new impetus of the infinite.

If the believer can so fully embrace the secular, how is he still distinct from the non-believer? In his theory of "hidden interiority" Kierkegaard shows that there is no visible distinction between the true believer and the unbeliever. "The knights of the infinite resignation are easily recognized: their gait is gliding and assured, those on the other hand who carry the jewel of faith are likely to be delusive, because their outward appearance bears a striking resemblance to that which both the infinite resignation and faith profoundly despise ... to Philistinism."[18]

There is great danger in this disguise, for without external manifestation the distinction between faith and paganism may disappear altogether. In order to maintain the honesty of faith, true resignation is indispensable to the believer. Without a constant resignation of the immanent, the transcendent simply disappears in the immanent. Resignation is the constant preliminary to faith. "The infinite resignation is the last stage prior to faith, so that one who has not made this movement has not faith; for only in the infinite resignation do I become clear to myself with respect to my eternal validity, and only then can there be any question of grasping existence by virtue of faith."[19] Faith which has not gone through the reflection of total resignation remains "aesthetic," an "immediate instinct of the heart, the vital fluidum—the atmosphere we breathe in."[20]

In his later doctrine of the imitation of Christ Kierkegaard will go even further and give up the principle of hidden interiority altogether. Faith, he will say, must reveal itself outwardly in the works of faith.[21]

FAITH AS THE PERFECTION OF FREEDOM

The novel character of the sphere of faith is indicated by the difference between the believer and the tragic hero. Tragic heroes such as Agamemnon or Brutus sacrifice one universal ethical value to another: love for one's child is made subordinate to the interests of the country or to the sacredness of the law. Abraham, on the contrary, has no universal value to justify the sacrifice of his son. "He acts by virtue of the absurd, for it is precisely absurd that he as the particular is higher than the universal."[22] Abraham is alone with his decision; he can only hope that he was not mistaken in his belief.

"The paradox of faith has lost the intermediate term, i.e.,

the universal. On the one side–it has the expression for the extremest egoism (doing the dreadful thing it does for one's own sake); on the other side, the expression for the most absolute self-sacrifice (doing it for God's sake). Faith itself cannot be mediated into the universal, for it would thereby be destroyed. Faith is this paradox, and the individual absolutely cannot make himself intelligible to anybody."[23]

What Kierkegaard is expressing here goes far beyond the mere distinction between the ethical and the religious. It touches on the nature of the religious "object." For Kierkegaard a transcendent God can never be an "object" and, consequently, a correct relation to him cannot be objective—universal. The only alternative is that man's relation to God be subjective. This implies that faith is a way of being, a choice, rather than an intellectual acceptance. The truth of such a relation lies in the authenticity of the relation itself, not in its conformity to a certain object.

The emphasis on subjectivity in this position must not be confused with the subjectivism of pre-reflective religious feelings in which the *relatum* is either absent or indifferent. In the case of revealed religion as Kierkegaard understands it, the transcendent *relatum* determines the entire relation. This *relatum* cannot be a cognitive process; its transcendent nature excludes any objective relation. Of course, if there is to be any relation at all, the transcendent relatum must adopt some objective form in the revelation. However, this "objectivity" is such that it cannot be assimilated by a simple cognitive process. In the *Philosophical Fragments*[24] Kierkegaard expresses this by saying that the revelation is paradoxical. Its content is such that it throws the mind back upon itself where acceptance or rejection of the revelation is decided by the choice of the subject rather than by the compelling nature of the object. The point of this objectively repelling truth is not to provide information but to oblige man to bring himself to an inwardness which he can attain in no other way. "The paradoxical character of the truth is its objective uncertainty; this uncertainty is an expression for the passionate inwardness, and this passion is precisely the truth."[25]

The paradoxical, repulsive character of the object of faith, then, turns out to be its most valuable asset for the attainment of subjective truth. Objective certainty draws the subject away from itself toward the object. No commitment, no return upon oneself is required for the understanding of an objective truth. If the self is a free subject which constitutes itself in passionate interiority, then all objective certainty must ultimately disappear and make room for the subjective certainty of freedom. In the Christian revelation this paradox has a double aspect. First, it reveals to man that he has become so untrue to himself as to become irreconcilably opposed to his own transcendent foundation. Second, Christianity teaches that the absolutely unlike has become absolutely alike. After existence in time has severed its link with the eternal, the eternal itself becomes temporal. That God exists in time is the core of Christianity; it is also the absolute paradox.

This subjective nature of man's ultimate stage of existence can be expressed in still another way. Being a subject himself man can conceive of what transcends him only as a subject. He must address the transcendent and communicate with it as if it were another, more powerful subject. The moment he ceases to relate to God as to a person, transcendence disappears. The subject, however, which pre-exists the relation itself, simply cannot be related to as an object, for it is essentially openness, indetermination, and freedom. Only by concentrating on the relation itself rather than on what is already "given" can man do full justice to this openness. Any other approach to a subject or person, degrades him to an object, a fixed and closed entity, and is therefore essentially untrue. This does not deny that the other has an objective aspect as well, for at least the human being is perceived in a world of objects. Yet, beyond this objectivity, a true understanding of a subject must account for the openness and self-determination of the other.

Of course, all this is true for man's relation to another, finite subject, but is it also true for God? God is there, complete in his entirety from the beginning, and my relation cannot change him into something that he would not be independently of me. Nevertheless, God in his relation to man is more "subject" than any fellowman could be. Although God does not need my relating to him to be free, the simple fact is that his very being is freedom. His "completeness" never adopts the given objectivity inherent in a created freedom.

This is eminently true for man's relation to God, because God alone is entirely free. He is so free that he transcends any objective expression. He cannot be captured in even the highest objective form, and any attempt to make him into an object of rational knowledge reduces him to a finite god, an idol. For that reason, Kierkegaard can say that whether I have a relation to the true God matters less than whether I have a true relation to God.

> If one who lives in the midst of Christianity goes up to the house of God, the house of the true God, with the true conception of God in his knowledge, and prays, but prays in a false spirit; and one who lives in an idolatrous community prays with the entire passion of the infinite, although his eyes rest upon the image of an idol: Where is there more truth? The one prays in truth to God though he worships the idol; the other prays falsely to the true God, and hence worships in fact an idol.[26]

◇

1. Soren Kierkegaard, **Either/Or,** trans. David and Lillian Swenson (Garden City, N. Y.: Doubleday, 1959).

2. **Ibid., p.** 184.

3. **Ibid., p.** 188.

4. **Ibid., p.** 182.

5. Soren Kierkegaard, **Repetition,** trans. Walter Lowrie (Princeton, N. J.: Princeton Univ. Press, 1941).

6. Soren Kierkegaard, **Fear and Trembling,** trans. Walter Lowrie (Garden City, N. Y.: Doubleday, 1954).

7. Kierkegaard, **Either/Or,** p. 26.

8. The English word "repetition" does not have all the connotations which **gjentagelse** has for Kierkegaard. In an unpublished commentary which can be found in Soren Kierkegaard's **Papirer,** ed. P. A. Heiberg, V. Kuhr, and E. Torsting (Copenhagen: Gyldendal, 1909-1948), IV B, 117, he interprets **at gjentage sig** as **at tage sig selv tilbage,** which Lowrie in the Introduction to the English version of **Repetition** translates as "to withdraw," but which I would rather translate as "to recapture oneself," or "to resume oneself." I would even suggest that **Resumption or Reassertion** might be a better title than **Repetition.**

9. Soren Kierkegaard, **Diary** (New York: Philosophical Library, 1960), IV B, 177. Cf. Walter Lowrie's Introduction to **Repetition,** p. xx.

10. Job 1:21.

11. Kierkegaard, **Repetition,** p. 157.

12. Jean Wahl, **Etudes Kierkegaardiennes** (Paris: Aubier, 1959), p. 200.

13. Kierkegaard, **Fear and Trembling,** p. 152.

14. Wahl, **Etudes Kierkegaardiennes,** p. 200.

15. Kierkegaard, **Fear and Trembling,** pp. 153-54.

16. **Ibid.,** p. 150.

17. **Ibid.,** p. 51.

18. **Ibid.,** pp. 51-52.

19. **Ibid.,** pp. 65-66.

20. Kierkegaard, **Diary, IA,** 273.

21. On this subject one may consult Louis Dupré, **Kierkegaard as Theologian** (New York: Sheed, 1963), pp. 156-70.

22. Kierkegaard, **Fear and Trembling,** p. 83.

23. **Ibid.,** p. 93.

24. Soren Kierkegaard, **Philosophical Fragments** (Princeton, N. J.: Princeton Univ. Press, 1936).

25. Soren Kierkegaard, **Concluding Unscientific Postscript,** trans. David Swenson and Walter Lowrie (Princeton, N. J.: Princeton Univ. Press, 1944), p. 183.

26. **Ibid.,** pp. 178-79. The fact that Kierkegaard talks about the "true God" in one case, and an "idol" in the other, shows clearly that the matter is not entirely left to the individual subjectivity. There is, indeed, an objective datum, but it is not made objective by a self-sufficient process of knowledge: it is given by a transcendent revelation, and in that sense it is not objective at all.

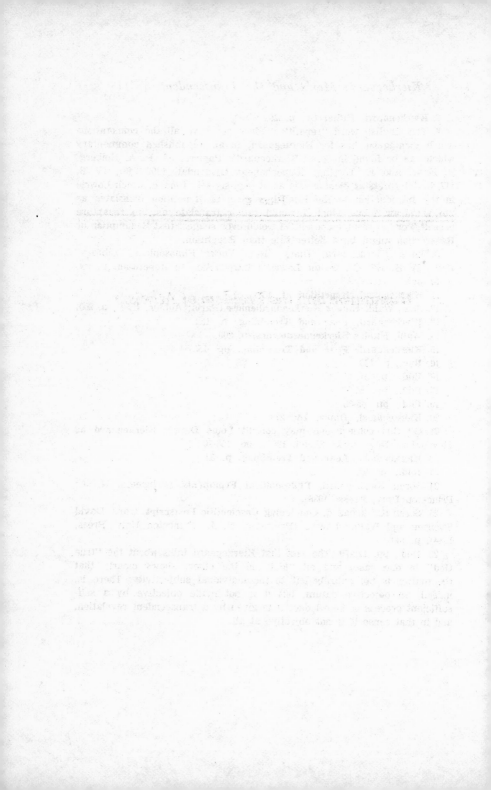

PART II

Humanism and the Problem of Atheism

God and Psychological Man

◇

Daniel Callahan

IN THE SHORT run, the most striking characteristic of social change are visible and tangible. They may involve changes in dress, mode of work, styles of architecture, forms of government, types of entertainment, and patterns of speech. The industrial revolution, for instance, radically altered the landscape, sundered the connection between place of residence and place of work, forced the development of fresh technical skills, and led to new forms of housing. These were changes which everyone could see; they assaulted the senses and the sensibilities.

The visible marks of our technological society are such things as super-highways, an international style of architecture, the presence of myriad gadgets and devices, a rise in the level of noise and air pollution, and the obvious presence of bustle, activity, and speed. Human beings may grumble at such changes or may welcome them. Either way, people soon learn to adapt their social behavior to the life around them, if only because constant exposure tends to dull the sensibilities and wear down resistance. Before long, everyone begins to act, speak, and dress more or less like everyone else. The clothes a person wears today rarely provide any clues about his religious beliefs, his political position, his ethical values, or his view of the world. Nor can one tell much by knowing where someone lives or what his occupation happens to be.

RELIGION AND SECULARITY

Religious Interpretations of the Secular

Nonetheless, external changes of this kind can be very misleading and suggest a more dramatic cultural revolution than may be the case. It is quite possible for people to alter their behavior patterns and yet remain essentially the same in their way of looking at the world. They can change their clothes, their work, their house, their entertainment, and yet retain, relatively intact, a traditional set of beliefs and values. Thus, for centuries Christianity was able to adapt itself to the gradual development of secularity. It learned how to live with the Copernican revolution, with the separation of Church and State, with the shift from an agricultural to an industrial economy, and with the rise of the revolutionary values of liberty, fraternity and equality. Of course, adjustments had to be made which were sometimes painful and confusing. Yet they were made, and at relatively little cost to the traditional Christian world-view and consciousness of the divine.

In making these adjustments possible, Christian theologians, philosophers, and hierarchs did splendid work. At first, they mirrored the shock of the faithful, proving from their axioms, exegesis, and speculation that the social changes were the work of the devil. However, as people became accustomed to changes and found that they could live with them, the savants graciously returned to their sources and discovered that the changes were actually the work of God. It is the fate of western secularity to have been scorned at first by the Christian wise men, who saw only arrogance, destruction and immorality, but now to be praised and extolled, celebrated and enjoyed. This kind of radical turnabout is not as hard to manage as it might seem. "Threats" are turned into "challenges," "dangers" into "opportunities," incarnation into eschatology or eschatology into incarnation (whichever is required), immutable dogma into developing doctrine, and old fears into new liberations.

It takes considerable work to make these shifts smooth and plausible, but the great advantage in favor of the transformers is that the people, at least the educated and affluent, want desperately to see the philosophical and theological transformation succeed. They have a stake in a reconciliation of religion and secular developments and ask only three things: that their fears be allayed, that their contemporary experience be legitimated, and that a minimally decent nod be made in the direction of the tradition. The art of the religious thinker is measured by his ability to meet these requirements. In principle, his task is to find the truth; in practice, his public acclaim depends upon his talents in reconciling traditional claims and one or more aspects of contemporary experience. This is only another way of saying that theological speculation and its public acceptance are conditioned by culture.

Secular Interpretations of the Religious

What works in the short run, however, does not necessarily succeed in the long run. Sooner or later, a decisive social change will begin to affect the consciousness of a people. If at first they adapt only their superficial behavior to the changes around them, preserving in the process traditional principles, eventually these latter redoubts will be influenced as well. Beginning with the Renaissance, religion was able to stave off any radical impact of the emergent secularity. Within the established religious frame, it baptized the social, political, and cultural shifts which secularity brought with it. These baptisms succeeded in integrating the social transitions while preserving an unshakeable core of convictions and ultimate perspectives.

Lately, however, there have been disturbing signs that the time-honored process of baptizing the fruits of secularity has begun to fail. Rarely in the history of religion has there been a moment of theological and philosophical creativity comparable to what we are experiencing today. Rarely have so many products of an evolving civilization been so rapidly blessed and so smoothly worked into a traditional frame. Technology, automation, contraception, ethical relativism, mobility, and anonymity—to mention only a few examples—have all found their religious apologists. Yet, for all this frantic activity, the religious malaise has increased rather than decreased. The reason should by now be apparent. So deeply has a secular consciousness penetrated within the walls of the religious consciousness, so thoroughly has a secular ethos come to replace a religious ethos, that all of the usual methods of baptism have begun to fail.

Why is this happening? The essential requirement for effective baptism, I contend, is the presence of a religious consciousness at least as strong as the secular consciousness produced by the rapid social change. Along with the secular consciousness there must be a consciousness of what has been variously described as the transcendent, or the infinite, or the ground of being; there must be a consciousness of something which seems to point beyond immediate biological and social experience. As Mircea Eliade has put it, "... religious man assumes a humanity that has a transhuman, transcendent model. . . . This is as much to say that religious man wishes to be other than he is on the plane of his profane experience."[1] Or, in the words of Thomas O'Dea, "The religious experience is an encounter with a beyond, with a power beyond the appearances of things and events, with an ultimate power seen as ground of existence. Such an ultimate ground of being is experienced as sacred—that is, as eliciting intense awe and exercising a strong attraction."[2]

However one might care to further characterize the religious consciousness, it must at any rate be a live presence in man if there is to be any hope of baptizing a secular consciousness within a religious frame. If it is absent, then no amount of manipulation and ingenuity on the level of conceptual development, or scriptural exegesis, or doctrinal change will continue for long to be effective, and the secular consciousness will win the field. People will experience the secular with a vividness, meaningfulness, and persuasiveness unmatched by an equally powerful experience of the sacred. The secular will be seen and felt as a closed, self-sufficient reality, requiring neither justification nor completion in a reality that is other than secular. At that point the dualistic consciousness necessary for baptism dissolves and a secular consciousness is all that remains.[3] In its own way this consciousness may be very rich, with many different streams and emphases. However, so long as it does not include within it a sense of transcendent possibilities, some lively degree of dualistic thrusts, the very ground of the religious consciousness and enterprise is destroyed.

In fact, one might suggest that the final triumph of a secular consciousness comes when the privilege of baptism passes from the hands of the religious establishment into that of the secular establishment. This is happening before our eyes. Where it was once the acknowledged task of religion to integrate social, cultural, economic, and political change into its transcendent, holistic scheme of ultimate truth and value, this has now become the self-appointed task of the secular consciousness. Hence, we now see in the higher reaches of the academic and intellectual world a new toleration of the religious consciousness and even of religious institutions. However, the obvious condition of this toleration is that the churches make a contribution to the solution of some of the problems posed by technology, nuclear weapons, underdeveloped countries, racial conflict, and the like. Religion is welcomed into the secular life so long as it demonstrates its relevance for that consciousness and life.

It used to be the other way around; the secular was welcomed on the condition that it could demonstrate its relevance to the religious mind and life. It is no mere coincidence that those religious thinkers most celebrated in and out of the churches and synagogues are those who have tried to show the pertinence of a religious perspective to man's secular needs, desires, and hopes. One would have to be blind not to see in these reversals of prestige—with the religious consciousness now in the position of a minority trying to justify its value to the interests of the majority—the all-but-complete triumph of secular consciousness.[4]

Further evidence of the triumph can be seen in the frequent use of words like "meaningless" and "empty" when traditional religious concepts are discussed. Despite what a primitive positivist might think, words and concepts do not make sense to people on the basis of some formal criteria of meaningfulness. They make sense because they have a place and a function within a cultural context or a broad world-view. As long as the context and the world-view remain intact, they retain their significance. Traditional religious language becomes meaningless when it lacks a culture to support it, a consciousness to provide it with referents and uses, and a unified intellectual scheme in which it can play a part. Religious language is culturally syncategorematic.

Faith and the Secular Consciousness

The great faith of the contemporary religious thinker is that, despite the triumph of a secular consciousness, man still possesses the capacity to experience within himself or within the world those powers, inclinations, and depths which point beyond a closed secular consciousness and perspective. This faith may take the form of an assertion that man desires a "meaning" in his life which transcends the routine satisfaction and significances of daily life, or that man still has latent within him the possibility of experiencing "the other," or even that man's affirmation of the secular can be traced to a religious drive.

No present religious thinker of any stature, however radical his posture, has been able to give up that faith. Leslie Dewart has been able to let go of traditional Hellenic concepts of God, but he cannot let go of talk about the "presence" of God. Thomas J. J. Altizer has been able to let go of a concept of the "sacred" understood as radically separated from the "secular," but even he looks forward to a rebirth of the "sacred" at some unspecified point. Michael Novak has been able to let go of a transcendent God, but not of the existence of an "unrestricted drive to know" which enables man to transcend himself. Harvey

Cox can suggest that we cease to use the word 'God,' but not that we cease to believe that a new word may be found which will better express what has always been meant by the term so far as basic human experience is concerned. William Hamilton finds in the person of Jesus a power and a mystery not exhaustively encompassed by an experience of the secular. However strongly Karl Rahner has pleaded for a Christian acceptance of profane secularity, his final faith is that the very progress of secularization will lead to a reopening of the religious question in the end.

Other examples could be supplied, but what is common to each of the thinkers mentioned is their refusal to give up the last bastion of religion. That bastion is precisely the belief that even in the most secularized consciousness and society, man can find the presence of experiences and intimations which are potentially able to point to something of ultimate meaning beyond man. We should not be misled by the frequent assertions that a valid philosophy or theology of God must today be cast in terms of a philosophical or theological anthropology, that we must know man before we can know God. Even this strategy, imposed in part by a secular consciousness which seems to know only man, is meant eventually to find a way beyond man.

When there is talk, then, of "radical" theologies it is necessary to keep in mind how well defended is the last bastion. An outsider might, indeed, see radical theology as the choice of that battle plan which gives up all such outer defense perimeters as institutional religion, Hellenic concepts, feelings of dependence and finiteness, and political privilege in order better to defend the last stronghold. To extend the image, the real struggle between the conservative and the radical is whether religion can afford to raze the perimeter defenses; this is a question of tactics. On the central question of the ultimate validity of the religious quest there is no dispute at all, even though different ways of talking and acting may make it appear so. However shocking the language, the proposals, and the attacks of "radical" theology, they all rest on a very traditional premise: that the religious quest has a permanent human validity and will not be in vain.

RELIGION AND
THE PSYCHOANALYTIC CONSCIOUSNESS

The Question

My question is this: why has this premise of the permanent validity of the religious quest endured? Why, given all the retreats and redeployments, all the linguistic, conceptual, and institutional maneuvering, has the religious mind remained comparatively so serene about the religious premise itself? In the face of an apparently regnant secular consciousness, why has it been able to stall a radical critique of the religious consciousness in its most fundamental human roots? There are a number of possible explanations. Among them might be the possibility that the secular ethos is still not so overpowering as to stifle altogether the religious drive; man's religious history and heritage lingers in his bones. Still another possibility might be that the secularity present in our times still depends on profoundly religious roots; religion is only hidden, not dead. A case could be developed for each of these possibilities, or some combination of them.

I want to raise and develop another possibility: that one should envisage the revolution of secularity not as a single revolution but as a host of concurrent and interrelated upheavals. There are the revolutions of an emergent political consciousness, of historical awareness, of technological power, of urbanization, of the desacralization of nature, morals, and politics, of biological evolution, and of work, leisure, and recreation. There has also been a psychological revolution, the revolution signalled by the emergence of a "psychoanalytical consciousness," to use Norman O. Brown's phrase.[5]

About this last revolution it is important to note that it is the one revolution of secularity which, on the theoretical level, has not attracted much attention on the part of religion. This is a curious fact, for it is the one revolution specifically centering on the workings of man's conscious and unconscious life. Needless to say, religious counselors and guidance experts have made use of psychoanalytical tools, and religious thinkers have pondered Freud, Jung, Adler, and other figures in the psychoanalytical pantheon. However, I cannot think of a single important theologian or philosopher of religion who has adopted a basically psychoanalytical perspective to investigate the religious premise, though Paul Tillich went very far in this direction. At most, psychoanalytical insights have been employed around the fringes of the religious question, their deepest penetration coming in the field of ethics.

Should not this strike us as somehow odd? One or more major religious thinkers have arisen in response to every other aspect of the secular revolution in order to show how a reconciliation with the religious premise might be effected. Teilhard de Chardin did this for an evolutionary consciousness. Whitehead did it for a process consciousness. Cox did it for an urban consciousness. Bonhoeffer did it for the consciousness of human autonomy. Paul Van Buren did it for secularity as a general phenomenon. The problem here is not whether each of these men did it successfully, or whether each is of equal historical importance. My only point is that each showed some promising ways in which a religious consciousness could be joined with some element of a secular consciousness. Yet there is no candidate at all for the area marked "psychoanalytical consciousness." Is this merely an historical accident, sheer chance in the distribution of talents among religious thinkers? Such an hypothesis is not very plausible. My own guess is that religious thinkers have instinctively recognized that a "psychoanalytical consciousness" poses such consummate dangers to the religious premise and to a religious consciousness that they have preferred to avoid it. On the evidence, I would not hesitate to call this avoidance the expression of an unconscious desire to flee from the threat of a potentially cataclysmic danger.

Psychoanalytic Consciousness

What is a "psychoanalytical consciousness" and what danger does it imply for the religious consciousness? By a "psychoanalytical consciousness" I mean that way of looking at man's language, intentions, concepts, attitudes, and behavior which tends to find their meaning in subconscious or unconscious drives and attitudes that may be at odds with their professed or conscious meaning. The danger to religion posed by such a consciousness is evident. It threatens the belief that religious drives, institutional structures, and theological systems are the product of a healthy, conscious, controlled, self-aware, and rational attempt to arrive at truth. It threatens to introduce into religious analysis and discourse a tool of discovery which could create the utmost confusion and chaos, changing the *ad hominem* argument from a fallacy to a revelation. It threatens the myth that the only requirement for productive theology and philosophy is sound scholarship, clear thinking, and a decent sensitivity to criticism and counter-suggestions. It threatens, in other words, to turn our whole world of conventional requirements and expectations, norms, and criteria in this field upside down.

The time has come for these threats to be accepted, and there is no better place to begin than with Freud himself. The fate of Freud's small book, *The Future of an Illusion*,[6] is a good example of the evasions of religious thought. On one level, it is perfectly true that Freud's analysis of the origin of religion is open to innumerable criticisms. There is no historical evidence to support his hypothesis of a primal father and a primal horde. There is no reason to suppose that simply because it is conceivable that religious belief displays some marks of an infantile regression, it must necessarily be reducible to nothing but infantile regression. It does not follow that because there is a large amount of wish fulfillment in religion, religion can logically be seen only as wish fulfillment. Further, as religious philosophers have been fond of pointing out, in the end psychological reductionism tells us nothing about the truth value of beliefs; to suppose otherwise is to become trapped in the genetic fallacy. Finally, since two can play the psychoanalytical game, it is plausible, as Gregory Zilboorg showed, to see Freud's analysis of religion as itself influenced by Freud's own psychological history.[7]

Against such an array of objections, coming from every angle, it is hardly surprising that religious thinkers have felt comfortable in dismissing Freud. The most anyone has been willing to concede is that Freud may have been perfectly correct in noting that some projections of God are, indeed, infantile or represent an earlier stage of human evolution. Once this concession has been made, the conventional sequel is to urge the need for, and the possibility of, a less infantile response and set of images. Leslie Dewart's handling of *The Future of an Illusion* in his recent book *The Future of Belief* provides a sophisticated example of this technique.[8] It is a very disarming technique, conceding almost everything—except the validity of the religious premise itself, which remains unanalyzed and preserved in full purity.

Freud and Religion's Cultural . Context

There is needed a fresh approach to Freud, of which only the outline can be sketched here. I would suggest that the place to begin is the recognition, obvious from the texts themselves, that Freud's analysis of religion is only part of a broader analysis of civilization, its needs, problems, and discontents. As Freud insists, his aim in *The Future of an Illusion* is to point out the need for an *"education in reality,"* the main purpose of which is to improve the life of civilization. His hope is that human beings, "by withdrawing their expectations from the other world and concentrating all their liberated energies into their life on earth . . . will probably succeed in achieving a state of things in which life will become tolerable for everyone and civilization no longer oppressive to anyone."[9] The first step needed to put mankind on the way to this future is the renunciation of religious illusions. Freud does not contend that religious belief is necessarily harmful to individuals, or even that it has been wholly without value for civilization. His main contention is that religious beliefs stand in the way of the most urgent need of mankind, which is for men to reconcile themselves to civilization.[10] While Freud saw the origin of religion in the human need for a defense against nature, on the one hand, and against the shortcomings of civilization, on the other, he also observed that the former motive has become largely anachronistic. Once nature was discerned to be autonomous and the gods expelled, the main function of religion centered upon providing compensation for the suffering and privation which a civilized life in common imposes.[11] In a passage in *Civilization and Its Discontents,* Freud speaks eloquently of man's coming of age in his relationship to nature.

> Long ago he [man] formed an ideal conception of omnipotence and omniscience which he embodied in his gods. Whatever seemed unattainable to his desires—or forbidden to him—he attributed to these gods. One may say, therefore, that these gods were the ideals of his culture. Now he has himself approached very near to realizing this ideal, he has nearly become a god himself.[12]

Unfortunately, man's success in conquering nature, or coming progressively closer to that goal, has not solved all his problems. "The human being of today," wrote Freud, "is not happy with all his likeness to a god."[13] What remains to be done poses difficulties far exceeding those posed by the brute force of nature. In fact, the very tools with which man has learned to conquer nature exacerbate his remaining tasks. "The fateful question of the human species," Freud wrote in the last paragraph of *Civilization and Its Discontents,*

> "seems to me to be whether and to what extent the cultural process developed in it will succeed in mastering the derangements of communal life caused by the human instinct of aggression and self-destruction. . . . Men have brought their powers of subduing the forces of nature to such a pitch that by using them they could now very easily exterminate one another to the last man. They know this—hence arises a great deal of their current unrest, their dejection, their mood of apprehension.[14]

In Freud's terms, the question is whether Eros, the life instinct, will triumph over Thanatos, the death instinct. A closely related question concerns the relationship between the individual and the community.

> A great part of the struggles of mankind centers round the single task of finding some expedient (i.e. satisfying) solution between . . . individual claims and those of the civilized community. It is one of the problems of man's fate whether this solution can be arrived at in some particular form of culture or whether the conflict will prove irreconcilable.[15]

The citation of even a few passages like this—usually neglected when *The Future of an Illusion* and *Civilization and Its Discontents* are discussed—should show how little the religious community can afford to continue ignoring Freud's analysis of the dilemmas of civilized life. Secularization has presented itself as a question of the function and value of religious belief in an age where man seems on the verge of successfully creating his own values and meaning; the problems that remain once man has "come of age" are those of avoiding self-destruction and realizing the rich possibilities of human development. The problem of God and religion fundamentally presented itself to Freud as the problem of human beings living in community. In its own too narrow way the religious community has tried of late to begin what Freud hoped someone would eventually undertake, i.e., a "pathology of civilized communities."[16] Thus, the questions most alive today within religion concern the relationship between the individual and the community, the problem of God as it relates to temporal life, the nature of love, the body and secularity, and the devising of strategies for warding off a final technological disaster. These were exactly the questions which concerned Freud in his later writings. The religious mind, by slighting these writings simply because it found in Freud's critique of religion some logical and historical blunders, ignored a beautiful forest out of resentment for one tree which seemed ill-planted. The problem of God cannot be solved until believers have relinquished their fear of the psychoanalytical consciousness in trying to think about God; nor can the problem of civilization be met until those believers, intent upon taking reality seriously, begin examining the psychological sources of aggression, domination, and destructiveness, particularly as they bear on the question of God.

RECENT INTERPRETERS OF
INDIVIDUAL-COMMUNITY RELATIONSHIP

One must admit, however, that much will depend upon the way Freud is used and on the way one chooses to go beyond Freud. There have been too many effective criticisms levelled at Freud by further psychoanalytic research to give full allegiance, even on the secular level, to all the details of his speculations about individuals and civilization.[17] However, what is required is not full allegiance but only a willingness to make as creative a use of Freud's initial probings as possible, and then to profit from the later criticisms and refinements of those who have followed him. Within the past decade, for instance, there have been a number of attempts to take seriously Freud's analysis of the discontents of civilization and to find, within Freud's general framework, a way of surmounting his essential pessimism about the possibility of a peaceful civilized life. The three attempts I would like to mention here are those of the sociologist Philip Rieff, the classicist Norman O. Brown, and the philosopher Herbert Marcuse.

The source of Freud's pessimism is not difficult to locate. According to his theory of the instincts, their essential aim is pleasure and, left to his own resources, the individual would seek full instinctual gratification. However, individuals live not in isolation, but in communities of other individuals. The price they have to pay for that common life which is necessary, among other things, for libidinal satisfaction and protection against nature is sublimation of instinct. The very basis of civilization is this common renunciation of instinctual gratification,[18] but its absolutely necessary price is ever-increasing guilt and aggression. That is why a highly developed civilization, such as that of the West, is notable for its close correlation between, on the one hand, technological progress, which results from ever more refined forms of sublimation, and, on the other hand, aggression. This analysis in itself was one source of Freud's pessimism.

A further reason for pessimism was that Freud believed he could discern within the individual an "intimate, independent, instinctual" tendency toward aggression, an instinct, in brief, toward destruction and death. He urged:

> The meaning of the evolution of culture is no longer a riddle to us. It must present to us the struggle between Eros and Death, between the instincts of life and the instincts of destruction, as it works itself out in the human species. This struggle is what all life essentially consists of and so the evolution of civilization may be simply described as the struggle of the human species for existence.[19]

Freud could imagine mankind finding ways of alleviating this struggle, mainly through a diligent application of science, reason, and experience. However, alleviation was the most mankind could hope for. By giving up his religious illusions and educating himself to reality, man could learn to live with his individual and cultural limitations. With ingenuity, the aid of reason, and science—Freud's God "Logos"—the individual could learn how to bargain with civilized community and thus find a satisfactory middle-ground between the claims of his instincts and the claims of the community. For those nurtured on a more glorious vision of man's future, Freud's restricted, hardly ecstatic vision of the Kingdom to Come can only appear as somber.

Philip Rieff

If I may be allowed to use the phrases, the work of Philip Rieff can be characterized as a right-wing response to Freud's pessimism and that of Brown and Marcuse as a left-wing response. By this I mean that Rieff accepts, with relatively minor variations, Freud's pessimism. Rieff does not envisage mankind making a great leap; that to him seems unimaginable. The psychological *status quo* will continue in force and be emeliorated only by a growing affluence. By contrast, Brown and Marcuse envision a civilization where Eros will have decisively triumphed over Thanatos, however difficult this is to bring about. They allow themselves the kind of messianic dreams which Rieff, with Freud, would have mankind abandon.

For Rieff, the distinguishing mark of contemporary civilization is that the purposes of the individual self, rather than those of the community, are becoming central. As a result of spreading affluence, once the privilege of the few but now a mass phenomenon, men are finding ways of bargaining more effectively with a repressive culture. The discernible movement of civilization is toward the creation of a post-communal culture, though such a culture may never actually be achieved.[20] In *The Triumph of the Therapeutic,* Rieff wrote:

> Faith is the compulsive dynamic of culture, channeling obedience to, trust in, and dependence upon authority. With more or less considered passion, men submit to the moral demand system—and, moreover, to its personifications from which they cannot detach themselves except at the terrible cost of guilt. . . . Now, contradicting all faiths, a culture of the indifferent is being attempted, lately using the rhetoric of 'commitment' with which to enlarge the scope of its dynamism. Such a credo of change amounts to a new faith—more precisely to a counter-faith.[21]

That passage, with its ironic observation on "the rhetoric of 'commitment' catches the flavor of Rieff's style and his anti-visionary philosophy. Indeed, his style is beautifully matched to his counter-faith: ironic, self-critical, playful, and uncommitted. The full power of the "counter-faith" is caught in the following lines.

> Our cultural revolution does not aim, like its predecessors, at victory for some rival commitment, but rather

at a way of using all commitments, which amounts to loyalty toward none. By psychologizing about themselves interminably, Western men are learning to use their internality against the primacy of any particular organization of the personality.[22]

If traditional cultures, and particularly Western Christian culture, are seen to be dominated by a symbolic of control, then the new culture is dominated by a symbolic of release from communal identities and purposes, ascetic moralities, normative institutions, and from all god and faiths.[23] In this new culture, the "spiritualizers" will have lost all power of persuasion. To the extent that religion espouses the organization of communal purposes, it will lose its grip on a culture which repudiates commitments beyond the purposes of the private self.

The regnant man of our day is "psychological man,"[24] the critical, detached, self-serving man. Psychological man adopts the "analytic attitude"[25] toward life, which is neither hopeful nor hopeless, but only realistic. He does not scorn commitments but, more cleverly, sees them as fluid and shifting, amusing or boring, and to be used for the enhancement of a private life. The goal of psychological man is to live in a "therapeutic" culture, "with nothing at stake beyond a manipulable sense of well being."[26] Inevitably, for this kind of man with this kind of attitude and aspiring to this kind of culture, the distinction between a "meaningful" and "meaningless" life ceases to exist. "Dichotomies" of that kind "belong to the eras of public philosophies and communal theologies"[27] when the promise of salvation lay in community. In Rieff's view, the death of these eras is at hand.

Can any religious believer hear words like this without feeling chilled, not only because of the confidence behind Rieff's descriptions and predictions, but even more because one can see many signs of the presence of psychological man within the religious communities themselves. The line is exceedingly fine between, on the one hand, psychological man as sketched by Rieff and, on the other hand, a contemporary religious man seeking "self-fulfillment," that is, freedom from a legalistic morality, acceptance of sexual pleasure, and liberation from ascetical doctrines and practices.

Norman O. Brown

With Norman O. Brown one enters, once again, a world of passion and commitment, though one that is perhaps no less disturbing than Rieff's. For Brown, man's great passion must become the victory of Eros over Thanatos, a victory which would require the enthronement of a psychoanalytic consciousness. By such a consciousness Brown means a number of things. It is a consciousness which is dialectical, going beyond the "normal" and sane law of contradiction. It is a consciousness which seeks a Dionysian, bodily ego; it seeks in the overflowing of limits the way of wisdom. It seeks once and for all to give up the way of negation, of repression, and of sublimation which, by denying the body in a quest for spiritual transcendence, actually nourishes the death instinct and turns man against himself and other human beings. As Brown put it in *Life Against Death*:

> The human ego must face the Dionysian reality, and therefore a great work of self-transformation lies ahead of it. For Nietzsche was right in saying that the Apollonian preserves, the Dionysian destroys self-consciousness. As long as the structure of the ego is Apollonian, Dionysian experience can only be bought at the price of ego-dissolution.[28]

The Dionysian can only be faced with a consciousness which embraces and affirms instinctual reality.

Culture, as we now know it, is neurotic. Its sickness stems from the thus far irreconcilable conflict between an instinct toward death and an instinct toward life within the depths of man. The existence of the conflict, however, is what makes men different from animals. Man has the privilege of being neurotic, a privilege which is at the same time his curse and his burden. In Brown's eyes, the truly radical impulse of Freud lay in his willingness to take the body seriously. He differs from Freud, however, in his belief that man need not be alienated from his body and its instincts. To escape this alienation a way must be found beyond repressive sublimation, a way of accepting the reality of death and a way of turning work into play. According to Brown, certain streams of the Christian mystical tradition, together with the doctrine of the Resurrection of the body, provide many clues. The mystical tradition which is of value here is not that of sublimation-mysticism, but of Body-mysticism as exemplified in the writings of Jacob Boehme who, as did Freud, acknowledged "the potent demand in our unconscious for an androgynous mode of being and a narcissistic mode of self-expression. . . .[29] The consciousness of history, which looms so large in recent religious thought, is dealt with by Brown in a devastating way.

"If historical consciousness is finally transformed into psycho-analytical consciousness, the grip of the dead hand of the past on life in the present would be loosened, and man would be ready to live instead of making history, to enjoy instead of paying back old scores and debts, and to enter that state of Being which was the goal of his Becoming."[30]

In the end, the redemption of man, the neurotic animal, entails nothing less than a reconstruction of that psychological reality which Freud felt to be given, but which Brown believes can be transmuted. In the end, all antinomies will be nullified, "the antinomy between mind and body, word and deed, speech and silence, overcome."[31]

Herbert Marcuse

Herbert Marcuse also looks forward to a transformation of psychological reality, but for him the first step is a political revolution. According to Marcuse, Freud's mistake was to assume that the reality principle was fixed and permanent; it was this assumption which led to his pessimism about the human condition. The reality principle, in the form of the irreconcilable conflict of the life and death instincts within the biological nature of the individual, and of the conflict between the individual and community at the level of culture, could only seem to Freud a permanent datum of human existence. Marcuse's counter-thesis is that the reality principle, while having deep biological roots, is nonetheless historically conditioned.[32] In the technological West, it has taken the historical form of what Marcuse calls the "performance principle." Reality presents itself to Western man as requiring acquisitiveness, competitive economic performance, domination, control, and aggression.[33] The performance principle springs not from the nature or the requirements of civilized life, but from "the prevalent social organization of labor"[34] which produces an alienated man, living in an alienated civilization, and doing alienated work. Where Rieff sees "psychological man" coming to dominate society, Marcuse sees the rise of "one-dimensional man,"[35] closed to the body, closed to the transcendent,[63] closed to play, closed to the life of Eros, and closed to the full range of his talents, instincts, and visions.

Marcuse accepts Freud's conviction that civilization depends at least to some degree on repression and sublimation. However, he differs with Freud in seeing the mode of repression present in late industrial society as "surplus-repression."[37] By this phrase Marcuse means a repression which springs from social domination, based upon historically conditioned modes of labor, technology, and competition, rather than upon fixed, biologically instinctual sources. The problem for mankind is to rid itself of the performance principle and to do away with surplus-repression. Were this to be accomplished, the prospect of a non-repressive civilization would begin to appear. Indeed, Marcuse holds that it is already beginning to appear because the performance principle has pushed mankind so far along the road to self-destruction that Eros should be ready, barring an ultimate disaster, to reassert itself. The advent of automation, a product of technological society, gives special promise of providing the material tool necessary to take man beyond surplus-repression.

None of this can occur without a political and a psychological revolution; the two go hand in hand. The political revolution will lie in a decisive rejection of social domination and alienated labor. Marcuse looks to those outside the technological reward system, for example, the Negro masses, as a possible source of the political revolution. Though the traditional proletariat is dead, domesticated by technology and diverted from revolutionary goals, this is not true of the Negro masses.

The psychological revolution must come in the form of a rejection of the Logos of domination in favor of a Logos of gratification. "Whatever the implications of the original Greek conception of Logos as the essence of being," Marcuse writes in *Eros and Civilization,*

> since the canonization of the Aristotelian logic, the term merges with the idea of ordering, classifying, mastering reason. And this idea of reason becomes increasingly antagonistic to those faculties and attitudes which are receptive rather than productive, which tend toward gratification rather than transcendence—which remain strongly committed to the pleasure principle.[38]

Only a new reality principle can reverse the direction of Western history and re-establish a Logos of gratification. The present late industrial civilization is dominated by a value system characterized by delayed satisfaction, restraint of pleasure, toil, productiveness, and security. A non-repressive civilization would show the marks of immediate satisfaction, pleasure, joy, receptiveness, and the absence of unnecessary repression. Together with Norman O. Brown, Marcuse would have man cease trying to transcend himself and instead come to accept himself.

PSYCHOANALYTIC CONSCIOUSNESS AND THE FUTURE OF RELIGIOUS THOUGHT

This brief tour through the writings of Rieff, Brown, and

Marcuse only begins to suggest some of the implications and alternatives which spring from a psychoanalytical consciousness.

General Implications of the Psychoanalytic Consciousness

There is, first, a far more systematic attempt to take account of man's biological nature than is characteristic of religious thought. For a psychoanalytical consciousness the quest for transcendence, which is the basis of the religious premise, lies within man's biological nature. Instead of this quest being seen as the source of man's glory, it is seen as the source of his unhappiness and self-destruction. In the hands of a Rieff, a psychoanalytic consciousness becomes a mode of thinking about man with the air of immunizing him against an obsession with "meaning" and "purpose." In the hands of a Brown, it seeks to enable man to become reconciled to his body, restoring that unity and polymorphously perverse sexuality which man lost through his attempt to consciously master reality and to live a life of reason. In the hands of a Marcuse, it seeks to restrict man's drive for transcendence to the sphere of the historically possible and imaginable; man can transcend his present political and economic modes of organizing and manipulating reality. Common to all three thinkers is a desire that man accept a "reality principle" which would place a limit on any pretensions that human beings can escape from this world by finding a meaning which lies beyond it.

There is, second, an attempt to locate the enduring sources of human community. For Rieff, this takes the form of arguing that affluence at least makes possible the cultivation of a human community oriented toward individual rather than communal interests. There need no longer be any pretense that man finds his salvation in a sacrifice of personal goals for the sake of the common good. Instead, the community is so structured as to do away with all communal goods save that of the narcissistic self-realization of each individual. In the hands of Brown, community is located in the drive of Eros to encompass an ever-greater range of libidinal pleasures and relationships. For Marcus as for Brown, community is to be found in an expanding circle of libidinal bonds together with the constant effort needed to transmute the historically conditioned reality principle.

Religious Implications of the Psychoanalytic Consciousness

The difficulties this kind of psychoanalytical consciousness poses for a religious consciousness and for the religious premise do not need to be underscored. No religious confrontation with secularity can pretend to completeness until this consciousness has been acknowledged and dealt with. Can the religious mind, with Philip Rieff, begin to contemplate a culture which is releasing rather than controlling, uncommitted instead of committed? Can the religious mind, with Norman O. Brown, envision an individual who has moved beyond sublimation, beyond attempts to transcend himself, and who has ceased to reject the body? Can the religious mind, with Herbert Marcuse, imagine a civilization which has ceased to be repressive, which has ceased to let humans dominate each other, and which has ceased to allow material progress to become the instrument of its own destruction?

The problem of God must have a central place in any attempt to provide answers to these questions. Any future formulation of the nature of God and his meaning for human life will require simultaneously the formulation of an ideal civilized life. The problem of God and the problem of culture are as inseparable as are the problem of God and the problem of the body. Freud saw God as the infantile projection of a humanity unwilling to adapt itself to the reality principle. In so doing, he made it possible for the religious community to reject literally infantile images of God and regressive ways of speaking of and responding to God. The way out of that trap has almost been found. However, Freud saw another trap lying in wait, into which contemporary religious thought is all too unwittingly and unconsciously falling. That is the belief "in a higher spiritual being, whose qualities are indefinable and whose purpose cannot be discerned."[39] Freud has thus far not been proved correct in his prediction that such a spiritual being will lose its "hold on human interest."[40] But then it is only very recently that religious thinkers have tried, to use Freud's words, "to preserve the God of religion by substituting for him an impersonal, shadowy, abstract principle, and say, 'Thou shalt not take the name of the Lord thy God in vain!' "[41]

Is it not suggestive, from a psychoanalytic point of view, that one major stream of contemporary theism has of late resorted to a hidden, or absent, or dead, or silent God? Does not this kind of a God sound strikingly like Freud's "impersonal, shadowy, abstract principle?" Is not this God psychologically congenial for the contemporary mind because he enables man to assert his autonomous dignity and freedom all the more easily; because, since nothing can be known or said of him, he is proof against the criticism of unbelievers; because he is compatible with any direction humanity may take; and because he allows the religious mind to continue to justify itself without having to pay a high price for its belief?

Similarly, is it not suggestive that those categories most frequently employed today, when attempts are made to speak of God, are precisely those categories useful to a contemporary mind? In an era of great social change, of flux in every direction, it can hardly be coincidental that some theists would be attracted to a God in process. In a period where man has come to a sense of his power to shape his future and to create his own history, it can hardly be an accident that some theists find God's revelation to be manifest in history. In an era when the believer finds his identity uncertain and feels beleaguered by the success of a confident secular humanism, is it sheer chance that some theists contend that the believer and the unbeliever are brothers under the skin in that they share a fundamental desire to know?

It might be replied that there is no coincidence or accident in these correlations and that the theist today is only doing what has been required of theists in every generation: using those concepts and categories available to him as he tries to speak of God. It is a time-honored practice, resting on the apparently impregnable principle that the only language available to man as he tries to speak of God is human language. On that score there can be no particular objection, for what else can human beings do?

Psychoanalytic Projection and God

There can be an objection, however, to the way in which working models and linguistic probes soon become reified and presented as firm, enduring principles. There are two ways of objecting to this kind of development. One way is the more traditional protest against the creation of idols based upon the fact that as soon as we reify our concepts and ways of talking about God we have created idols to put in the place of God. A second way of objecting can be called the "psychoanalytic" way and is based upon the fact that the language and concepts employed in speaking about God serve to fulfill certain cultural needs and may have nothing whatever to do with a deity who purportedly transcends these needs. This seems to me the most promising way of criticizing contemporary attempts to re-formulate the theistic problem. Thus, the notion of a hidden or dead God, on the one hand, or the notion of an historical or process God, on the other, can all be shown to have their psychological roots in the theist's attempt to find a way of reconciling his position to contemporary cultural developments. In short, a God is being fashioned who will enable man to be at one with his times.

But is this necessarily an objectionable procedure? It seems objectionable to me, if I may so put it, only when it is done in perfect innocence. If the theologian or philosopher does not recognize what he is up to, if he does not realize the way in which the culture is shaping his response to the problem of God, then there is danger that his hearers will believe something is actually being said about God. In fact, what is being said will only be a disguised statement about the aims and needs of the culture and of the theologian himself. Another drawback in such innocence is that the full possibilities of creating a viable culture God will not be realized. Without intending paradox, let me put matters in the following fashion: (1) it is wrong to fashion a God who is only a projection of one's cultural needs and ideals if one is unaware that it is a projection; (2) but if one is aware that it is a projection, then one has the obligation to make it a good projection. This proposition rests on two assumptions: that the source of idol-worshipping is the erection of an adequate projection, and that a good projection even while remaining a projection, need not fall prey to the perennial temptation to erect idols.

It is at this point that the value of a psychoanalytical consciousness becomes evident and this value is both therapeutic and propaedeutic. It is therapeutic in that it can help make clear the extent to which theistic formulations are a function of cultural needs and pressures; in so doing it helps expose the roots of projection. It is propaedeutic in that it can help to locate the genuine needs of society, as distinguished from false or unhealthy needs; in so doing it can prepare the ground for adequate, viable projections. To say this is merely to repeat a previous point: the problem of God is one with the problem of culture. This is what Freud saw and what theists are prone to neglect. An adequate projection of God will be culturally valuable, that is, valuable to the individual who is part of a community and valuable to the community of all individuals in their attempt to live together. It will be a valuable projection insofar as it is open to further revision, serves as a source of prophetic criticism of the culture, draws the culture forward to higher norms and values than those of the status quo, is psychologically meaningful for people without pandering to destructive and escapist inclinations, and leaves open the question of whether there is a God who stands behind, or is the ground of, man's persistent tendency to fashion projections.

The work of Rieff, Marcuse, and Brown gives a hint of the possibilities. Rieff's "psychological man" poses the question of whether it will remain necessary to posit a God who is the God of demand rather than release cultures. This question, in turn, serves to turn the eye toward the contemporary religious belief that "commitment" is somehow a central question for religion. Are belief and "commitment" correlative terms, or is their relationship only an historical accident? Brown's Dionysian man, for whom all opposites are reconciled and all dualisms dissolved poses the question of whether the religious premise—that man must transcend himself—is, unbeknownst to us, the source of his self-destructiveness. Marcuse's politico-psychological man poses the question of whether the religious drive to go beyond history may not actually lead man to make himself the victim of history.

There is not sufficient space here to attempt a thorough explanation of the many points made in this paper. Specifically, there is required an elaborate argument for a Christian theist like myself to make plausible the view that the way to a viable contemporary theism is to cultivate the art of projection (or, better, to turn what is an unconscious process into a conscious art). There is also required a lengthy discussion to show that it is a mistake to attempt to isolate the problem of God from the problem of creating viable cultures. I will be content, however, if I have done only one thing: to have made plausible the suggestion that a failure on the part of theologians to come to grips with a psychoanalytic consciousness will be the kind of failure which can jeopardize everything else they do. If I am correct in stating that the theological community has evaded a full confrontation with a psychoanalytic consciousness, then I hope I have also added enough to show that this consciousness could, in the end, turn out to be the most valuable of all. Whether it turns out to be all that valuable, however, will depend upon a willingness to suffer the pains and shocks it will surely bring to the quest for God.

◊

1. Mircea Eliade, **The Sacred and the Profane,** trans. Willard R. Trask (New York: Harper and Row, 1961), p. 100.

2. Thomas O'Dea, **The Sociology of Religion,** (Englewood Cliffs, N. J.: Prentice-Hall, 1966), p. 28.

3. My use of the word "dualistic" does not imply that there is any necessary dichotomy between an experience of the sacred and the pro-

fane. I am using the word to specify only that convention whereby a long tradition of religious philosophy has tried to characterize the difference people have reported between their ordinary, mundane experience and certain intense experiences which seem to take them beyond the mundane. Cf. Rudolf Otto, **The Idea of the Holy** (London: Oxford University Press, 1923) for a classic description, and Abraham H. Maslow, **Religions, Values, and Peak-Experience** (Columbus: Ohio State University Press, 1964) for a more recent discussion.

4. Cf. Peter Berger, "A Sociological View of the Secularization of Theology," **Journal for the Scientific Study of Religion,** VI (1967), 3-16, for an interesting, though at times hostile and misleading, account of the way contemporary theology has allowed itself to become overly enamored with secularization.

5. Norman O. Brown, **Life Against Death** (New York: Vintage Books, 1959), p. 176. I am using the phrase "psychoanalytic consciousness" here in a broader and somewhat different sense, however, than Brown.

6. Sigmund Freud, **The Future of an Illusion,** trans. W. D. Robson-Scott (New York: Anchor Books, 1964).

7. Gregory Zilboorg, **Freud and Religion** (Westminster, Md.: The Newman Press, 1958).

8. Leslie Dewart, **The Future of Belief** (New York: Herder and Herder, 1966), p. 20ff.

9. Freud, **The Future of an Illusion,** p. 82.

10. **Ibid.,** p. 73.

11. **Ibid.,** p. 25.

12. Sigmund Freud, **Civilization and Its Discontents,** trans. Jean Riviere (Garden City, N. Y.: Doubleday, 1958), p. 35.

13. **Ibid.,** p. 36.

14. **Ibid.,** p. 105.

15. **Ibid.,** p. 41.

16. **Ibid.,** p. 104.

17. See especially Dieter Wyss, **Depth Psychology: A Critical History,** trans. Gerald Onn (New York: W. W. Norton, 1966).

18. Freud, **Civilization and Its Discontents,** p. 43.

19. **Ibid.,** p. 75.

20. Philip Rieff, **The Triumph of the Therapeutic** (New York: Harper and Row, 1966), p. 11.

21. **Ibid.,** p. 12.

22. **Ibid.,** p. 21.

23. **Ibid.,** p. 20.

24. Cf. Philip Rieff, **Freud: The Mind of the Moralist** (Garden City, N. Y.: Anchor Books, 1961), p. 360ff.

25. Rieff, **The Triumph of the Therapeutic,** p. 50ff.

26. Ibid., p. 13.

27. Ibid., p. 52.

28. Norman O. Brown, **Life Against Death**, p. 175.

29. Ibid., p. 310.

30. Ibid., p. 19.

31. Norman O. Brown, **Love's Body** (New York: Random House, 1966), p. 266.

32. Herbert Marcuse, **Eros and Civilization** (New York: Vintage Books, 1962), p. 34.

33. Ibid., p. 41ff.

34. Ibid., p. 117.

35. Herbert Marcuse, **One-Dimensional Man** (Boston: Beacon Press, 1964).

36. "Transcendent" in Marcus's usage refers only to the historical possibilities of human existence and society. Cf. **ibid.**, p. 220.

37. Marcuse, **Eros and Civilization**, p. 32 and **passim.**

38. Ibid., p. 101.

39. Freud, **The Future of an Illusion**, p. 89.

40. **Ibid.**

41. Freud, **Civilization and Its Discontents**, p. 14.

Atheism and Man

◊

Howard L. Parsons

ATHEISM AS AN attitude, belief, and practice has had a long
and complex history within the whole of human history. It is
doubtful, in fact, whether human history can be adequately
understood apart from the dialectical engagement of theism and
atheism, one with another. This engagement has taken place in
thought, for every form of theism and atheism represents a
doctrine concerning the nature of human values and ways of
realizing them. But it has also taken place in the field of social
practice where commitments are expressed and fought out, for
both theisms and atheisms include the conviction that such
values ought to be realized and a disposition to realize them.

Theists have asserted that, because the gods or a god exist with
certain characteristics, certain things or acts have value, and,
therefore, that man is commanded or forbidden to act in certain
ways with regard to values. While disputing overtly about the
gods, theists and atheists have in actual practice met and opposed
one another principally at those points where human values were
at issue, both in theory and in practice. Though disputes over
the gods cannot be dismissed as having no metaphysical or
epistemological import, they have represented the forms through
which men's real and living struggles for values in history have
symbolized themselves. Thus, while the question of the nature,
character, and import for man of the gods or God remains the
religious question, it is also a value-question; as such it is easily
transformable into human terms for the nonreligious imagination.

[149]

In the same way that atheists have attacked theists and theism precisely because they wished to challenge the value-claims of the latter, theists have defended their religions against atheists and atheism because they saw in the latter a competing claim concerning what is of ultimate significance or value for man. As a result, the interlocking struggle of theism and atheism is woven into the fabric of human thought and action. It is one form of the general struggle for human values and human fulfillment that defines human history. Theism, as a claim concerning what is divine for human decision and living, inevitably generates a question and counter claim. If the counter claim goes far enough it is labelled atheism, though atheism may itself use the term "divine" to refer to its ultimate value. The two are inseparable. Atheism arises as a critique of a theistic value-claim, and proposes its own answer to the question of what is of great or supreme significance for man; theism responds in a critical and constructive manner to the negative and positive claims of atheism. This is the dialectic of moving unity and opposition which defines the development of all theistic and atheistic ideas. The present efforts at Christian-Marxist dialogue mark an implicit recognition of the dialectic; they hold promise of widening the dialectic in a conscious and non-violent way to a world scale.

In this I shall limit my discussion of the complex issue to the following: (1) the meanings of the term "atheism," both negative and positive; (2) the origins of atheism and its development leading up to and through Marx's atheism; and (3) atheism's humanistic critique of religion and theism. This discussion will be confined chiefly to theism and atheism in the Western, European world, and to their development and relation in the milieu of Western Christianity.

THE TERM 'ATHEISM': NEGATIVE AND POSITIVE

The term "atheism" may be taken in two major senses, one negative and the other positive.

The Negative Meaning of 'Atheism'

In its negative sense, 'atheism' signifies a belief or doctrine that denies the existence of god, gods, or a particular deity such as God for Christianity. In this sense the term has referred to what certain men did *not* believe, that is, a-theism. It has usually been employed by theists to characterize atheists in a negative way, as the absolute opposites of theists. This usage has taken a variety of forms.

(1) 'Atheism' has meant that a person did not use the term 'God' or its equivalent to characterize an object of his belief concerning what is supremely significant. This failure to speak of 'God' might be a deliberate attempt to distinguish one's belief from theism as, for example, when Comte spoke of the "religion of humanity." It might occur also because of a person's ignorance of the term or concept, in which case theists might debate whether the person can really worship and believe in a deity without attaching this term to the object of his belief. Some of the Apostolic Fathers, for example, held that the souls of the righteous who died before the Ascension of Christ and hence could not know God in that particular form, received salvation and might eventually see God.[1] Paul Tillich has maintained that the "ultimate concern" gripping the ardent atheist must necessarily direct him toward God.[2]

(2) Atheism has meant a deviant concept concerning the quantitative character of deity. Ikhnaton, who was perhaps the first monotheist of history, was an atheist in the eyes of the polytheistic priests of his own day. Atheism was alleged against the Christians during the first centuries.[3] In the early Christological controversies the Arians who separated God from Christ, the modalists who denied the personalities of the Trinity, the Nestorians who affirmed separated natures in Jesus Christ, the monophysites who denied the human nature of Jesus Christ, and the Apollinarians who denied the human character of Jesus' mind or spirit, all were rejected by the early Church Councils as being mistaken concerning God. They were variously described

as "impious," "blasphemous," and "godless." Similarly for the Jews, an atheist was anyone not a Jew, that is, a Gentile. Finally some Jews and Muslims, with their emphasis on the unitary character of the deity, Yahweh or Allah respectively, might be inclined to view the Christian trinitarian belief in God as mistaken and hence atheistic.

(3) Atheism has also signified a mistaken concept concerning the qualities of God. For example, from the point of view of prevalent Christian or Judaic theology, the term 'atheistic' might be applied to the mystical view of God such as that of Eckart which holds that man becomes God, to Spinoza's concept of God as naturalistic and impersonal, and to Mill's notion of God as limited.

(4) Atheism has meant an explicit disavowal of the supernatural, including any supernatural God. Because orthodox theology has been identified with a supernaturalistic world-view, it has been assumed that all forms of naturalism or materialism would be forms of atheism, as, for example, in the expression "godless materialism."

(5) Finally, atheism has meant not only a conceptual denial of God but a correlative denial of certain important values in both theory and practice. Theists have held that, if man did not believe in God and worship him, he could neither really understand the order of values which ultimately is created and sustained by God, nor in practice fulfill those values.

The Positive Meaning of 'Atheism'

The second major meaning of the term 'atheism' pertains to the positive side of human thought and action with respect to religion, that is, to the effort of men to realize and reconstruct values. Most, if not all, atheisms have contained not only a negative and critical, but a positive and creative movement.

(1) This has been true of those atheists standing outside the religions. The Milesian naturalists were not content merely to attack the popular concept of anthropomorphic gods; they went on to propose their own ideas of "the divine." Thales remarked

that all things are full of gods; having stripped away all myths in his cosmology, Anaximander characterized the infinite all-pervasive matter of the universe as "divine" (το Θεῖον); and Xenophanes, whose iconoclasm is striking, identified deity with the universe. If not most, certainly many atheistic critics of religious concepts of God have proposed positive alternatives to the traditional religious views concerning the meaning of the world and history and the significance of human living. Such influential atheisms of ancient times as early Buddhism, Jainism, early Taoism, and Epicureanism were constructive and affirmative on the issue of human values and fulfillment. In modern times such principal atheists as Marx, Nietzsche, Freud, and Sartre have all expressed both negative and positive moments in grappling with the question of values, the meaning of "God," and his relevance to that question. In his early writing Marx considered atheism abstract and negative,[4] and Engels warned against the sectarian atheism of the Bakunists.[5] Camus chose to argue not against the affirmation of the existence of God, but against "the logic leading to that affirmation" as a flight from honest confrontation of the absurd.[6]

(2) Within the religions themselves there has been an analogous critical-constructive development which joins to the movement against the traditional concepts and practices concerning God an effort to reformulate the meaning of the divine and its implications for human thought, behavior, and values. In Asia, in part at least, the Upanishads represented an effort of non-Brahmins to bypass the traditional ritualism of the esoteric, caste-dominated, Brahmin religion, and to simplify Vedic polytheism.[7] Buddhism and Jainism were originally heresies which denied the existence of the gods, challenged religious privileges of caste, and made the disciplines of self-release available to all. But in the context of Indian culture they remained "religions" and affected Hinduism. Early Taoism was probably a revolutionary movement against the feudal class society of ancient China.[8] It offered a communal and naturalistic way of life to the people, in contrast to the static, status-bound society of traditional religion.

In Asia Minor, in the face of the polytheism, animal sacrifices, and ceremonial magic of Iranian religion, Zoroaster lifted up and transformed one of the many existing old gods, Ahura Mazda, into a moralized deity. In Judaism, the prophets and men like the author of the main part of Job progressively questioned and refined the concept of Yahweh. Simultaneously they denounced what they considered to be defects in the reigning concept of God and in man's putative efforts to obey God, and articulated new and often more humanistic concepts. Muhammad took one God out of Arabia's great congeries of nature gods and, with his armies, forged a single, monotheistic religion.

(3) Jesus himself, consciously placing himself in the line of the Jewish prophets, embodied a radical criticism of existing religious practices. His message was that God is not only a stern Judge but a loving and forgiving Father, and that as his children all men are brothers. As the Jews were generally more concerned about attitude than about theory Jesus was not accused by his enemies of being an "atheist," but he was charged with being in league with the devil,[9] out of his mind,[10] and blasphemous.[11]

(4) The critique of idolatry and the impulse to purify devotion within the history of Christianity has been a forceful and productive tradition. It is marked by such figures and movements as the Cathari, the Waldenses, the Franciscan Spirituals, Wycliffe, the Lollards, Conciliarism, Huss, and others. Christian theology has changed and evolved in response to critical challenges both inside and outside the faith. The first great challenge came from the Greek thought during the first four centuries of the Christian era, when the orthodox lines of Christian theology were laid down. The second challenge came in the thirteenth century with the revival of Aristotle's thought and the simultaneous threat of Muslim thought, mysticism, and secularism. The answer then was the theology of St. Thomas. The third challenge was the capitalistic and bourgeois democratic reaction against feudalism which generated a widespread secular criticism of religious institutions, traditions, and hierarchy. Protestantism represented a partial accommodation to this reaction, while Catholicism represented a conservative movement against it.

The fourth challenge and the one which is currently being experienced is the challenge of the modern world of science, technology, and socialism. This has its repercussions in the domains of human rights and duties as among laborers and women, of individuals in relation to public authorities, of relations between states, and of international relations such as the problem of war and universal genocide. Catholicism has responded to this challenge in recent years by the ecumenical policies of Pope John XXIII and Pope Paul VI, and by such developments as the thought of Teilhard de Chardin and theologies focussing on community and history.

Atheism vs. Theism

Thus the atheistic attitude and method of thinking has normally been a dialetic of negation and affirmation. Both inside and outside religious communities, it has functioned in relation to theism not by absolute opposition, but by dialectical unity, interpenetration, interdependence, and mutual opposition and modification. Sometimes the relation between theism and atheism has been one of constructive opposition, while at other times it has been one of destructive antagonism; but by the very nature of the case it has never been a relation which either side could escape. The present effort of communists and Christians to bring theism and atheism into dialogue is a recognition of the dialectical opposition of the two.

The atheist inside a religious community, while directing his criticism toward the beliefs and practices of his religion, at the same time accepts certain basic beliefs shared by the members of that community. Thus his affirmation of theism undergirds his a-theism and, so far as possible, justifies that a-theism as a possible constructive contribution to an ongoing tradition of belief and practice. Whether he remains within the community or is called "atheist" and anathematized depends on the members of the community and their threshold of toleration. Sometimes a belief declared to be "false and altogether opposed to Holy Scripture," as Cardinal Bellarmine described the Copernican hypothesis in 1616, is later sanctioned, as in 1822 the Papacy sanctioned that same hypothesis. Pronounced a heretic, Jeanne d'Arc was burned in 1431, but some 500 years later was canonized. Here it is a question of terminology as to whether a critical theist is to be called atheistic; it seems to be a matter of degree and of the judgment of generations.

This criticism, as one of the moments in the movement of human thought and action, is necessary not only as an inevitable fact, but for human improvement. It would be contradictory to assert that God possesses all value and that human improvement is either not important or not possible, for every assertion implicitly affirms the ability of man to know truth and hence entails a standard of better and worse with regard to truth, and to that extent the ability of man to improve.

The term "atheist" applies quite unequivocally to those who have separated themselves from a religious community, criticize its concepts, beliefs, and practices, and reject its basic beliefs. But even here a more important distinction is suggested by some of Jesus' parables, such as that of the good Samaritan. Such distinctions as theism vs. atheism, faith vs. unfaith, and belief vs. unbelief may be made and do describe the difference between men in their intellectual life. However, the more profound and determinative issue is how men meet the day-by-day decisions that confront them: do men in their conduct commit themselves to creating and sustaining certain values in human living and history? Among so-called theists and so-called atheists, men differ widely in this respect. It has been one of the contributions of atheists to religious thought and living to call attention to the contradiction between the professed beliefs of men of religion and their day-by-day commitments concerning values. They have insisted that religious belief and practice meet the secular and human test of serving men's values.

THE ORIGINS AND DEVELOPMENT OF ATHEISM

In order to see atheism in perspective, we turn now to its

origins and its relations to theism in history. We have already seen that the meanings of atheism and theism are complex and changing in consequence of the dialectical relations that they have borne to one another. A brief historical treatment will serve to elaborate these relations and to clarify the meaning of atheism.

The Origins of Theism

We have no evidence that the animals on our planet, including the primates, are religious in any sense of that term as applied to human behavior. However, the continuity of evolution implies some *Anlage,* some groundwork or natural tendency already in organisms and environment which makes possible the later emergence of religious behavior in man. Man's religions both primitive and sophisticated, seem to arise out of a need to relate and commit himself in a meaningful way to something other than the presently conceived being and value of either his self, his group, or his species. This other is conceived to be, have, or provide a commanding unity, wholeness, or supreme significance for which he feels a need. This sense of need for identity and direction, a sense of separation, and reaching out for what transcends present limits takes various forms in feelings of finitude, loneliness, frustration, impotence guilt, meaninglessness, and mortality.

We cannot deal here with such questions as whether these feelings and the underlying need for supreme significance in human living are uniquely "religious"; whether they are uniquely human but expressible in many different ways including the religious; or whether they are contingent and removable deviations from man's genuine nature, or forms of an inescapable alienation. These questions lie at the heart of any discussion between theists and atheists, and most would agree that historically they have defined the religious transaction. As Teilhard de Chardin put it, we are engaged in religion "when we turn towards the summit, towards the *totality* and the future."[12] Such an attitude arises in part because man is a symbolizing animal capable of creating a multi-dimensional domain of meanings, a noosphere. In becoming conscious of his world and rendering it meaningful to himself, man becomes conscious of himself and asks about his meaning and his life, his order and his significance in relation to that world.

The primitive religious answer of Paleolithic peoples was not, strictly speaking, theistic; at best it was proto-theistic. Thrown into an antagonistic but dependent relation to nature, they found that their ultimate relation to things was that of adjusting to those impersonal forces in the world by whose activities they lived or died: animals, plants, sun, moon, totem spirit, anima, mana, etc. When, after approximately a million years of food-gathering, men began to form agricultural and pastoral communities, the form of their religion gradually shifted from the impersonal to the personal.

Subsequently, new and complex social relations provided the basis for the rise of new religions directed toward the personalities of the "gods." The stages in this transition are not clear and were probably uneven in their development, as is suggested by the variety of competing theories.[13] However, the transition from the primitive nature religions to the humanized religions of the gods can be discerned in ancient writings such as the Upanishads, and is indicated by terms like "divine" (Latin *divus*, Sanskrit*divya*) which means day, heavenly, shining sky, or sky-god. The term is based both upon a direct evaluation of the sky and sun as grand, commanding, exalted, numinous, and mighty, and upon their metaphorical interpretation as symbols of those qualities. Thus, "divine" points both back to that nature from which man's primitive body was palpably emerged through the misty millennia, and forward to civilized life and the values of the human spirit. In this light it can be said that the gods are born at the threshold of the human community.[14]

These gods, originally conceived in the image of tribal chieftains and kings, reflected the level and type of dependence which men had to their increasingly important social and eventually urban environment. In this they were similar to the numinous beings which were worshipped during the food-gathering period and which reflected men's profound sense of dependence on nature. As Neolithic man by domesticating plants and animals changed his relation to natural creatures from being primarily that of dependency to that of control, men lost their attitude of awe toward creatures. It was gods who were worshipped, while animals were sacrificed. The distant, mysterious objects on which they began to depend were not principally natural objects but the human who ruled the early civilized societies, i.e., kings and their auxiliaries, such as members of the royal family, priests, scribes, and officials.[15] In this way theism emerged in human history.

The Origins of Atheism

The critique of the gods, or atheism, arose in response to the basic economic and social conflicts in ancient slave societies. Intimations of new gods and new religions, proposed as alternatives to traditional gods and religions, appeared as early as the 14th century B.C. in the thought of Ikhnaton and Moses. The Iron Age, with its relatively cheap tools and weapons made available to large groups of men, evoked widespread demands for justice.[16] In the 6th and 5th centuries B.C. these demands reached their climax as articulate laymen gave voice to new religious and philosophical ideologies which proposed radically new ways of thinking and living, regardless of whether they retained the older symbols and concepts. This group of men included the Greek philosophers, Jewish prophets, Persian Zarathustra, Indians Gautama Buddha and Mahavira, and the Chinese Lao Tzu and Confucius.

The Jewish thinkers concentrated their criticism on the moral aspects of the gods in the manner of Job who boldly challenged the arbitrary, punitive character of Yahweh. The prophets and their predecessors passionately insisted that the regal divinity had the human qualities of a personal being with whom men might enter into a reciprocal covenant—something impossible with despots.

The pre-Socratic Greek philosophers were concerned more with the natural, metaphysical, and rational character of the divine. Anaximander, for example, in speaking of the first principle or "Boundless" was reported to have said: "This is the divine for it is deathless and indestructible."[17] Although these Greek philosophers accepted the criterion for divinity previously applied to kings, they returned to nature in order to locate it. Their theism thus signified a sharp departure from the general development of ancient religions, being in some respects closer to primitive animism than to the personalized gods of the Greek pantheon or the popular mystery religions. Thus, it was a-theistic both as a recrudescence of a naturalistic outlook and as an anticipation of the modern scientific perspective. At the same time, it expressed the rising critical spirit and new rationality which was suffusing religious thought.

This critical spirit had gripped Jesus, who applied it not to nature but to men and to their interpersonal relations in a radical, concrete and shocking way: the ultimate reason for our life is unconditional love. On the basis of the older view that God is an unbending despot, the view of Jesus was, of course, atheism. Judged in terms of the despotic, self-righteous, and hypocritical religious leaders, whom he denounced, Jesus seemed heretical. It is true that he consciously placed himself in the mainstream of the Law, the Prophets, and the Psalms, which he frequently quoted or to which he often alluded. But in the eyes of contemporary religious and political leaders he represented a radical departure from tradition. As he did not fit the categories of the dominant theism, the result was his crucifixion.

Precisely because of this radical break with the theism of the ruling groups, the faith of Jesus in a loving Father who cares for all his children and calls them to care for one another became the chief challenge to existing religious and political ideologies and systems. When the Roman empire of unbending despots collapsed, the conviction which this outcast from Nazareth embodied and for which he died, catching fire among the dispossessed of the empire, became the dominant theism and the center of ideological and political struggle in Western civilization. It provided a criterion by which men measured and judged their fellow men, their rulers, and the classes around and over them. It became the final appeal for resistance to tyranny and the clarion call for revolution. The early Church was built on the stone that the builders had rejected.

Repeatedly critics or "atheists" objected that the Church herself had rejected that foundaton stone of her temple; they called for its restoration. Whereas Greek atheism struggled to break free of superstition and to assert the claims of natural science, subsequent to Jesus and the emergence of the Christian Church atheism became intensely ethical, concerning itself with the values of love, brotherhood, and justice which had been upheld by the prophets and Jesus but often ignored or crushed by the Church. As he himself said, Jesus introduced into history a new power and hence a new dialectic.

Jesus rejected "the God of the dead," the God of empty words and rituals, the narrow God of a class and nation, the God of armed hosts and war and human oppression. The conflict between the followers of the God of arbitrary and cruel force and the followers of the God of forgiveness and mercy, was an old one in Judaism. Who were the true believers and who atheists? Historically the term "atheist" and kindred terms have been used as terms of opprobrium both for those criticizing some established order of religious thought and practice and, by the critics, for those defending that order. Among numerous historical examples we may cite the conflict between Elijah and the Baal priests, the Cathari and the Papacy, and the reformers and Rome.

Thus the conflict between atheism and theism must be seen as a reflex of contending social forces each of which has stimulated, called forth, and changed the other. In symbolic form the doctrinal struggle has expressed a deeper struggle over values which must be examined on their own merits. The examination, moreover, must deal with unique and concrete instances of the dialectical engagement of the two viewing them in their historical development. For example, the skepticism of the Ionian philosophers toward received religious ideas was a consequence of their own practical experience, the development of new techniques in their society,[18] the variety and pluralism induced by a wide maritime trade and commerce, and the confident speculation of a new dominant social group. The "free thinking" of the eras of the Renaissance, the Reformation, and Enlightenment mirrored the rise of a new, independent, and individualistic class of merchants and entrepreneurs. Marxist atheism grew out of the needs and demands of nineteenth century intellectuals, artisans, and industrial workers.

Where "theism" developed its strongest and most systematic expression as an ideological reflection of a privieged ruling class, its "atheistic" criticism emerged as the main weapon in the hands of an oppressed or neglected class. Especially in the context of the Christian tradition, such criticism has proceeded by an appeal to a selected set of values which transcended class concepts and were professed but not practiced by the ruling class. In order to find, in written or oral tradition, an ideological leverage for change all radical and revolutionary movements have had to build upon the accumulated wisdom of their own society, for their guidance and inspiration they have tended to rely upon the great and exalted dreams of the past. Until recent times, these dreams have taken their origin and form from the Judaeo-Christian tradition, with its ideals of a single source and goal for man, brotherly love, mutuality in all things, messianism, millennialism, and apocalypticism.

By laying claim to what they considered to be the core of theism itself, both religious and secular critics of prevailing theism have sought to overcome that theism by transforming the world onto a new base and thereby transforming theism itself into the reality of its redeeming dreams. This was the meaning of the young Marx who wrote that while religion is fantasy it is also "the *expression* of real distress," a "protest" against it, and "the heart of a heartless world"; and that therefore "the *task of history*" is to "establish *the truth of this world*."[19] In his vision of a new world, the critical and prophetic imagination foresees the dissolution of all artificial distinctions of thought and all antagonisms of practice between religion and philosophy, theism and atheism, the divine and human, and their replacement by the creation of unified men in a unified society. In sum, whether inside or outside a religious community, atheism has taken its stimulus and ideas from theism, then criticized its values, and in turn elicited and responded to the criticism of theism.

This ideological struggle of atheists and theists has been one way in which the major conflicts in social practice in Western Christian societies have worked themselves out. In its intensity and range, this struggle appears to be peculiar to Western societies. In China, until recently an agrarian society with a relatively stable empire, the divine omnipresent power was conceived as gently enfolding, sustaining and harmonizing the individual with other persons and the universe. In India, the divine was thought to be interiorized in the depths of individual consciousness. By contrast, both the early Jews and Greeks dared to picture men in dynamic dealings with deity or ultimate cosmic reality, with whom they entered into covenant and cognitive relation. Dialogue, negotiation, questioning, and even challenge and defiance (Job, Prometheus) were possible.

Both theists and atheists grew to demand that men have a dialectical relation with God, with other men, and with nature. Thus, an essential reason the atheist could not conceive of God's existence was that he did not appear to be a being with whom man might interact or communicate. Increasingly, neither theist nor atheist could maintain his position apart from this dialectical posture in relation to the object of his concern and in parallel manner they have stressed the dialectical development of truth as it emerges in man's relations with the persons, things, and events of his world.

The Jewish and Greek peoples developed their unique forms of dialectical interchange around their own social tensions. The prophetic, popular, and strongly humanistic strain of religion to which Jesus repeatedly appealed established itself in Judaism over against the priestly, hierarchical one. In Greece a long-standing tension grew up between the Ionian, naturalistic, scientific, and atheistic outlook and the Pythagorean, Platonic, teleological, and supernaturalistic position. Since the fusion of the Jewish and Greek traditions in Christianity, these dialectical tensions have been at work, fructifying thought, dividing kingdoms, and producing new syntheses. Depending upon the social situation, these tensions have taken different forms. The tension between the naturalistic and supernaturalistic positions was quiescent for nearly a thousand years because of the decline of Greek science and the lapse of western Europe into barbarism and feudalism. With the revival of the Greek classics in science and philosophy in a religious culture tension revived, and the synthesis of St. Thomas was an initial response. The tension became critical in the sixteenth century with the rapid development of the activities of the theoretical and practical sciences. Finally the advance of capitalism upon the foundations of applied science accelerated the tension by inducing a widespread naturalistic and atheistic outlook in masses of people. The next section will study the resulting development of atheism in the modern world.

Development of Modern Atheism

As can be seen from the above, modern atheism is the child of two genetic lines. Empirical atheism, founded upon a criticism of final causes and supernatural entities, can be traced back to the Ionian philosophers of the sixth century B.C. It was sensory and materialistic in its leanings, and allied itself with the developments in technology, science, and hence empiricism in fifteenth century Europe.

Greek civilization generated another kind of atheism. This operated within a speculative and teleological framework, but, in figures like Socrates and Plato, raised serious questions about the existence and character of the divine. The vigor of Scholastic philosophy depended in large part upon its inheritance from this tradition of critical rationalism. As a result it produced numerous controversies and deviations from received religious teachings, for then, as now, it was not always easy to categorize certain thinkers as "theistic" or "atheistic." In the Scholastic period rationalism concerned with theological matters was not overtly or evangelically atheistic; unlike earlier and later empirical atheism, it did not normally quarrel with most basic articles of belief in traditional theology, but ordinarily expressed itself in theological form. From Scotus Erigena through Bruno and Hegel, however, such innovative and critical rationalism has been invariably viewed with suspicion and alarm by orthodox theologians.

Marx was influenced by both forms of atheism. He received his empirical atheism through the Greek atomists, the French philosophers, and Feuerbach, and his rational atheism through Kant, Fichte, and Hegel. Thus Marx took both a negative and a positive attitude toward religion and theology. He rejected those elements in religion that were non-empirical, or in his terms, "fantastic" and "ideological.' At the same time in his rational critique of religion he sought to incorporate its viable human values while transcending their previous expressions both in theory and in social practice.

Depending on their particular temperaments, personal histories, countries, and situations, Marxists have emphasized one of the two kinds of atheism. Modern empirical atheism represents the earlier, more simple, direct, and naive approach to the problem. It stems from a bourgeois reaction against a feudal idea and social organization. The materialist d'Holbach and the empiricist skeptic Hume reasoned that because God cannot be sensed, he cannot be an individual substance; therefore he cannot exist. Moreover, if in fact deity does exist, it cannot be a patriarch, feudal lord, or monarchic king, but only a supreme principle of cosmic, benign Reason as the Deists concluded.

Were this not so, pantheists would be correct in considering the deity to be a universal presence throughout nature and man, pervading your being and mine no less than that of Jesus. Thus, to say that the world and man are divine is but the last step toward a simple materialism and humanism. Such atheism in its masked and naked forms was one of the great themes of the Enlightenment and led men to abandon an institution that held them more by force of blind habit than by the illumination that is drawn from reflection and experience.

Empirical atheism attracted men and drew them from the enchantments of the Church for those same reasons that a child leaves his parents or a traveller deserts the myths of his home tradition. It substituted the immediacy and certainty of the sensed object for the authority of symbol and ritual, of ideology and custom, by returning to man the simple gifts of sight, sound, and touch. Accordingly, deity either disappeared in the insensible ether or was transformed into natural and human bodies, excruciatingly concrete and fearfully and wonderfully made.

Though the Deists proudly insisted that their religion was "true Christianity," the atheism of the Enlightenment was a child of the bourgeois transformation of Western Europe. Because in many ways it never grew up, it had to be superseded in order to be improved. The *philosophers,* for all their vitriolic attacks on the clergy, their passion for "reason," their unrelenting, but amateur devotion to science, and their worship of autonomy, were the creatures and the captives of the great age of national capitalism. For the most part they were dependent on the men in power, both secular and religious, whose favor they cultivated and with whom they formed shifting alliances.[20] Their critique of things was essentially literary, esthetic, philosophical, and theological, not political, social, or economic. When they engaged in social criticism, they were not, nor could they be, aware of the system which made and sustained them. Following such seventeenth century revolutionaries in science and philosophy as Newton and Locke, they spoke for the capitalistic revolutions that overturned things in England and then in America and France. They were radically opposed to the feudal Church, which resisted such revolution at every turn. Their cry, "God is dead!" was not so much a battle-cry as an announcement, a delighted, prolonged elegy, flung toward the past and toward an institution whose influence in social affairs was being outstripped by the onrushing movement of the bourgeoisie.

The arguments of the *philosophes,* even before the sophisticated reasoning of Kant which closed the age, have the air of those who, having found a gaping hole in the enemy's line, will exploit it until the enemy is completely destroyed. If the Church seemed dazed or powerless to strike back, it was not because she lacked the talents or resources, but because the tide of general opinion with its spreading skepticism was running against her. Though the warriors did not realize it, the victory had been secured. Europe was leaving feudalism behind, and with it, a feudal theology.

Historical and Social Background of Marx's Atheism

The antecedents of this change go back to beyond the eleventh century, when the urban revival began to overtake Europe generating one heresy after another, beginning with the Cathari. Over the centuries the Church, weakened but intact, weathered these shocks, remaining mortised at its base to the rock at Rome, and developing at its peak great university centers. However, in northern Europe industrial changes inaugurated the Protestant Reformation and other dissent. These changes were reflected by Luther's doctrine that "I have faith, therefore I am saved," and by Descartes' declaration that "I think, therefore I am." The bourgeois spirit was one of individual priesthood, individual philosophy, and individual authority, fighting free of tradition. Though Luther was often crude and Descartes was sometimes hesitant and equivocal, they paved the way for the refined and confident men of the Enlightenment. Neither was a strict empiricist, but their challenge to tradition and their example of independence remained permanent influences on the thought of men long after the particulars of their teachings had been forgotten.

The empirical atheism of the Enlightenment (*Aufklärung*) had its positive side, being secular, humanistic, and cosmopolitan, and it called on the individual to be responsibly autonomous in thought and action. With its accent on freedom from all external restraints and its enthusiasm for the release of men's capacities, it played on the borders of nihilism. Even Voltaire thought it would be dangerous to have atheistic kings, business men, or servants. Capital at once created, and capitalized upon, this emphasis upon individual autonomy.

Because the old authority of the Church stood blocking the way of the new freedom of the State, the intellectualized ideology of freedom as expressed in the *philosophes* was infected with negative qualities. Individualistic, sensate, positivistic, it swept all relations, all authorities, all hallowed gods before it. As Marx and Engels put it in the *Manifesto,* before the revolutionary onslaught of the capitalists "all that is holy is profaned" (*entweiht*).[21] The attack of the intellectuals on feudal theology was simply the ideological *avant-garde* in this revolution. Though the intellectuals thought they were using those who were providing them pensions, they in turn were being used by the new class who needed justification for their exploits in enterprise at home and abroad. They were the counterparts of Calvin, who two centuries earlier had provided an ideology for the entrepreneurs in need of a post-feudal theology to suit their post-feudal money-making. Today, the ideology of the empirical capitalistic national states sometimes seem to require no external authority, insofar as such states act as a Law or God unto themselves.

Devastating as it was, the religious critique of the *philosophes* was destined to lose some of its force. While liberated from feudal theology and hierarchs, sensible men could increasingly see that they had only passed from the tyranny of the fief under the God of faith to the tyranny of wage labor under the God of free trade. Rousseau and his contemporaries saw this before the French revolution, and once the reaction set in, others saw it even more clearly. Some prophetic souls, like Winstanley and Baboeuf, representing the needs of the lower classes, had pointed out that changes more far-reaching than mere political ones were required to rid the mass of men of institutionalized deprivation and cruelty. As feudal religious ideology signified only a symptom of the radical dislocation in society, so atheism seemed to be only the first step in the diagnosis.

By the time Marx and Engels arrived on the scene, the industrial system in countries like England had advanced deeply into its antagonism of mounting surpluses and deepening miseries. What was to be challenged was the immediate existence of capitalists and their exploitations of workers in practice, not remote and theoretical questions such as the status and nature of a feudal deity. The new authority was not the free thought of *philosophes* cultivating their gardens or conversing urbanely in the glittering salons of emperors, but the rising anonymous mass of workers in the great industrial cities. If the divine power was to be relevant to men, it had to be at work in the depth and breadth and length of human history. Hegel saw this, as did Marx later in his own way. Before Hegel's time the Jewish prophets, Jesus and Christian thinkers like Joachim of Fiore and Bossuet also had been aware of it.

Throughout its history, in one place or another, the lower classes in Christianity had nourished this vision and hope. Periodically the dream of a Kingdom of equals living in love broke forth, but was suppressed when acted upon. While they believed in the transcendence of God, these communal, apocalyptic movements in Christian history, took his immanence seriously. They believed that in his own good time God would fulfill the needs of man. Like a few warm days of spring, the urban revival simply brought these slumbering seeds, scattered througout Christendom, to sprout. As spring moved into summer, Europe was teeming with ripening discontent and expectant hope. The imminent coming of the Kingdom led men to identify their own aspirations with the divine nature and fulfillment. "No one can believe in Christ," said Müntzer, [if he does not first become] "equal to him."[22] For him God was working in history through his elect to bring the millennium to pass. Secular thinkers like Condorcet took up the theme of the perfectibility of man and the progress of history. It was not a great step from the Holy Ghost *(Heilige Geist)* of Müntzer to the World Spirit *(Weltgeist)* of Hegel, who complained of the "bacchanalian revel"[23] of the world of the multiple and of appearances and inveighed against "the frenzy of self-conceit."[24]

Thus while bourgeois, atheistic intellectuals were rejecting the feudal God of Christianity, the prophetic and radical thinkers of Christianity were rejecting both the theism of feudalism and the atheism of capitalism, both the exploitation of the serf and the exploitation of the wage laborer. These thinkers tended to be idealistic and utopian like Saint-Simon, but they laid bare the defect in the atheistic approach to the problem of society and provided the beginnings of an ideological foundation that would transcend the ideology of capitalism.

Marx's Atheism

It was Marx and Engels who first saw the problem clearly. As young Hegelians they had acquired a sense of history and later an acquaintance with the history of socialist movements. It was their encounter with Feuerbach's materialism that showed them the way in which history can be seen as meaningful. Where Hegel and his predecessors had been theistic, the materialists were atheistic. Marx and Engels absorbed, synthesized, and transformed both, going beyond static materialism and idealistic dialectics, beyond crass individualism and utopian organicism. For this reason any religious rejoinder to Marxism must start with the immanentism of Hegel.

However, where Hegel for all practical purposes had historcized but idealized the divine by portraying it in the dramatic colors of a dialectical process, Marx transformed this portrayal by insisting that the drama be real, material, natural, and human. As historical materialists, Marx and Engels rejected an ultimate reality and value, or what has traditionally been called the divine, conceived as an individual spiritual substance, that is, as a static being independent of the world, disembodied, and completed. To them it seemed merely a reflection of man's individualized, loveless, falsified relations to his fellow man and to nature. A true conception of the world and man, they argued, requires the triadic category of creative interaction, of dialectical relations, or, if you will, of love. Thus, the old conception of God must be replaced by a material, secular dialectic which is immediately experienced and which we suppose, on the basis of the sciences, to be the basic character of all reality.

Marx and Engels carried Hegel's view to its logical conclusion. Insofar as history is the increasing self-consciousness or freedom of man, the distinction between the divine and the human is destroyed in principle. What is important is evolutionary movement or change, development, and transformation in both nature and history. Man makes himself under given historical conditions,[25] but he is also made by the materials and processes of nature and history. It is these materials and processes, in part independent of man as individual and species, that displace the absolutely arbitrary and independent divine substance of feudal theology and redefine the "transcendent" factor in the world. Disowning a metaphysical or divine transcendent, Marx and Engels affirmed a spatio-temporal process which is forever transcending itself, and whose transcendence is a function of its immanence. Their view is the major offspring of Christian theology and its chief challenge.

Where Feuerbach tended to make the divine a predicate of man and Hegel to make man a predicate of the divine, Marx saw the alienation in each position: the former collapsed the Other into the human I, while the latter, though dialectical, absorbed man's otherness and outwardness into the Divine I. For Marx man is simply man, unchangeably interpersonal and interactional; he is in the process of self-creation and self-fulfillment through his other-creation and other-fulfillment. Whereas Feuerbach repudiated the God of individual substance and historicized God, Marx repudiated all religious alienation and absorbed the divine into the natural and the human. In this sense Marxism is an effort to conquer religion by joining itself to the essential aspiration of religion, that is, to the effort of man to surpass his solitude and emptiness.

In its dialectical method, as contrasted to the Feuerbachian stance toward religion, Marxism has concentrated more on criticizing the values of religion than on refuting the existence of God. With the shift of society from feudal and other-worldly concerns to the secular concerns of capitalism and socialism,

Marxism shifted the ground of the argument. To the extent that religion enters into the dialogue on this ground, it must accept the reality and value of the secular world. It has no choice but to do so unless it is willing to let history pass it by. However, once it accepts the value of the secular, the critical question becomes that of values and how they are realized in human history.[26] Marxists and Christians both take history seriously for they are respectively opposed to phenomenalism and Gnosticism; both believe in a real incarnation of value in history. The challenge of secular Marxism, in its aim "to unmask self-alienation in its unholy forms"[27] and to reconstitute the ideals of religion upon their secular basis, is to recall Christianity to its secular origins and aims. In this dialogue, Christianity can contribute from its long and rich history its distinctive perspectives on a question which in principle has been central to its thought and concern.

Thus Marx integrated into his outlook the humanism and the historicism of early Christianity, coming to these through their secular and philosophical translations in German philosophy and French socialism. In his doctoral dissertation, Marx saw the inadequacy of Democritean atomism, individualism, and fatalism, and held aloft the standard of Epicurus' "energizing principle" and his militant struggle against the tyranny of superstition and religion. Christianity had developed a different kind of humanism directed toward a Kingdom in but not of this world; it was emotional and mystical, and essentially personal. Like Epicurean humanism it resisted the reduction of man to the status of merely one natural object amongst other natural objects relentlessly governed by the laws of nature. Through the heritage of Kant, Fichte, and Hegel, Marx grasped the prime fact about man, namely, his own creative power as conscious, purposive, active, social, and quite distinct from that of the animals. This humanistic perspective was balanced by a deep respect for the sciences of nature and the material sub-structure of man and history. The peculiar richness of Marx and the divisions among Marxists themselves derive in part from this combination. In addition, by combining both humanism and science, and historicism and naturalism, Marxism possesses a subtly complex relation of both convergence and divergence to Christianity. This can best be elucidated by examining this relation in a series of particular issues.

ATHEISM'S HUMANISTIC CRITIQUE OF RELIGION AND THEISM

Atheists have been impelled by diverse motives, ranging from self-indulgence, vanity, and revenge to the desire to serve mankind, and they have proposed many different arguments and conclusions. Many have taken a stand for such basic human values as truth, consistency, honesty, and justice in opposition to the theism of religion. The reason for this is not hard to find: normally the dominant religion in western societies has been associated with the rule of a dominant class, with the result that in many respects both in thought and in practice the dominant religion has been anti-humanistic. The persecutions, wars, superstitions, and thought-control of religions, particularly Christianity and Islam, have placed them against basic human values and the welfare of the great masses of the people. Hence both inside and outside religious communities the critics of religion have tended to take up the defense of those basic values.

These criticisms have often indicated the class situation of their origin. Early Greek atheism, among the Milesians and others, reflects the unrest of the age and the tendency of commercial transactions and money to moderate aristocratic privileges. The radical religious humanism of Thomas Müntzer expresses the cause of the oppressed peasant against the feudal lords. The atheism of Hume and d'Holbach speaks for a bourgeoisie already repudiating the ideology of a feudal religion. The atheism of Owen and Marx has broadened the base of humanistic protest against a religion often indifferent to or allied with capitalism's exploitation of industrial workers.

Truth

In their humanistic criticisms of religion, one of the standards held aloft by atheists has been truth. "There never was, nor ever will be, any man who knows with certainty the things about the gods . . ." wrote Xenophanes.[28] Truth for atheists has meant not only those propositions that can be confirmed by observation, but also what might be reasonably inferred from observation in a consistent way. Atheists have pointed out not only that the gods cannot be observed (Hume, Ayer), but also that man's conceptions of the gods are in many respects contradictory (Hume, d'Holbach). They have also judged the truth of religion in a broader and pragmatic sense, inquiring whether theists in the way they lived really meant what they said and said what they meant. "Scribes and hypocrites!" has been the recurrent judgment.

In this way the atheistic critique has thus tended to move from a concern with the truth claims of religion to an analysis of the human situation in which these claims are embedded. From Epicurus to modern positivists, atheists have argued that the idea of a supernatural being is an illusion; they have supposed that pointing this out would free men from its grip. This frontal tactic of the free-thinker has not always been as successful as wished. Religious men have continued to hold certain illusions, such as the ideas of heaven and hell as physical places, even though such beliefs have been abandoned by their leaders. Although critiques of the emotional and social roots of religious belief had been made in the past by Hsun Tzu, Cicero, and others, it was Marx who most forcefully made the point that false ideas and contradictions, religious and otherwise, spring from men's false and antagonistic relations to one another and to the non-human world. Intellectual truth, as a reflection of man's mobile reality, cannot emerge until man's exploitations of man are rectified. Only then will men be freed from relations to one another and to the rest of their world that are false, in the sense of dehumanizing. Hence "the demand [on the part of a people] to give up the illusions about its conditions is *the demand to give up a condition which needs illusions.*"[29] Similarly Freud found religious ideas to be generated by psychological need or "childhood neurosis":

> When the growing individual finds that he is destined to remain a child for ever, that he can never do without protection against strange superior powers, he lends those powers the features belonging to the figure of his father; he creates for himself the gods whom he dreads, whom he seeks to propitiate, and whom he nevertheless entrusts with his own protection.[30]

Probing the roots of self-deception, Marx and Freud demanded that religious men be absolutely honest in their dealings with the universe and with themselves, that they suppress nothing in their efforts to find, articulate, and act on the truth, and that they take no refuge in a flight from reality. Camus echoed this same demand for the whole truth of the human situation which avoids metaphysical "escape" and illusory "hope."[31]

From the viewpoint of such atheism, theism is in bad faith and disingenuous in dealing with man and his world. It refuses to be honest in confronting the meanings and the meaninglessness of man's existence. It betrays man by having a lack of faith in man's power to know himself and his world, to discover truth and value in relation to others and his world, and to cope with his problems in the world. It was this humanistic faith that was displayed and taught by such great religious figures of history as Gautama Buddha, the Jewish prophets, and Jesus; it is a faith which can make us whole.

Fear, which, we are told, love casts out, takes hold of men and gives rise to ideas about gods which promise reward and threaten punishment here and hereafter.[32] Fear and ignorance arise together and are dissipated by courage and truth together. In reaction to the weakness and partiality of the religious life, atheists have called for the strength and wholeness of an affirmative faith in man and his relation to himself, to others, and to nature. In this way the atheist's demand for truth leads to the demand for courage to seek and face the truth; both call for a sound and healthy man in a sound and healthy society.

Humanism

The basic criticism directed at religion is its dehumanization of man. As penetratingly as any other, Nietzsche's psychoanalysis of Christianity revealed it as a sickness, an "anemia,"[33] a "physiological depravity."[34] The Christian God is a dead God, decaying in the charnel house of man's own morbid sentiments, and reeking of defeat, weakness, and decay. That God for Nietzsche is the symbol of all that is anti-human: the denaturing of nature, the denial of life, the devaluating of genuine values, and the despising of reality, time, change, variety, opposition, and struggle. "What I am not, that to me are God and virtue!"[35] For Nietzsche it was not enough merely to negate God as an idea, because this idea was a clue to man's deepest bondage to all that cripples and destroys. The idea of God was but a symptom of his dehumanization.

The rationalistic critique of religion has normally been rooted in the reaction of some educated men to the evident irrationalities of established religions. The articulate, rationalistic atheists have come from such groups. Heraclitus, for example, like many philosophers of his period, came from the aristocratic, wealthy class, and was critical of both the gods and the mob. The philosophers of the Renaissance, who were in the pay of their despots and wealthy patrons, tended to fuse reason and nature, and to worship both. If a conflict threatened to rise between the reason of nature and God, it was usually solved by identifying God with nature. In this way Leonardo da Vinci defined "force" as "a spiritual power,"[36] and argued that "in Art we may be said to be grandsons unto God,"[37] reproducing the form and movement of natural things created by God.

A strain of humanism underlay the Greek critique of the gods. Aeschylus, writing with a moral purpose in *Prometheus Bound*, had Prometheus say,

In one word, all gods are my enemies.
They had good from me. They return me evil.

Euripides likewise judged the gods by a humanistic criterion:
"If the gods do aught that is shameful, they are no gods."
Plato, concerned about the conditions of education in the ideal
society, declared:

> . . . that God being good is the author of evil to any one
> is to be strenuously denied, and not to be said or sung
> or heard in verse or prose by any one whether old or young
> in any well-ordered commonwealth. Such a fiction is suicidal,
> ruinous, impious.[38]

It is true that prophets and others like the chief author of Job
substituted certain non-humanistic qualities of Yahweh with
certain humanistic qualities. Jeremiah spurned abstract com-
mandments and arbitrary punishment, for which he substituted
God's personal relation to an individually responsible man and
God's forgiveness.[39] Nevertheless, they did so under the spell
of religious consciousness and remained unconscious of the
inescapably *human* modes of conceiving the divine. For the most
part the antihumanistic character and effects of God as conceived by theism did not come under conscious and explicit
criticism until late feudal times.

The popular revolts against ecclesiastical feudalism marked
the beginnings of widespread, militant, and broadly humanistic
atheism. Wycliffe proposed his fourteen century doctrine of
"dominion by grace" whereby spiritual or temporal lordship is
derived from God and not through intermediaries. Müntzer held
that man must become equal to Christ and die with him in
revolutionary struggle: "The living God is sharpening his scythe
in me, so that later I can cut down the red poppies and the blue
cornflowers."[40] These criticisms of a God associated with class
privilege and exploitation represent a criticism of the inhuman
effects of theism and mark a turning point in the history of

atheism. They are efforts to overthrow these effects by overthrowing their causes in thought and in social institutions. Although Wycliffe, Müntzer, and other reformers were theistic in the broad sense of that term, their criticism of feudal theism opened the church door to the rising tides of secular criticism and revolutionary change. Men asked whether a God who is altogether on the side of man's oppressors was of any value to them, and whether he was not even their enemy. This atheistic criticism deepened as it became more humanistic, that is, as attention shifted from ideas concerning God and his properties to the causes and consequences of these ideas in human living.

This changed perspective or new *point d'appui*, was itself of great significance, for it manifested that the criterion of judgment in matters of reality, value, and knowledge had been converted from abstract, esoteric, remote "reason" to the concrete human situation of man's well-being and fulfillment. This new atheism incorporated the reason of traditional atheism but rendered it applicable to man's sufferings under injustice and to his aspirations; atheism had become emotional, social, and often revolutionary in its demands. Man made demands of God, requiring that his standard of value be compatible with, instead of independent of man's.

D'Holbach identified with the rights and struggles of the French people against tyranny during the period of the Revolution. He measured traditional theism by such a humanistic test and found the notion of God to be the cause of the most inhuman effects (I use his own strong words): terror, melancholy, afflicting ideas, inquietude, inflammation of imagination, consternation, inebriety, mental ravages, exasperating and souring of temperament, despair, alarm, spleen, animosity, unrealism, benumbing, stupefaction, fanaticism, fury, fear, trembling, appeasement, dread, tears, misery, unreason, a state of infancy or delirium.[41] Once having had it pointed out to him, the worker or peasant would see that the heavenly "absolute monarch" of the Church did not differ in his despotism from the absolute monarch on the French throne. Both were "unjust, severe,

capricious, and implacable."[42] Whereas Greek atheism had tended
to be metaphysical, this analysis of the Enlightenment revealed
the social, human effects of theism.

It was not until Nietzsche and Freud that theism was explicitly linked with the human, psychological condition and
viewed not only as an error in thought but as the symptom
of a defect in personality. However, whereas Nietzsche and Freud
appealed to the bourgeois mentality of the individual man already
emotionally alienated from his religion, Marx analyzed theism
on a broader, historical scale. Since he considered theism to be
a symptom of social repression and massive dehumanization,
he appealed to the broad class of industrial workers. Many
other critics in the nineteenth century laid the groundwork for
class atheism, and in 1874 Engels observed that "atheism is so
near to being self-obvious with European working-class parties
nowadays" that it is unnecessary to propagate or decree it.[43]

Naturalism

The reason for this lay in the fact that by the end of the
nineteenth century the world view or the *Weltanschauung* of the
European population had appreciably shifted from medieval
supernaturalism to naturalism, whereas the Church continued
to cling to earlier viewpoints and practices. Naturalism, which
had its roots in Judaic and Greek thought and had been quiescent
during the decay of the Roman Empire and the isolation of most
of Europe, revived at the end of the first millennium when commerce and urban life began to develop. It took the realities and
values of "this life" to be final and irreducible, and explored
and cherished what the human senses and reflection could find.
The economic revolution against feudalism had reverberations
in all other dimensions of culture. Thus, though they remained
oriented to the "other world," the Cathari, Waldensians, and
Franciscans were moved in part by a communal and humanitarian
spirit. The growing pantheism, mysticism, urban piety, and early
rumblings of the Reformation that appeared in the Lollards,

the first peasant revolts, Wycliffe, and Huss were all simply diverse ways of responding to the demands of the emergent order of human life.

These demands called for: (1) the use of the senses and the mind in knowing and predicting the things of the world; (2) the expression and satisfaction of impulses and appetites; (3) the development of muscular skills in exploring, forming, and controlling things and events; and (4) opening up of the whole domain of communication, not only in the national languages but in the arts, the sciences, and elsewhere. In a word, this was the secular revolution whereby men discovered that they belonged to an age (*saecularis*) and were limited both by time and space and by the materials and processes of this life. Of course, this discovery came gradually, as did the transition from supernaturalism to naturalism as a popular outlook on things. During the transitional period, the doctrines of dualism and double truth served to satisfy both the demands of the new era and those of the old. Men were not always conscious of the historical forces moving them. For example, when the fourteenth century Utraquists fought for the right of all Christians "not precluded by mortal sin" to drink of the Eucharistic cup,[44] they were not fully aware of how and why they, like the mystics and violent revolutionaries, were asking for a democratizing of God.

Some religious spirits sought to find God in the individual depths or communal life of the new secular order, or even to identify God with that order. For St. Francis of Assisi, how alive was the whole of nature with the love and loveliness of God! Indeed, the secular emphasis in Judaism and Christianity on the immanent presence of God in the world had been a leading article of faith and a source of strength and inspiration in times of affirmative action and struggle in the world. However, that secular faith was almost forgotten during the decay of Roman civilization, the rise of barbarism, and the first feeble centuries of feudalism. When later faced by the anti-feudal, commercial, secular revolution inside and outside its walls and estates, the Church by and large chose to continue its alienation from the secular, with the result that God was separated from the renaissance of the common life. (On its part, Protestantism simply substituted the gospel of work for the Church ritual, so that the God of capitalism remained as remote from man as had the feudal Lord.) The choice reflected the alienation of the existing economic rulers from the life of most men and had the predictable consequence: God being alienated from men, men alienated themselves from God. As "the criticism of theology" turned into "the criticism of politics,"[45] the need of the ruling hierarchy for an alien God became evident: revolution from below is always followed by counter-revolution from above.

Secularism

The secular revolution, of which atheism is one intellectual reflection, thus set itself against the world of religion. It did so, first, because that world seemed to it unreal and illusory, outdated and alien, a world of the past, of the distant and antique, of irrelevancy. Religion was its "spiritual *aroma*,"[46] the incense of an imaginary world that had never existed, the spirit of a quite non-spiritual and secular situation. Laplace understated the contempt of the eighteenth century European intellectual when he said, "I have no need of that hypothesis." ("Je n'ai pas besoin de cette hypothèse.")

Second, the world of theism seemed to the secular mind unknown and unknowable. Its methods were faith coupled with revelation, mystical experience, and a Scripture allegedly revealed by God. In the natural world of family life, farming, industry, commerce, technology, and science, these methods are unusable, They represent modes of knowing that appear to transcend public inquiry, ways of fixating belief and protecting it against criticism: "sacred" means, beyond criticism. For the secular mind, nothing is exempt from criticism: the fully secular man desires to perceive and know everything, from every angle.

Third, for the secular mentality theism represented an obstructive force to man's existence and his method of fulfillment. It was not merely an illusion hiding behind a "mystical veil."[47] It also opposed social criticism and change, and was allied with social institutions and practices which crippled and weakened man. In short, it was anti-progressive and for this reason anti-human, for even in a good society something cannot be pro-human if it contravenes man's direction toward progress.

CONCLUSION

We have called attention to the necessary historical and logical interdependence of theism and atheism. This dialectical opposition and development of theism and atheism in Western Christianity has reflected the more pervasive social opposition and change; in turn, it has helped to shape an outlook and style of thought that is perhaps distinctive to the west. This outlook is perhaps best summed up in the single word, "Progress," with all that it implies for man and his attitude toward other men, history, and the universe.

The notion of progress in its very broad sense had its origin among the Jews and Greeks. As a result of their own repeatedly precarious position in history, the Jews conceived the notion of a Power progressively revealing himself in history. This implied man's responsibility to respond in a progressively more moral way to the unfolding Being and Truth of that Power. The Greeks also had a notion of being and truth as unfolding. In this light they developed their understanding of forms as these are revealed in nature (Ionian philosophers, scientists), in the events of human history (the great dramatists, Thucydides, Herodotus), and in the domain of ideas (Plato). Accordingly the Greeks felt that man must respond to his world in a progressively more cognitive way. Early Christian theology fused the moral emphasis of the Jews with the cognitive emphasis of the Greeks, with the result that they conceived the divine Logos as universally at work in man, history, and nature, and called upon man progressively to do and to know the good.

One strand of Christian thought has stressed the progressive revelation of the Divine both as a moral power and as an ontological presence yielding up the various facets of its Being and Truth in human history. It also stressed the demands for a progressive sensitivity and responsiveness on the part of man to this occurrence, and for a dialectical correspondence between the two. Because this viewpoint has its secular counterpart among atheists, both theists and atheists alike share the common tradition: that through man's creative interaction with other men and things in the processes of history and nature truth is refined, expanded, and integrated and human living improved; that the truth will make man free; that the truth is ultimately one; and that man can grow in his grasp of the truth and in moral character. Though many have not shared these convictions, they seem to us distinctive and valuable. Both the convictions and the facts to which they refer have helped to provide a matrix in which have developed certain distinctive institutional practices: the method of question and answer in law, philosophy, and other disciplines; the rights of the minority, of the accused, and of individual conscience; the processes of the sciences; the democratic practices of freedom of expression and voluntary association; and, indeed, the theist-atheist dialogue itself.

Without denying or minimizing the real and significant differences between theists and atheists, it is important to call attention to the fact that both share an origin and an orientation. In this tradition neither an authentic atheist nor an authentic theist can rest content apart from a continuing and faithful effort to communicate his truth to the other, to receive his truth, to correct error on both sides, and to integrate all truths in his progress toward the ultimate unity of truth in both theory and practice, where the truth of being would be inseparable from the being of truth. This is the inspiring goal toward which many theists and atheists have moved, and to which men today remain committed both by their common history and their humanity.

◊

1. See, for example, St. Clement I, **Epistle to the Corinthians.**

2. Paul Tillich, **Dynamics of Faith** (New York: Harper and Brothers, 1958), pp. 46, p. 127.

3. As indicated by **Athenagoras** and in **Martyrium Polycarpi,** cited in Henry Bettenson, **Documents of the Christian Church** (New York and London: Oxford University Press, 1943), pp. 4, 13. See also Tertullian, **Apology.**

4. Karl Marx, **Economic and Philosophic Manuscripts of 1844** (Moscow: Foreign Languages Publishing House, 1961), pp. 103, 114.

5. K. Marx and F. Engels, **On Religion** (Moscow: Foreign Languages Publishing House, n.d.), p. 142.

6. Albert Camus, **The Myth of Sisyphus and Other Essays** (New York: Alfred A. Knopf, 1955), pp. 31ff.

7. John B. Noss, **Man's Religions** (Revised edition; New York: Macmillan, 1956), pp. 128-29.

8. Joseph Needham, **Science and Society in Ancient China,** Conway Memorial Lecture (London: Watts and Co., 1947).

9. Matthew 12:24.

10. Mark 3:21.

11. Matthew 26:65.

12. Pierre Teilhard de Chardin, **The Phenomenon of Man** (New York: Harper and Brothers, 1959), p. 284.

13. Mircea Eliade, **The Sacred and the Profane** (New York: Harcourt, Brace and Co., 1959), pp. 229-32.

14. But the gods retained their link with animal life. See George Thomson, **Studies in Ancient Greek Society. The Prehistoric Aegean** (Third edition; New York: The Citadel Press, 1965), pp. 50-51.

15. For an account of these stages, see V. Gordon Childe, **Man Makes Himself** (New York: New American Library of World Literature, 1951).

16. Gordon Childe, **What Happened in History** (New York: Penquin Books, 1946), Ch. X.

17. Charles M. Bakewell, **Source Book in Ancient Philosophy** (New York: Scribner's, 1939), p. 5.

18. Benjamin Farrington, **Greek Science** (Harmondsworth: Penquin Books, 1944), Vol. I.

19. Karl Marx, "Contribution to the Critique of Hegel's Philosophy of Right," in **On Religion,** p. 42.

20. Peter Gay, **The Enlightenment: An Interpretation** (New York: Alfred Knopf and Co., 1966), pp. 23-27.

21. Karl Marx and Friedrich Engels, **Manifesto of the Communist Party,** authorized English translation, edited and annotated by Fried-

rich Engels (New York: International Publishers, 1948), p. 12.

22. **Of the Fantastic Beliefs.** Quoted in Sanford A. Lakoff, **Equality in Political Philosophy** (Cambridge: Harvard University Press, 1964), p. 56.

23. G. Hegel, **The Phenomenology of Mind** (New York: Macmillan, 1931), p. 105.

24. **Ibid.,** pp. 391ff.

25. Karl Marx, **The Eighteenth Brumaire of Louis Bonaparte** (New York: International Publishers, 1964).

26. See the comments of Leslie Dewart in **Initiative in History: A Christian Marxist Dialogue.** An occasional paper published by The Church Society for College Work (Cambridge, 1967).

27. Marx and Engels, "Contribution to the Critique of Hegel's Philosophy of Right," in **On Religion,** p. 42.

28. **The Fragments,** p. 14. In **Source Book in Ancient Philosophy,** p. 9.

29. "Contribution to the Critique of Hegel's Philosophy of Right," in **On Religion,** p. 42.

30. Sigmund Freud, **The Future of An Illusion,** translated by W. D. Robson-Scott, revised and edited by James Strachey (Garden City, New York: Doubleday, 1964), p. 35.

31. Camus, **The Myth of Sisyphus and Other Essays.**

32. Cf. P. H. D. d'Holbach's statement: "The human mind, whose invincible ignorance and whose fears reduced it to despair, gave birth to those obscure and vague notions with which he has decorated his god." **The System of Nature,** trans. W. Hodgson (Philadelphia: R. Benson, 1808), Vol. III, Ch. III.

33. Friedrich Nietzsche, **The Antichrist** (Berlin: Nordlan, 1941), pp. 59, 62. In **The Portable Nietzsche,** translated and edited by Walter Kaufmann (New York: Viking Press, 1954).

34. **Ibid.,** p. 47.

35. Nietzsche, **Thus Spoke Zarathustra,** in **The Portable Nietzsche,** p. 206.

36. **The Notebooks of Leonardo da Vinci,** edited by Edward MacCurdy (New York: George Braziller, 1954), p. 68.

37. **Ibid.,** p. 853.

38. Plato, **Republic,** p. 380.

39. Jeremiah 31:27-34.

40. Quoted in Norman Cohn, **The Pursuit of the Millennium** (Fairlawn, New Jersey: Essential Books, 1957), p. 255.

41. d'Holbach, **The System of Nature.**

42. **Ibid.**

43. Marx and Engels, **On Religion,** p. 142

44. Articles of Prague, 1420, Article II.

45. Karl Marx, "Contribution to the Critique of Hegel's Philosophy of Right," in **On Religion,** p. 42.

46. **Ibid.**

47. Karl Marx, **Capital** (Moscow: Foreign Languages Publishing House, n.d.), Vol. I, p. 80.

Catholic Theology and the Death of God

◊

Thomas J. J. Altizer

THE TIME HAS passed when new expressions of Catholic theology could be considered to be radical simply in terms of their negative relationship to the dominant forms of post-Tridentine Catholic scholasticism. One has only to observe the overwhelming impact which Teilhard de Chardin, a more radical thinker than any Protestant theologian of the twentieth century, is having upon most Catholic theological circles to realize the revolutionary state of the contemporary Catholic theological situation. At least in the United States and perhaps in the world at large, Catholic theology is passing through a revolutionary transformation which has no real counterpart in either past or present forms of Protestant theology. Naive Protestants often assert that this is simply the price which the Roman Catholic Church must pay for its long delayed entrance into the modern world, with the corollary that Protestantism has always been modern and contemporary. Yet the mere fact that the great majority of Protestant theologians remain bound to the final authority of sixteenth century Protestant dogmatics should dispel one side of this illusion. At the same time, it makes it possible to realize that it is Christianity itself which must undergo not merely a reformation but a revolution if it is truly to exist and be real in the modern world.

Why should not Catholic and Protestant theologians join hands in the great challenge lying before us? If ecumenical

[187]

theology has moved to the practical stage and now poses few theoretical problems of serious interest, has the time come when Catholic and Protestant can occupy common theological frontiers? I propose to examine one such frontier, the possibility of an atheistic or death of God theology, with the purpose of ascertaining whether or not it is closed to the Catholic thinkers. Many critics have charged that a death of God theology can have no possible ground in the life of the Church, that it ignores or simply negates the Christian tradition, and that it collapses theology into a naturalistic or humanistic anthropology. If these charges are true, I can see no possibility of a Catholic death of God theology, nor for that matter of any form of Christian atheism. However, believing them to be untrue, I shall approach these charges by discussing the question of the inherent possibility of a Catholic atheistic theology. Inevitably, I shall be forced to conceive the nature of Catholic theology from a somewhat novel point of view. Nevertheless, I intend to be loyal to the intrinsic Catholic ground of Christian theology, even if I believe that that ground can never be given either a definitive or an exhaustive definition.

CATHOLIC THEOLOGY AND HISTORY

Church, World, and History

Obviously, Catholic theology is first a Church theology, incorporating the life and teachings of the Roman Catholic Church; as such it clearly must be subordinate to the life of the Church. However, unlike most Protestant dogmatics, Catholic theology is not and cannot be bound to a single form or image of the Church, nor even to its widely varying scriptural images. This is so because Catholic theology is the product of a Church living simultaneously in the historical past, the contemporary present, and the apocalyptic future. That the Church is organic and moves through an evolutionary process of development is a distinctively modern idea, though rooted in patristic dogmatics.

It is the inevitable consequence of a Church claiming an ultimate or divine authority not only for its past, but for its present and future acts. Moreover, Catholic theology increasingly conceives the Church in terms of its necessary and integral relationship with the world. Like a biological phylum, the Church can neither exist nor develop autonomously; it can be truly organic only to the extent that it opens itself to incorporate its total environment. Consequently, it is non-Catholic to think of the Church as apart from or opposed to the world: to think of Catholic theology as being bound to the life of the Church one must recognize that it is likewise bound to the life and movement of the world.

Another distinctive note of Catholic theology is its analogical method, rooted in a Catholic conception of the integral relationship between nature and grace. This manifests simultaneously the influence of both the sacramental religious life of Catholicism and the world-affirming ground of the Catholic Church. Genuine Catholic theology has always attempted to set itself against all forms of dualism, resisting every polar dichotomy between nature and grace, reason and revelation, and God and world. Catholic conceptions of God have been basically analogical, if only because they have refused the idea of a purely negative relationship between God and the world and have attempted to establish a balance or harmony between the distance and nearness or the transcendence and immanence of God. Today these traditional Catholic conceptions of God seem to be in crisis because of their apparent bondage to the static categories of pre-modern Western thinking. As yet, however, there is no decisive sign that the analogical method is in crisis.

What is requisite in our situation is an application of the analogical method to the dynamic or process categories of contemporary scientific and historical thinking. We no longer can think in terms of an analogical relation between two eternally given or unchanging forms of being; we must think now in terms of a moving or evolving series of analogical relationships between the integrally related poles of a forward-moving process. A truly Catholic theological method will always ground its understanding of God in an understanding of the world which is actually available to it, just as it will understand the world in terms of a Catholic apprehension of the integral or analogical relationship between the world and God.

Modern thinking has reached both a new understanding of the evolutionary movement of nature and the cosmos, and a new understanding of the historicity or integral reality of the various situations and conditions of man. This confronts us with the challenge of reaching a new conception of the relation between cosmic evolution and the historical movement of humanity or human consciousness. This challenge has at least partially been met by Whitehead and Teilhard de Chardin. It would seem to be peculiarly open to the Catholic thinker, for Catholicism grounds its anthropology in ontology and its understanding of man in a prior understanding of being itself, thereby requiring a natural or philosophical theology as the foundation of theological thinking.

At no other point has Protestant theology reacted so negatively to Catholicism. Most Protestant theologians have insisted that to understand God by way of his analogical relation to the meaning of being which is present in consciousness is to subordinate the God of revelation to purely human thinking, and to make the God of faith a demonic idol. In part, such Protestant critics are questioning the integral or open presence of God in the world. Confining the meaning of God to that meaning which is present in the special revelation of the Bible, they refuse any kind of general revelation which is present in nature or history.

Christ and History

Precisely because the Catholic thinker is open to such general revelation he must take with ultimate seriousness the movement of history and the cosmos; he must foreswear every temptation to erect a chasm between the God of faith and the God manifest in nature and consciousness. Above all, the Catholic theologian knows that God the Creator and God the Redeemer are one God, that there can be no irreconcilable opposition between the Word of revelation and the world of Creation. A redeemed humanity is as much the product of creation as of salvation, for the Christ who is the primordial Logos is identical with the Christ who is the Incarnate Word. Therefore, the Catholic thinker can never truly isolate the reality of the cosmos from the reality of Christ.

The Catholic thinker must refuse the Christ who is neither cosmic nor historical, who cannot be apprehended in the reality of cosmic process, and who is neither active nor present in the actuality of human consciousness. Since both the cosmos and the consciousness are moving or evolving, it would seem that the Catholic thinker must posit a dynamic or evolving Christ who is in process of development or evolution. This is not to say a Christ who is identical with the process of evolution, but one who is in some genuine sense evolving or moving from a beginning or a primordial state to an end or eschatological consummation.

Similarly, the Church, identified as the Body of Christ, must be known as an evolving Body, inseparable in its reality from the total body of humanity. It must undergo a process of development or self-transformation which is at least fully analogous to that undergone in the evolution of the human body and consciousness. Only a generation ago Catholic theologians were asking whether there was revelation and salvation outside the Church. Now we can see that, at least from a Catholic point of view, the form of this question is erroneous, because to be Catholic is to recognize the presence of the Church wherever there is revelation and salvation. The only question for the Catholic is where is the Body of Christ active or real. This, in turn, is to ask where is the fully active or wholly real body of humanity, for the true body of humanity is ultimately the Body of Christ.

By refusing any kind of purely negative dichotomy between God and the world, the Catholic thinker adheres to the God who is actively present in the world. This means that he is bound to the God who can appear in a present and contemporary state of consciousness, itself the product or consequence of the present stage of evolution and history. To speak of God under the impact of historical and evolutionary thinking is to recognize not only that distinct times or periods imply distinctively different ways of apprehending God, but that God Himself is present in quite different forms at various points of time and history. Of course, the Catholic believes that the God who is manifest to the Church today is identical with the God who is manifest to the Church in all ages. But just as the Catholic does not believe in a single form or image of the Church, he need not believe in a single form or image of God.

Indeed, unlike the classical Protestant, the Catholic is not even fully bound to the biblical images of God. As the Catholic Church moved far from these biblical images in absorbing Hellenistic philosophy and religion, it is able to move still further from them by absorbing the thinking and sensibility of the modern world. Such a movement need not be thought of in any sense as a betrayal. In Catholic terms it is an evolutionary movement of organic development and but a further step toward the Church's goal of becoming incarnate in the fullness of the world. The true God of Catholicism is neither simply biblical, nor confined to the historical world of Christendom, nor wholly linked to any past forms of human consciousness. From the perspective of a forward-moving and evolving Church, it must be said that all images of God, even biblical ones, are limited and provisional. To give a final authority to any given image of God would be to turn away from the forward and evolving movement of God Himself.

Development and Transformation

A decisive problem of contemporary Catholic theology is the meaning of the development or evolution of dogma. That John Henry Newman's *The Development of Christian Doctrine*[1] was written before Charles Darwin's *The Origin of Species,*[2] demonstrates that the idea of organic and evolutionary development originated in Catholic theology independently of its birth in scientific thinking. It is not a secular motif being incorporated into Christian thinking, but a fundamental factor in Catholic understanding. Moreover, as the idea of organic development is thought through to its theological conclusion, it will surely become obvious that any genuine evolutionary understanding is incompatible with the idea of an original deposit of faith which is absolute, unchanging, and immobile. New Testament scholarship, through historical investigation, has demonstrated that a variety of "original" forms of faith are present in the beginnings of Christianity. I cannot even imagine a modern historian maintaining that there is no substantial dogmatic distinction between the faith of a Paul or a Peter and that of an Ignatius or Irenaeus, to say nothing of an Augustine or a Thomas Aquinas. Among other things, to think historically is to recognize a transformation in consciousness in accordance with the movements of history. Such thinking leaves no room for the naive supposition that historical or organic development is simply the progressive enlargement of an original and never changing form. The cry of conservative Catholics today: development, yes, but transformation, no, is basically a refusal of both the modern and the Catholic idea of development, for there can be no organic or historical development apart from transformation.

PROTESTANT CHRISTOCENTRISM AND EVOLUTIONARY MOVEMENT

Evolutionary Movement in God and World

One notable obstacle to theological progress in our time is the secular and profoundly unchristian view that faith is simply a human phenomenon, that it bears no necessary or integral relation to its presumed object, and that the question of God and of faith are wholly distinct since God exists independently of what faith apprehends him to be. I suspect that this idea is a peculiarly Protestant aberration, although it seems to have clear parallels in modern Catholic scholasticism. In any case, here we may observe a theological appropriation of secular thinking for purely defensive purposes. At a time when everything which was once manifest as faith in the Christian world is withering away, it becomes vitally important for the theological conservative to insist that the human reality of faith bears no essential relation to an eternal and unchanging God. Some Christian theologians have even ventured to assert that God is eternally unnameable or unsayable, without pausing to consider what this assertion does to the theological logic of their sentence or to the whole question of revelation.

If the Christian faith has undergone an historical transformation, then the theologian cannot truly maintain that God Himself remains unchanged, for the Christian believes that God has fully revealed Himself in Jesus Christ and that that revelation is present in the Bible and in the Church's original deposit of faith. Thus, the theologian cannot look upon the historical transformation of faith as the product of a simple growth or coming to maturity of faith. If faith itself is passing through an evolutionary transformation, then we must regard that transformation as a consequence of the evolutionary movement of God.

Theologians must also take far more seriously than is their habit the identity of the Church as the full Body of Christ or the universal body of humanity. When this is done, there can be no pretension that faith is confined to the institutional bodies of the Church or to that sphere or realm which is sanctioned by ecclesiastical authority. Indeed, if Christ is present wherever there is full human energy or life it would seem apparent that He is more fully present outside than within ecclesiastical bodies. Why this idea should bring offense to a theologian today is beyond my imagination, but that it apparently does so should warn us ever to be on our guard against all forms of theology which are merely church or ecclesiastical theologies.

If, in the context of the present stage of history as the expression of a total evolutionary process, we take the world or the full body of humanity seriously, we must face the possibility that the ever more pervasive inability of modern man to speak the name of God is a consequence of a movement of God Himself. Innumerable voices in the institutional churches now are crying that they cannot evoke God's name, not even in their rare moments of prayer and meditation. The fact that Catholic artists have all but ceased to envision a redemptive or life-giving image of God should be of unusual significance to theologians both Catholic and non-Catholic alike. One might well presume that it is the increasing impotence of the confessing Christian today to speak the name of God which has led so many theologians to speak of our time as a time of the silence or the eclipse of God.

If ours is indeed such a time, is it then the duty of the Christian to be silent about God? This is a weighty question which many Christians are now answering affirmatively. But are all Christian thinkers called to follow this way, limiting their work to assaults upon the idolatries about them, or, at best, confining their inquiries to pragmatic and specialized problems? Is it possible that many of us have followed this way because of a deep fear of the consequences of a full theological inquiry in our world? Above all, is it inconceivable that atheism could be a Christian destiny, a culminating movement of the Christian faith itself?

Protestant Christocentrism

Catholic theology stands to gain new life and understanding from the positive achievements of modern Protestant theology. That theology has been in the process of reaching a conceptual formulation of a totally Christocentric form of faith, directed totally to the life-giving name and reality of Christ. It refuses every word about God which is not a reflection of the judgment and redemption present in Christ. Simply stated, modern Protestant theology has in large measure given itself to a transformation of theology into Christology. It has attempted to transform all our inherited language about God into a language reflecting solely the meaning of God incarnate or embodied in Jesus Christ. We should not regard this project as simply an idiosyncrasy of the modern Protestant theologian, or even as a peculiarly Protestant quest. Much the same could be said about the work of Teilhard de Chardin, who carries his thinking to more radical conclusions than those of his Protestant counterparts. This all too modern theological motif might more properly be considered an attempt to give systematic conceptual expression to a uniquely modern form of the Christian faith.

DIALECTICAL NEGATION AND DIVINE IMMANENCE

Negation and Dialectical Evolution

Does such an approach entail a simple negation of the Christian tradition? It does, if we regard that tradition as being monolithic and eternally given. It does not, however, if we regard the Christian tradition as a series of evolving movements, not necessarily juxtaposed in a simple chronological or sequential sense, but embodying a progressive estrangement of the name and image of God from every source of life and energy in the world. Everything depends upon understanding the nature of such movements: how an evolutionary process could reach its goal by moving beyond its original source; how, moreover, it would be forced to transcend both its beginning and its successive expressions if its own initial momentum is to be carried to its intrinsic resolution.

It would be false to process thinking and to the evolutionary perspective to entertain the supposition that because a given form or expression is transcended it is thereby quite simply negated, as though each point or stage in the forward-moving process was isolated and autonomous or wholly enclosed within itself. It must be understood that everything is carried forward in this process, or, rather, that life itself moves forward. As it evolves into new forms and its former life is redirected and transfigured by its expression in these new modes, it leaves its earlier forms and expressions behind as mere fossils. As we can see in our example from Protestant theology, the life and power once symbolically evoked by the name of God become present once more in the name of Christ. However, the life and power are not simply the same, but have assumed a more immanent and in-carnate expression. As a consequence the name of God now points to a darkened and emptied transcendence, as the life and energy of an original transcendence wholly passes into the in-carnate immanence of Christ.

Increasingly, theology is abandoning its former static ideas and images of God. As it does so, it is beginning to grasp the integral relationship of the evolutionary movement of cosmos and consciousness to that of God. The Catholic Christian must inevitably assume that God's movements are reflected in human consciousness and experience, if only because of his belief in the analogical or positive relationship between God and the world. Thus, if human consciousness, including the explicitly Christian consciousness, has been progressively abandoning its former ground in the life-giving power of the name and the image of God, the Catholic Christian can only conclude that God Him-self is in some sense moving through a process of the self-negation or self-emptying of His former epiphany or self-mani-festation.

Once we are liberated from the root idea that the biblical and apostolic images of God have an absolute and eternal author-ity, we can be open to the possibility that everything which orthodox Christianity has known as God is but a particular stage of God's self-manifestation, which must in turn be transcended by the forward movement of God Himself. If the Christian God is truly an evolving God, then we must understand that He evolves to new forms or manifestations by negating His past expressions. He must leave them behind as empty and lifeless shells, as His whole energy completely moves forward to a redemptive and apocalyptic goal. An evolutionary understanding of God under-stands him as evolving by means of a gradual series of self-transformations. This implies the realization that God cannot fully and forever be identified with any one of His manifestations, or even with a particular series of such manifestations. Instead, he must be known as a forward-moving process continually transcending and thus moving beyond each one of His particular epiphanies or expressions.

A literal and unimaginative mind resists the idea that God could negate or transcend Himself because it clings to a simple and uncritical conception of identity. Obviously the formal logical law of identity, A is identical with A, is either invalid or irrelevant in any thinking which would apprehend process or evolution, unless it is assumed that A does not have an unchanging or an unmoving identity. Once the mind is directed to the arena of process it must abandon all static categories, including logical categories. It must open itself to a dynamic or flowing movement in which nothing remains wholly the same from one moment to the next, and in which there is always the possibility that a movement from one stage to another will entail a movement of radical if gradual transformation.

Moreover, if we assume an evolutionary movement or a forward-moving process, it must follow that process or being undergoes a continual transformation in which nothing at all remains eternally or substantially the same. How could the Catholic thinker, who accepts process or evolutionary thinking, assume that God is the one exception to the self-transforming movement of process? Such an assumption would entail a renunciation of the principle of analogy and a regression to a purely negative conception of the relationship between the world and God. Would it not be far more Catholic for the Catholic thinker to assume that God Himself passes through a continual process of self-transformation wherein His life or energy continually transcends or negates itself as it moves to a final or apocalyptic goal?

Dialectical Negation and Immanent Presence

An inevitable objection to the theological project is the question of how God could remain in continuity with Himself if He evolves by negating and transcending the particular moments or points of His evolving self-expression. We can attempt to answer this question by realizing that as God moves forward His full life and energy are carried into new forms or expressions, so that His energy remains itself even while undergoing trans-formation. At this point we are touching upon the most difficult problem of contemporary atheistic theology: can God remain Himself if He passes through an ultimate act or movement of self-negation or self-annihilation? If God dies as God, how can He remain God; or for that matter, how can He then be known as an eternal process?

First, we must note that the biblical tradition, and Christianity in particular, has a unique understanding of God insofar as it apprehends him as the transcendent Lord who is immanent in His creation. In its Christian expression, faith knows God as being at once both radically transcendent and radically immanent, even though the meaning and reality of transcendence and immanence assume different forms in different moments and periods of Christian history. Furthermore, Christianity has al-ways proclaimed that the fullest meaning of God is present in Jesus Christ, that in him God has fully and finally become in-carnate, and that all things will be made new in the event or process of the Incarnation. The Christian would seem hardly able to escape believing that an event of ultimate significance has and is occurring in Christ, and that this event has and is making God present or immanent in an absolutely novel and decisive manner. Indeed, insofar as the Christian believes that the fullness of God is present in Christ, he must believe that here transcend-ence has or is passing into immanence, unless he heretically be-lieves that Christ is not fully flesh. It would appear that, at the very least, the Christian must believe that in the Incarnation the transcendence of God has undergone a genuine transformation. May we not say that in the Incarnation God empties Himself of His original power and glory, thereby negating and trans-cending His pre-incarnate Being, so as to make possible a new or apocalyptic union between Himself and the world?

If the meaning of the Incarnation is approached in this man-ner, we can see that a negation or emptying of God's transcendent manifestation makes possible a total realization and fulfillment of His immanent presence. It is precisely by negating Himself as transcendent Lord that God is becoming all in all. Only as that negation becomes embodied in history can the cosmos fulfill its movement towards an apocalyptic end.

In what sense can one speak of such a movement of God as a self-negation or movement through death? The Christian does so because he is bound in faith to the Christ who fulfills the movement of Incarnation in the Crucifixion as a passage through the actuality and finality of death. Unless the death of Christ is thought to be ultimately a facade or a Gnostic mirage, it cannot be considered a mere transition to a higher realm, or symbolically linked with an ascent into a transcendent realm or heaven. The Christian would more truly and more consistently understand the Crucifixion as a final negation of that transcendence which is pure transcendence. Thereby God might be understood as freeing Himself from every dichotomy or opposition between His transcendence and His immanence, making possible the apocalyptic triumph of a transcendence which would finally appear and be real as total immanence.

If the pure or radical transcendence of God is to be understood as passing into a pure or apocalyptic immanence, the symbol and reality of death must be evoked to speak of the finality of God's movement. Accordingly the symbol of the death of God will become a portal through which to pass to the realization of the meaning of God's evolutionary and apocalyptic movement. By this means it is also apparent that to limit the meaning of God to that which is present in Christ is to accept God's self-negation in Christ and to pass with him, through the death of God's transcendence, toward the fulfillment of the apostolic promise that God will be all in all.

Death of God and Christian Life

There is here the danger of understanding God's self-annihilation or self-negation as a simple or literal negation of His transcendence. This would imply understanding God's transcendence as a purely negative or demonic pole or potency of the Godhead. However, this danger can be avoided if it be seen that God's self-negation is consumated in the transformation of transcendence itself into immanence. Once God is understood as moving or evolving through an organic and evolutionary process he can be known as dying to His previous epiphanies or manifestations. He progressively ceases to be truly present in His previous forms, even if those forms remain embedded in human memory and tradition.

We must not, therefore, confine the death of God to a particular point or occasion, not even to Calvary. His death issues from the whole movement of revelation in the Old Testament and is successively and ever more comprehensively embodied in all of that history which is a consequence of Jesus Christ. As a result of that movement of history, transcendence has been manifest in progressively darker, emptier, and more alien forms, until, with the advent of the modern world, it has been real in consciousness and experience only to the extent that it is totally empty or alien. When Christian theology speaks of the death of God it is taking with full seriousness this revolutionary movement of our history. Acknowledging that it is the movement of history and consciousness which has made the name of God unspeakable as a source of energy of God's own act of self-negation in Jesus Christ.

Has the time come when the Church must confess that it can no longer speak the name of God? The Christian can hardly escape the historical truth that for him the name of God is inextricably associated with transcendence; to pass beyond even the memory of transcendence, he must cease to speak the name of God. Indeed, it could be said that the Church has already confessed the death of God in the witness of many of her radical prophets and seers. It has been initiated into a new form in which even the confessing Christian is ceasing to evoke the name or the image of God. More precisely, the contemporary Christian truly speaks the name of God only when he speaks the name of Christ; hence, he seeks a totally Christocentric form of faith.

CONCLUSION

Thus far theology has only begun the task of attempting to understand such a form of faith. May we hope that Catholic theology will move through a revolutionary transformation wherein it will come to accept the death or self-negation of God as a truth of faith? It is only Catholic theology which holds the promise of coming to understand the confession of the death of God as a consummation of the Church's historical movement of faith; perhaps it is only the Catholic thinker who can reach a consistently Christocentric conception of God. If there is no possibility of Catholic theology moving in this direction, then I for one will reluctantly be forced to concede that an atheistic or death of God theology is a destructive aberration. For the moment at least I am sustained by the fact that it was a Roman Catholic thinker, Teilhard de Chardin, who reached the most radically Christocentric theological conception of the divine life and energy. It is also consoling to know that it is in the Roman Catholic world that theology today is most revolutionary and alive.

The Protestant Tradition and the Death of God

◊

Manfred Hoffmann

THIS ARTICLE PROCEEDS upon the assumption that Martin
Luther's theological discovery, or rediscovery, provided the
characteristic principle of the Protestant tradition in contrast
to the Catholic and Free Church tradition. Consequently, this
principle is taken as both the distinguishing mark and the criterion of Protestant thought; it allows for modifications, but
not for total surrender.

LUTHER

Continuity: the Catholic Principle

Luther's theological insight grew out of his life experiences
together with their concomitant and subsequent interpretation.
Life and thought were intimately intertwined. It was rare that
thought preceded life or that ideas were developed strictly theoretically and metaphysically: rather, thought impressed itself
upon him out of history and existence. In his monastery situation Luther found himself confronted with the way of salvation
as it was conceived in the medieval system of unity and order,
encompassing God, man, and the world, and as it was practiced
in medieval sacramentalism and ethics. The analogy of being

(*analogia entis*), variously modified, guaranteed the character-istically medieval relation of both the macrocosm of the world and the microcosm of man to the metaphysical realm. This, in turn, vouchsafed the unity and relatedness of all things to the absolute—notions which particularly fascinate modern man in his mangled and disjointed world.

Though qualified by dissimilarities, the relation of man and his world to God could be seen, both epistemologically and ethically, as continuous from nature to grace, from law to gospel, from sin to salvation, from the particular to the general—or vice versa. To be sure, the unity rested in God, who initially and continually had to give his gracious assistance for the process from the old to the new. Moreover, in the end God would bring the new to perfection. In terms of the theory of cognition, the analogy of faith (*analogia fidei*) would eventually replace that of being, so that the mysteries of faith could be inte-grated into this holistic world view. Nevertheless, man was considered capable of moving, developing, and improving in ever increasing responses to ever increasing graces, gradually leaving thereby the state of condemnation and ignorance and eventually reaching that state of holiness which produced the greatest degree of unity with God.

Admittedly, sin would interrupt this process of sanctification; but reinstitution into grace by the sacrament could rehabilitate man to that place at which he had stopped in his own develop-ment. On the other hand, the process could be accelerated if man performed deeds beyond duty or works of supererogation. In the general run of medieval theology all this amounted to the teaching that man really can sooner or later attain the same level as God in the sense that some kind of unity with the absolute is achieved through mutual divine operation and human cooperation. It seems that the typically Catholic principle was, and still largely is, characterized by the prevalence of the cate-gory of unity and continuity rather than that of distinction and discontinuity in the dialectic of man's relationship to God.

Discontinuity: *Luther's Protestant Principle*

Whether Luther was forced to revolt against this system by the influence of late medieval Nominalism in which he was deeply schooled, or by personal scruples in the form of a stubbornness that drove him to unflinching self-appraisal is not the question here. What is clear is that he started out by taking seriously the view of the Church as it reached him. Indeed, he took the life and teaching of his proposition into his life. Neither a born rebel nor an indigenous trouble-maker, he attempted to tread the path which monasticism, in its intellectual existential form of medieval mysticism, pointed out to him. Yet, meticulous and consistent to the utmost degree, Luther had to admit in the face of his existential experiences that he could not reach beyond himself. Though he tried this way of organic development from the old to the new conscientiously and persistently, he failed because he took reality in his life equally as seriously as he did the word of the Church.

His theological thought, therefore, is characterized by the category of discontinuity. Every attempt to move away from the old makes the old grow even older and produces death. Man's attempt to approach God, reproaches God; his move to God removes him the more from God. His ethical ascent results really in a descent into himself. His intellectual overextension produces an idealized image of his own which he then projects into the absolute, inflates in the theology of glory (*theologia gloriae*), and adores as God. His mystical introversion into his soul makes him meet, not God who is beyond himself (*extra se*), but only his own innermost self, that is, his naked and frightening ego. Thus, in the light of the reality of his existence, Luther experienced the relativity of the Church's word. Though he takes the Church at her word, this word does not hold out against his historical reality.

This discovery of the radical distinction between the old and the new, law and gospel, death and life, introduced into the center of theological thought the criteria of the Protestant tradition: discontinuity, historicity, relativity, particularity, subjectivism, and contextualism. With its revolutionary impetus, this caused the tragic split in Western Christianity. Yet, it opened possibilities for a commensurable appreciation of modern man's self-understanding, unfortunately not realized by Lutheran Orthodoxy and Pietism. Luther demetaphysicized or historicized medieval theology causing a change in theological climate as fundamental as had the demythologizing and historicizing in St. Paul. As Gogarten correctly maintains, the post-Pauline metaphysics was basically an attempt at rationalizing ancient mythology in a Christian framework. By employing categories of the later Platonic philosophy, most of the Church Fathers had metaphysicized the historical nature of Paul's theology. In so doing they initiated a trend which was to prevail throughout of the middle ages, and this despite the reception of Aristotelian realism which was more challenged than altered by late medieval Nominalism.

Dialectical Unity: Luther's Revelational Anthropology

Luther did not carry his method of discontinuity vis-a-vis a metaphysical God to its radical consequence. To be sure, he was modern in that he placed God on the plane of history so that God can be found in man's faith or in his understanding of himself and his existential situation (faith as creator of divinity: *fides creatrix divinitatis*). In this way theology becomes anthropology. Nevertheless, because Luther retained traces of medievalism, his theology is still a revelational anthropology. Although grace is not nature perfected, life not death overcome, and righteousness not law fulfilled, nevertheless, he tried to bring the relative into some relationship of unity with the absolute. Though the meeting occurs on the same plane, history, the absolute remains totally different. Luther intended to be dialectical in order both to avoid absolutizing the relative and to relativize the absolute. Thus he holds them together in an absurd, paradoxical confession of faith against reality.

Luther professed not to be fundamentally concerned with a metaphysical or mythological God in his aseity, from which one would infer the death of such a God. Yet, even in confessing the life of the historical and existential God who appears in man's reality and is God for me (*pro me*), the category of distinction qualifies God's *pro me* revelation in history and existence as a revelation of God hidden under its contrary (*sub contrario*) (a theology of the cross: *theologia crucis*). The resurrection is in the cross, glory in suffering, strength in weakness, exaltation in humility, joy in despair, life in death, and the absolute in the relative, so that man exists simultaneously as just and sinner (*simul iustus et peccator*). It is precisely man's faith, his new self-understanding developed from the experience of discontinuity between these two realities, which holds them paradoxically together: faith conciliates contraries (*fides conciliat contraria*).

By this dialectical introduction of the category of unity, which does not impair the prevailing category of distinction, man's historical and existential reality is guarded against falling into complete relativity and particularity. At the same time the category of distinction keeps this concept of unity from being modified into one of continuity in its horizontal application. Nevertheless, a type of holistic view, albeit confessional and paradoxical in character, can be maintained. It is similar to the medieval universal world view in that it can embrace almost all phenomena of life. However, it is without metaphysical notions, for the revelation of God in human reality is never a matter of evidence, manifestation, and rational, ethical, psychological, ecclesiastical, or natural demonstration, but of faith, confession, and proclamation.

Lutheran Absolutism and Pietism

How historically important this safe-guard of the prevalence of the category of distinction against that of unity was, is evidenced by the relapse into a non-historical and consequently non-existential holistic concept in Lutheran Orthodoxy and Pietism. Lutheran Orthodoxy relativized the relative in an attempt at absolutizing the absolute, thereby establishing once again a metaphysical universal system. Lutheran Pietism absolutized the relative as well as the absolute in its dualistic subjectivism, and this created a similarly total, if negative, concept of the world.

Both movements represented a departure from Luther's own approach, since he endeavored to remain consistently dialectical and not to allow the category of unity to prevail over that of distinction. This is evident in his increasing disavowal of the language of continuity, that is, in his resistence to the concepts of growth, development, and evolution. If a secular theology were developed so radically that the category of distinction reduced that of unity to an utter and powerless paradox the prominence given the category of distinction could have marked a transitional stage to modern man's understanding of his and the world's historicity. This would have meant the death not only of the transcendent, metaphysical God in his self sufficient reality (aseity), but even of the immanent, historical, and existential God in his reality for me (pro-me-ity).

In fact, the change of the confessional and paradoxical character of the category of unity into one that allowed itself to be used as an instrument for rational, psychological, or ethical verification, reduced the category of distinction to an almost negligible significance. Thus, in Lutheran Orthodoxy and Pietism, this change allowed for a remetaphysicizing and consequently remythologizing of theology. The first, the secularizing modification of Luther's dialectic, risked the loss of wholeness and could fall into complete relativity, while remaining true to history and existence. The second, remetaphysicizing and remythologizing, imposed a holistic view on reality at the cost of abandoning the historicity of existence. It is interesting to note that the vast majority of Protestant theologians up to the present time have opted for types of the second alternative. However, the Luther-Renaissance since the beginning of the twentieth century recovered the genuine Luther, which reveals a remarkable affinity to existentialist philosophy. Yet it did not attempt to radically secularize his theology in a post-Christian age, and only a few such as Bultmann, Bonhoeffer, Braun, and, above all, Gogarten have become alert to the problems of modern secularity.

MODERN SECULARIZATION

Enlightenment Rationalism

The general process of secularization marking the Western history of ideas in its modern period is characterized by man's increasing emancipation from absolute, metahistorical authorities. Whether one finds its roots in Renaissance thought, the genuine philosophy of Plato, or even in the New Testament (Gogarten), this much is obvious: for the first time man is proceeding in his understanding of himself and his world from the premise: even if there were no God (*etsi deus non daretur*). In order to come to terms with his situation in the world and his obligation to order it, in law and political thought, philosophy and science, art, economics, and technology, and with ever growing measures of audacity, man has used his reason, unconditioned by supernatural absolutes. This whole development presents itself as an often confusing compound of both revolutionary and retarding moments, of advance and setback. Nevertheless, seen in retrospect and as a whole, the general trend can be recognized: man tried to make sense of himself, of his place in the world, and of his work in the community by employing a cognitive principle found in himself and verified by empirical experience and experiment. On this basis, he ventured to develop a universal system of values as well as generally applicable patterns of behavior. However, though modern man had set about constructing this holistic concept of his immanent reality with a carefree naivete and a disarming intellectual honesty, he succumbed to the illusion of having ascertained a center of unity in reason. Once he presumed reason to be better able to produce true knowledge and order than the transcendent ultimate authority of God he began slowly to proceed from the *etsi deus non daretur* to the elimination of God (*exitus dei*).

Nineteenth Century: Reactions and Historical Relativism

In the naive optimism over what he had discovered, man with the spirit of the Enlightenment hardly realized the fundamental fallacy in his approach, that is, that reason cannot serve such a unifying purpose. Reason itself is not ultimate, but relative to historical or inherited cultural, educational, and national conditions of particular stages in Western civilization, which in turn is only one among a variety of other civilizations. Furthermore, by restricting itself to empirical phenomena, reason forfeits the possibility of transcending itself. It is obviously empirical reality in its historical and temporal dimension that, through particular situations, contexts, contingencies, milieus, circumstances, and accidentals, determines man's rational faculty—not vice versa.

Therefore, the question of the nineteenth century was: "What basic common possession beyond reason can be assumed, how far is such a unifying principle universally applicable, and where is it located as the center of a total system?" The age of restoration produced ideologies such as Kantianism, Idealism, Romanticism, Evolutionism, Hegelianism, cultural Protestantism, Ultramontanism, or the Social Gospel, to mention but the most important. All of these movements represented something of a reaction against Enlightenment rationalism in that they increasingly endeavored to face up to the problem of history. Whether the unifying principle was discovered in practical reason (*praktische Vernunft*), emotion and feeling, the individual person, the organic or dialectical progress of *Geist,* social or cultural change, the *Übermensch,* morality, monarchical, hierarchical, or democratic political stability, or even in the reintroduced notion of a transcendent God, the last century seems characterized by the search for something to which a holistic world view could be affixed in the face of a threatening historical relativism.

In brief, the nineteenth century attempted to resist the process toward a radical secularization by looking for the wholeness of reality in history while largely ignoring its temporal character. As a result it was unwillingly remetaphysicized, and in turn remythologized. In order to protect this wholeness in historical reality the category of discontinuity, which would qualify the historical moment as punctiliar and relative, was eliminated. In addition the category of unity was horizontally applied to insure a historical absolute and consequently provide a possibility of finding truth and meaning in history. No wonder, then, that most of the nineteenth century ideologies employed the notion of continuity—variously called growth, development, evolution, and organic change—which Luther already had abandoned.[1]

Indeed, it was impossible finally to ignore the inevitable conclusion of the historico-critical method that the historicity of man's individual and corporate existence in circumstantial, temporal situations completely relativizes truth and meaning. Like a destructive fungus, historical science attacked any ideology of history, and it did so the more effectively as its validity was dramatically vindicated by the political, social, scientific, and cultural conditions of the twentieth century. Thus, through the process of secularization the relativity of man's existence came to assert itself so strongly that any total view claiming truth for all of reality was rejected once and for all. Historical relativism produced pluralism and finally indifferentism, because man was forced to see himself irredeemably caught up in the situation of compartmentalization, fragmentation, and eventually atomization of his reality. Hence, the pronouncement of the death of God must be interpreted as expressing the experience of the loss of any type of unifying principle beyond or in man that could be used as a criterion for understanding himself and the world as a whole, and consequently as an instrument to plan, order, and build this whole in the future.

Twentieth Century: Nihilism and Ideology

In the face of this radical secularity, twentieth century man's various attitudes appear to be variations on two basic options: the lapse into some form of nihilism and the relapse into some form of ideology. The nihilist resigns himself to the utter relativity of his existence, and accordingly his actions are mere responses to chance. He does not direct his decisions to any whole whatever, and thus retreats from the scene of general involvement, leaving the planning and ordering of larger contexts to others. The range of this attitude extends from complete fatalism and passivism, on the one side, to existentialism and contextualism, on the other.

The ideologist, on the other hand, relapses into a nineteenth century attitude. He takes his part for the whole (*pars pro toto*), claiming universal truth for that understanding of the whole which he abstracted from his segment of particulars. He forces the latter to fit into the mosaic of a general idea and then enlarges the scale of this idea to embrace all of reality. Neglecting the relativity and limitation of his set of particulars, either by confession or by pointing to an ideal functionalism in a particular framework, he insists upon the absolute general authority of their abstracted idea. Then he develops a plan for the overall realization of his idea, which assumes mostly a utopian form.

Since such a utopia is at best applicable to a restricted portion of reality, in a pluralistic situation its claim of universality cannot be realized against those advanced by other ideologies. Claims to totality have been rooted in anthropology (neo-Humanism), society, economics, and politics (totalitarianism, Communism, Capitalism), history (for example, Pannenberg), cosmology (Teilhard de Chardin), and theology (revelational positivism on the one side and ecclesiastical absolutism on the other side of this spectrum). In every case they all seem structurally similar to nineteenth century value systems, which in the light of historical relativism proved to be a failure. An ideological absolutizing of particular historical phenomena cannot deliver modern man from his dilemma, because it remythologizes his reality and leads to what Gogarten calls "secularism," that idolatrizing of the world which once again confers a religious quality on reality.

TOWARD A SECULAR PROTESTANT THEOLOGY

Dialectic of Continuity and Discontinuity

The Protestant theologian is led to believe that this drama of modern man's secularity is prefigured in Luther's spiritual and intellectual development, if stripped of its particular historical frame of reference and grasped at its elemental level. In Luther's agonizing attempt to experience the medieval claim of unity and continuity between the natural and the supernatural, the reality of his existence eventually forced him to face its total relativity, that is, its discontinuity from any absolute. As a result, Luther was placed between a medieval ideology and a modern nihilism: he had to find a way between the Scylla of abandoning distinction for unity, and the Charybdis of sacrificing unity for distinction. The surrender of the absolute would deliver him up to the complete despair of nihilism, whose logical consequence is self-annihilation. Conversely, the surrender of the relative by an unquestioning acceptance of the medieval ideology would demand an intellectual and existential dishonesty equivalent to the abandonment of the historicity of his real situation.

In his self tormenting search for identity, he finally came up with a dialectic that proceeds from the category of radical discontinuity. Only with this as a basis is the notion of unity introduced. In this light unity is a statement of faith or a word of proclamation which does not do away with discontinuity in an attempt at synthesis, but rather maintains this discontinuity in a confession that is absurd and paradoxical in the face of opposite evidence.

Secularity and Radical Discontinuity

The modern theologian who endeavors to radicalize this Protestant principle in secularizing theology will have to take most seriously the category of discontinuity that expresses the relativity and historicity of man's existence. He must recognize discontinuity not only in its negative sense of bondage to this real existence, but in its positive sense of freedom from any bondage to absolutes outside of the relativity of one's existence. Drawing out the lines more or less distinctly indicated by Luther, the modern theologian will have to think of a radical demetaphysicizing or demythologyzing of historical existence, which would necessarily include any nineteenth or twentieth century ideology. Immanent realtity loses thereby its demonic, religious quality as a realm where salvation or wholeness—the German *Heil* (savlation) equals "whole"—can be found or even approached. Historical reality can no longer be considered a stepping stone toward any metahistorical reality whatever. Any type of continuity from man to an absolute outside of, or in him, which could promise wholeness as the basis of an integral world view, must be disclaimed. There is no way for man to reach beyond his relativity by organically improving what he has and is, even in history. The only existent absolute is, paradoxically, his relativity.

The freedom which man receives by this loss of the demonic claim of historical reality means that he now can live and act in his relativity joyfully because it no longer requires him to establish an integrity of himself as well as of the world. Once modern man sees his existence to be void of religious demands, he is at liberty to take his reality for what it is. In meeting situations he is no longer constrained from analyzing them empirically, existentially, and historically, and from making his decision in a non-religious or secular fashion. Such an attitude implies neither libertinism nor nihilism. Making a responsible decision in the encounter with a particular situation, which in itself suggests a course of action and even one that is discerned by reason, one acts both in response to the situation and reasonably. He is kept from fatalistic nihilism by the quality of reasonableness by which he uses his reason, though not in the Enlightenment sense as an absolute, and by the quality of responsibility by which he takes account of a particular moment of decision, though not without judgment. At the same time these qualities keep him from the religious attempt to establish a whole. Since man can make such a reasonable and responsible judgment only in the moment of decision, any abstract ethics or general laws of moral behavior lose significance. Abstractions and generalizations, hypothetically anticipating patterns of decision, would necessarily redemonize reality by introducing absolutes.

Regarding the category of distinction, a modern Protestant theologian meets little difficulty in extending Luther's thought to a radical application. In fact, he may well find himself in unison with much of the twentieth century secular temper, and may even be tempted to consider it a "Protestant Era."

Paradoxical Unity

He finds the crux of his task in the notion of a confessed, paradoxical unity. If he wishes to remain a theologian, he cannot ignore the category of unity represented by an absolute. Yet the utter relativity of man's existence, demonstrated paradigmatically by twentieth century secularity, forces him to forsake any endeavor to claim such an absolute outside or within man. Any claim to an absolute unity would redemonize reality by imposing either a nineteenth century, or Enlightenment, or Lutheran Orthodox and Pietistic, or medieval ideology upon it. If there is any such unity at all, therefore, it must be found within the relativity of man's existence. It must be a relative, non-religious unity that does not allow for absolutizing into a utopian ideology.

Luther and Kierkegaard, who applied Luther's mode of thinking consistently in the face of nineteenth century ideologies, confess this paradoxical unity by way of its contrary (*sub contrario*). Empirically this unity can be neither fully experienced nor demonstrated, but it does introduce into man's existence wholeness, namely, salvation. What a modern Protestant can accept is their insistence that unity must be sought in man's historical existence. What must be questioned is their propounding of this unity in faith as a holistic view, for in that case faith, as an absolute, becomes the central problem. A secular Protestant theology must face the task of avoiding an absolutizing even of faith if it is to do justice to the genuine secularity of the twentieth century. Faith will have to be relativized even more radically than in Luther and Kierkegaard. On the other hand, if there is a relative absolute, it must be shown as empirically recognizable in man's existence. A simple claim can no longer do, because modern man cannot accept a non-experiential and non-demonstrable reality of faith confessed as a paradox. If modern man really is free in his relativity, that is, if his salvation lies in the fact that he no longer has to establish the whole, whatever relative unity does exist is in need of being discerned.

The presence of a non-absolute unity within the existential relativity would seem to have been adequately expressed by Gogarten's phrase "searching ignorance" (*fragendes Nichtwissen*).[2] We take this to mean man's stretching out toward understanding his reality as a whole, and thus toward an absolute. This reaching, however, is kept in check by the radical recognition of his relativity in his historicity. Here, the Protestant principle was applied more radically than ever before to the situation of modern secularity. Yet even Gogarten's thought needs to be pushed further. Although he admits the possibility of *fragendes Nichtwissen* by secular man who has given up the symbol "God," Gogarten is quick to add that this attitude may rapidly abandon the state of relativity and absolutize the relative world. This would create either ideological or nihilistic "secularism." For Gogarten, man's proper relativity as lord over the world can be maintained only if man sees himself in the relation of son of God who is his creator. This relation takes place in faith, which keeps man back both from absolutizing and from completely relativizing himself. This is faith as *Rückalt.*

Although he cautiously admits that the *fragendes Nichtwissen* is also possible in man without faith, one may judge from his insistence on faith as the relative unity in man's existence that Gogarten, in his published work, does not sufficiently supersede Luther. Nevertheless, he opens an avenue, and the task of the Protestant theologian after Gogarten would be, then, to explore this possibility of an atheistic *fragendes Nichtwissen.* This is especially true since to the more critically minded it appears that it is faith, rather than the secularity of modern man, which is more apt to lapse into claims of absoluteness and finality. The following will be confined to a tentative attempt to show how a secular Protestant theology might look if it explores the possibility of a non-theistic *fragendes Nichtwissen.* The experimental character of such a venture prevents a comprehensive presentation. Therefore, only the main lines will be drawn and in rough strokes, taking into consideration only the existential-historical aspect of this concept, not its noetic-ontological dimension.

Self Transcendence as Survival

The modern Protestant, proceeds within the propositions that he cannot make any claim to absolute unity and that secularity should not be allowed to degenerate into complete relativity. In view of this, he is able to introduce the proper relativity by recognizing that the absolute has its place in the eschatological dimension in man's future. This, in fact, is what Gogarten proposes. However, he expresses the future as ahead of man and "adventing" (*Zukünftigkeit der Zukunft*), and identifies this with God, in relation to whom alone man can have his proper relativity. In so doing he leaves himself open to being interpreted as introducing a metahistorical, divine absolute.

It would seem more appropriate to understand the future

only insofar as it evidences itself in man's present reality. This would eliminate the mention of God and substitute the concept of "faith" by other terms less encumbered by traditional notions. Man's historical transcendence from one relative moment to another can be taken as such an eschatological presence of an absolute in relativity, for the only unity to be discerned in man's historical relativity is that which binds his historical moments together in a continuity that is non-absolute or does not abandon their relativity. An appropriate term for such a "living over and beyond oneself" in self-transcendence, and yet a living from the same into the same, is survival. This concept should not be taken in its general meaning of the fortunate and passive outlasting of some previous disaster that struck others (continuity), but in its literal meaning, as implying the gift of a new future (discontinuity), which allows man to make use of his possibilities to the fullest that he is able. This eschatological character of survival as the gift of a future becoming present keeps the present, past, and even the future in their proper relativity, because in becoming present it becomes relative.

In the transcendence of his survival, man certainly does not leave the situation of relativity for one of wholeness. In his eschatological stretching out and extending beyond himself in quest for unity, the whole is present, not as a possession or even in anticipation, but as relative, that is, as that to which he aligns himself in his self-transcendence. Man's salvation and the very wholeness of his fragmented reality lies in survival, which never eliminates his relativity. The old relative is replaced now by a new relative according to which one and all are determined by the final relativity, death, as the ever-present future possibility. Perhaps the concept of survival could substitute for that of faith. Because such a transcendence means survival from his relativity, it prevents nihilism; because it also means the movement of surviving into a new relativity, it keeps man from absolutizing himself and the world into an ideology. Consequently, survival exercises the same dialectical function as faith, yet in a demythologized and thus historical setting.

Survival as Love

The recognition of the relative unity that is had in survival enables man to make full use of his human possibilities, for he is now aware both of his limitations and of his freedom. In the light of this relativity, taking himself and the world realistically, he will make religionless decisions. This will be done not in response to any absolute that may challenge him to establish or perfect a whole in and around himself, but in answer to the relative situations themselves. Intelligent analysis and reasonable action are the tools he employs to find and realize the best possible solution to his problems. As he still is limited largely by relativity, he uses in freedom the relative unity present in surviving himself to pass on survival to other persons. In love he shares his survival with his fellowman.

Just as man existentially lives beyond himself and leaves his past behind in the movement of survival, so in love as his ethical transcendence to the other he gives himself up in the movement of self-emptying or self-annihilation toward the other person.

Indeed, man who survives himself will realize that he is able to retain this freedom from himself only if he is willing to give it to the other in love. If he realizes that his own future surely means death and that he experiences self-unity only in the movement of survival toward death, he can joyfully anticipate it by giving himself up for the other. In so doing he can, with radical consistency, take upon himself his own relativity or death. Thus, in dying unto himself for the other, man offers the gift of survival to his fellowman. Although the unity of this gift of love, as that of his own survival, is relativized again by his own relativity, he need have no qualms regarding the totality of his gift if he gives as much as he is capable.

Survival as Hope

The place of relative unity in the relativity of man's existence becomes paradigmatically clear in terms of hope as man's historical transcendence. Hope is commonly understood as man's projection into the future of his desire to have his existence amplified and intensified, that is, to have perfected what he has and is.

Dominant in this projection is the concept of continuity toward unity. In the perspective of the Protestant principle of discontinuity, hope appears as an attempt on the part of man to transcend his historicity. It grows on the experience of his relativity in the face of death as the ultimate relativity; consequently, it means a longing and extending in quest toward the opposite of his reality, viz., life and unity. Again, this hope introduces unity, but a relative unity, present only in the act of historical transcendence. Even then, man's reality remains relative, for his hope is never fulfilled and its object can never become his property, but remains in the unattainable future. The paradoxical character of hope against hope must be strictly maintained. Particularly in this aspect of his non-absolute unity, man tends to absolutize the future in a present, proleptic anticipation of hope, thus producing various types of utopias. In view of this, the relativity of hope is essential in order to guard man's historical transcendence from being transformed into present absolutes of hope.

Death of God

Such a radical application of the Protestant principal to the secular self-understanding of modern man clearly implies the elimination of any transhistorical or ultimate absolute, that is, it recognizes the death of God. Furthermore, the historical action of such a God in the man Jesus of Nazareth also loses its quality of salvation, considered as beyond the possibilities of man and as something to be appropriated by the unquestioning surrender to its claim of absoluteness. Modern man no longer considers definitive that uniqueness attributed to God in Jesus: death and resurrection as love in surrender *(kenōsis)* to others, eliminating the past and opening the future. Man himself is capable of seeing and doing the same in his own existence and apart from such revelation. At best the significance of Jesus lies in the fact that his life and action demonstrate and illuminate man's existence. From the absence of the quality of salvation, Jesus is led to the vacancy of God himself, even of the historical God.

Similarly for any man who realistically takes his existence upon himself, no death could be so radical as to surpass the acceptance of his relativity; no resurrection in history so powerful as his transcendence in survival; no surrender of oneself so desperately unselfish as his ethical attempt in love to survive himself in order to live with the other; and no eschatological concept so realistic as the hope to which he clings in the face of opposite evidence. In his relativity and death he is crucified, in his survival he rises again, in his love he empties himself, and in his hope he aligns himself to a completely new future. Man finds his salvation in not trying to be more than he is— man. But recognizing squarely his relativity, he does the best he can to find and pass on the relative unity available to him.

◇

1. Seen from this perspective, the "Death of God" theology as applied in the preceding article to Catholic philosophy is but an element of this nineteenth century ideological approach. It does not recognize the full implications of a radical secularity, since it introduces the holistic concept of evolution, i.e., historical continuity. Despite its seeming radicality, such a "Death of God" theology is basically defensive and apologetic. In an attempt at a utopian ideology, it kills the transcendent God, thereby claiming discontinuity in this one respect. However, it revives this dead God on the plane of historical immanence by juggling Hegel's and Newman's categories of synthesis and evolution in order to preserve the concept of wholeness in the face of historical relativity. It is not surprising then that Altizer shows sympathy for Teilhard de Chardin's concept of a development toward cosmic unity or creation at the end.

2. Friedrich Gogarten, **Verhangnis und Hoffnung der Neuzeit**, (Hamburg: Taschenbrich, 1966), pp. 139 ff.

Alternatives to Atheism

◇

D. A. Drennen

ANY SEARCH FOR "alternatives to atheism" implies two fundamental but strangely conflicting assumptions: (a) that it is now possible to make a reasonable case in behalf of atheism; but (b) that it is neither reasonable nor emotionally possible to accept such a case without first exhausting every possible claim in behalf of theism. Posing the issue in this way appears to undercut the pretensions of the first assumption with the hopes of the second, for it would be presumptuous to imagine that there are alternatives to atheism unless one still clings to the realistic possibilities of some sort of theistic faith. The issue of alternatives might then be reframed in the question: "Is it reasonably possible to substantiate a case for theism, while at the same time admitting reasonable claims for the cause of modern atheism?"

BELIEF, DISBELIEF, AND UNBELIEF

The relation between theism and modern atheism must be understood largely from the point of view of theism itself, since the apparent success of atheism is usually attributed to the apparent failure of theism. Because, in the West at least, the greatest concentration of theists is to be found in or around established Christian churches, the situation which confronts

[223]

Western Church-related theism might provide a suitable context for understanding the implications of the problem. In its simplest terms, the situation appears to be that church-theism in the modern world has been assaulted from without and undermined from within. Indeed, to some observers it now appears in the process of being dismantled.

Admittedly, the phrase "church-theism" is not completely satisfactory, but is employed here in the sense of institutional-theism, and thus can equally be construed to refer to many of the problems confronting modern Judaism in the West, but no less those of Islam in most Muslim countries. Because the issue of atheism is so often related, both positively and negatively, to Christian themes, the phrase "Christian churches" is used without intentional bias.

One of the most persistently held reasons for the decline in recent decades of church-theism is that modern industrial society no longer looks to the churches for intellectual and moral leadership. Because religion has been eased from the center of modern secular life, it is asserted, the churches are forced to surrender any rightful claims to influence contemporary man. Some observers ascribe the failure of the churches to the prior failure of religion; others argue from an antecedent decline of the churches to a consequent demise of religion. Outside the churches, too, the once dominant role of religious faiths appears to have been replaced, on the one hand, by scientific humanism proclaiming the hopes of the future and, on the other hand, by classical humanism celebrating the glories of the past.

To many church spokesmen, the blame for this shift in allegiance rests entirely on the shoulders of modern secularist man whose never-ending quest for power has replaced an earlier search for salvation. To more severe critics, the winds of secular doctrine have penetrated even the mind of Christianity which has simply allowed itself to succumb to the "secular drift."[1] Hence, the shifts in external allegiance to church leadership have apparently been less painful than the dislocations of fidelity within church communities themselves. The erosion of formal belief, reflecting both the apathy of some and the hostility of others, is particularly evident in the increasing number of defections from active church-membership.[2] The situation becomes even more painful when one adds to this the growing mass of so-called "believers" whose Church attendance can be attributed more to the demands of social than religious ritual.

A still more significant deviation from church leadership has occurred among both laymen and clerics who, while still genuine and serious theists, no longer feel religiously at home in the churches. To express their innermost hopes and convictions they rely on secularist ideals rather than on churchly formulas. Socially and politically concerned where the churches have found little cause for alarm, morally disturbed by events to which the churches have been all too blind, while intellectually distressed by evils traditionally sanctioned as the wages of man's sinful estate, these disquieted theists, often maintaining church-affiliation against their conscience, suddenly find themselves in religious alliance with those whom the churches officially scorn as enemies of religion.

Yet to such disquieted theists it is not belief but credulity which symbolizes the actions of "believers" who either as militant defenders of the *status quo* unquestioningly accept church policy and action, or as religious socialites vainly club with ministers and monsignori. It is complacency and the "unbelief" as well as what has been called "absolute theism" which makes church-centered theism comfortless and even scandalous to such serious theists.[3] It is ironic that the loss of spirit within the churches has been a significant factor in driving from their shepherding influence many who inwardly doubt churchly competence and jurisdiction.

Other equally disturbing factors appear to threaten the inner stability of the churches. Not the least of these is the alteration in forms of theological thought and moral expression which have substituted secular learning for scholastic vocabulary and homiletic categories. Even "religious discourse," which once served to unify the convictions of many kinds of believers, no longer maintains its unchallenged prestige against charges that it is little more than ceremonial rhetoric.

Perhaps the most significant threat, however, is neither the increase of unbelief outside, nor the rising tide of disbelief within, the churches, but a growing sense of the churches' utter irrelevance to modern experience. Indeed, this irrelevancy appears to explain not only why churches have lost their impact upon contemporary men, but also to explain the startling decline in new religious vocations. It may also account for the dramatic increase in the numbers of those who are abandoning their religious vows. It is not unusual that so many church-goers should interpret these events as the wages of sin and secularism.

In the face of such serious external and internal threats to their existence, the churches have naturally sought ways to repair the damage of events. As could be expected, however, no single solution has found a majority of adherents. Therefore, responses to the "secularist heresy" have tended to converge along several different axes, which might be termed "outright opposition," "selective modification," and "radical transformation." The first elects forcibly to resist the secular heresy, the second modestly to blunt its criticism, while the last seeks radically to transfigure theism itself.

1. Until rather recently, the standard rejoinder among churchmen to the ideals and hopes of modern secularist society had been that of inspired resistance. Among Roman Catholics, for example, this took the form of militant apologetics. Usually entoned in neo-scholastic language, catechetical defense tended to equate all modern movements with anti-Catholic, and therefore anti-theist and irreligious, sentiment. From such a viewpoint, the Protestant Reformation was naturally an important target since it appeared to represent the opening wedge which divided "True Religion" from the moral and intellectual netherworlds of deism and atheism. Among Protestants, opposition normally took the form of fundamentalist or "confessionalist" reaction to Roman Catholic bureaucracy, often considered to be the real root of modern godlessness.

2. In contrast, those who follow the path of selective modification, simply because they represent a "moderate" approach, have something in common with both the paths of opposition

and of transformation. With the latter, they share a sense of the urgency in order to make them more accessible to contemporary audiences. With the former, they share the feeling that this need dates back to the passing of the medieval Christian hegemony and the rise of the modern world. Thus, for example, the seventeenth-century founder of the French Oratorians, Pierre Cardinal de Bérulle, sought to persuade Descartes to express perennial Christian truths in new and scientifically congenial forms in order to counteract the threatening effects of scepticism and *libertinage*. Again, at the end of the last century, such men as Von Hügel and Maurice Blondel attempted a similar *rapprochement* with modern social and intellectual challenges to Christianity, although this *rapprochement* was later condemned as the "modernist heresy" by Pius X's 1907 encyclical *Pascendi*.

Among Protestants, the path of modification found ready spokesmen, for instance, in a group of British clergymen and intellectuals known as the *"Septem contra Christum"* which included Mark Pattison and Benjamin Jowett. They argued that there was nothing genuine in the modern world not adaptable to Christianity and nothing in Christianity not modifiable by contemporary ideas. In our own times, such modifying sentiments expressed, for example, in the work of Emil Brunner and Paul Tillich drew attention to the unwisdom of many Christians who surrendered all relations with modern culture.

3. The theory of transformism is far more radical in its goals than that of modification. While admitting historical Christian influences on the modern temperament, it lays greater stress on the transfiguring, rather than the conforming, genius of Christianity. Transformists are less likely to ask: "What was it *once* like to be a Christian?" and more likely to inquire: "What must it now, and what will it in the future, mean to be a Christian?" The increasing influence of transformist opinion appears to explain the recent movement among many, particularly the younger radical theologians, to undertake a harder look at the issues involved in understanding a secularized Christianity.[4]

It seems evident that the attraction of each of these three reponses hinges on what one ultimately considers to be the relation between modern secularist society and Christianity. Each may, of course, take comfort in the view that secularism reflects an "indirect and unconscious influence" of Christian ideas,[5] or that secular thought "is not really so secular as it has supposed itself to be,"[6] or even that "in our own times our thought inevitably works on the lines laid down by Christianity."[7] But transformists are likely to ask whether these assertions refer to the inner spiritual reality of Christianity, or merely to the cultural forms which Christianity has used in order to express its genius. For them, the issue appears to be precisely the gap which separates Christian belief from modern thought. They argue that the real stumbling-block to the modern world is not Christianity, but the world-view upon which Christianity has so long rested. Such opinions have often been interpreted as signs which mark their adherents with the red pencil of atheism.[8]

The more fundamental question for each of these three views, however, lies in their judgment on the relation between Christianity and the advance of human consciousness. Can all agree on the principle that such an advance is not antithetic to Christianity? The real test of this principle resides in the way it is interpreted and applied. Thus, at one extreme, those who resist secularism may apply the principle not to Christianity but to its hellenistic categories, and so continue to await an alteration in the views and structures of secular society. At the other extreme, those who welcome the achievements of modern society may apply the principle, not to the cultural expressions of Christianity, but to its inner message, which then would barely be distinguishable from secular humanism.

The alternative responses within church-theism thus resolve into a choice between a *status quo*-theism on the one hand, and, on the other, an unknown *status ad quem*-theism which could turn out to be nothing less than a form of crypto-atheism. To those who point out that the best course of action would lie in the middle-road of slow modification, transformists reply that this course of action, which has been tried since the rise of the modern world, is no longer sufficient. What appears to be needed, they say, and what the theory of modification cannot basically admit is substantial alteration in the theory and practice of Christian theism.

Consequently, a modern theist is faced with the problem of seeking ways in which to maintain a theistic world-view which neither compromises the search for viable alternatives to present modes of theistic thought and action, nor forces him to confess that the search is pointless. Though perhaps initially attracted to the ideals of a radical transformation, he cannot long remain untouched by the uncertainty to which such a solution automatically commits him.

THE SEARCH FOR ALTERNATIVES

It is more likely that many Christian theists who deeply desire to live realistically and religiously in the modern world are attracted to the ideal of transforming Christian life and thought in order to make it not merely harmonize, but become identical with genuine secular life.[9] It is not difficult to see that such a theist is no longer satisfied with leading a split existence between the divergent ideals ultimately implied by any theory of modification. For this reason, those who lead a life identical with the aims of genuine secularism might become paradigmatic as a starting-point in the search for a unified religious life in the modern world.

For this reason, many observers have indicated that theists are becoming "increasingly aware of the nontheistic alternative" and deliberately desire to understand "alternative systems of value."[10] Thus, for perhaps the first time in the history of Christianity, theists are not merely listening "to reproaches offered by strangers" to their faith,[11] but are consciously seeking ways to realize within Christian theism competing systems of value. Hence, the question: "What are the alternatives to theism?" which might have been asked by serious Christians in the eighteenth century, is now replaced by the more radical question: "What are the alternatives to atheism?" This shift in emphasis indicates that for many theists today the burden of proof has slipped perceptively in favor of the new values to be found in the atheistic way of life. The question has indeed become so cogent—literally, so thinkable—that for some at least the first reaction might be that there *are* no alternatives to atheism. In any case, there can be little doubt that it is now consonant with the prevailing mood among many modern theists that atheism is a genuine alternative.

This remarkable inversion of the question particularly affects the lives of theists who have seriously entered into the spirit of their times. Yet it must be added that the underlying motive for this inversion is usually the search to justify not a less theistic, but rather a more realistic view of reality.

It should be noted, too, that the search for alternatives to atheism is also a search for alternatives to all previous forms of theism. Were it possible to demonstrate that any form of theism is incapable of embracing the world's value more genuinely than, or at least as genuinely as, atheism, theism would unmistakably be disqualified as a real alternative to atheism. Does this not then imply that it is necessary to determine in what way theistic and atheistic alternatives can be tested against one another?[12]

The first point to observe is that such a contrast is unworkable in terms of the formula: "God or Nothing," and equally unworkable in the formula Dostoevski might have phrased: "No-God or Everything." The important distinction to be made, then, is between the *viewpoints* of theism and atheism on the one hand, and, on the other, the question of the reality or unreality of God. The more immediate contrast thus becomes one between the formulas "Theism—or What?" and "Atheism—or What?" In other words, the important distinction is between the question of God's existence and competitive *viewpoint* about that question.

Though the question of God's existence or non-existence appears to involve contradictory alternatives, it does not follow that viewpoints in regard to that question must necessarily be treated as contradictory so that the truth or falsity of one automatically determines the truth or falsity of the other. There is no contravening reason to assume that the alternatives of these viewpoints are not contrarieties rather than contradictories. If this be so, then the issue is significantly reformulated so that a demonstration of the truth of one would necessarily invalidate the truth-claims of the other.

Thus recast, the theoretic resolution of counter-arguments claiming the falsity of theism or the falsity of atheism rests not on the inadequacy of one or the other to make a case *against* its alternative, but rather on the strength of either to demonstrate a case for itself. Hence, it could be said that the viewpoint of theism can be considered to be false only on condition that the truth of atheism is unanswerably demonstrated. Conversely, the viewpoint of atheism can be considered false if, and only if, theism is demonstrated to be true.

In withdrawing atheism and theism from the status of mutually exclusive alternatives and considering them as contrarieties, it becomes possible to avoid the temptation to conceive them as static positions. Consequently, it also becomes possible to search for a third alternative outside the merely apparent exclusivity of both. Such a search could be undertaken only by assuming that neither, as usually expressed, is completely satisfactory, and therefore that this search is undertaken only in order to reformulate both past and present versions of both.

This search for an alternative to both is also implicitly a search for the *alteration* of both, since the validity of the process of alternation implies the possibility of the alteration of present versions. Historically, the link between the concepts "alternation" and "alteration" is disclosed in the linguistic relation of these terms, which conveys the notion not only of "otherness" but, more importantly, of "change."

Before seeking an alternative to atheism-theism, it is necessary to examine the meaning of the correlative parties implicated in the search. The question of atheism or theism is fundamentally one of persons, that is of atheists of theists, and not merely of abstract positions. What exists is not atheism, but atheists: not theism, but theists. A confrontation with "atheism" produces in the theist a sense of uneasiness principally because of the perspectives and activities—that is, because of the way of life—of some atheists. Though lacking theistic motives, atheists are often more serious, more moral, more sincerely committed to an examined life, and more genuinely dedicated to creating new values for the world. In a word, they are dedicated to a more human life and, rather than resting securely in a faith which "stops asking questions,"[13] are unafraid to question both man and themselves.

It might be objected that a theist must also be a man of honesty, a man committed to values, a man who questions his experience; but then how would a theist differ from an atheist?[14] Were the distinction between theist and atheist merely one of behavioral patterns, the question might easily be resolved. But clearly, such is not the case. Furthermore, as already suggested, theists are not all alike; they present a spectrum ranging from genuine faith to indifference or uncomfortable toleration. Theoretically, a modern atheist who is genuinely involved in the affairs of the world would appear no different from many theists sharing the same involvement. How, indeed, do they differ?

One useful difference between the modern atheist and the "traditional" theist lies in the attitude of each toward the significance of present experience and its bearing on history. To the latter, present experience generally has an eschatological orientation to the future world which presumably will indemnify and redeem the shortcomings of the present historical world. Oftentimes this view has tended to act as an anodyne to present experience; it has been used to interpret the present merely as a fallen estate whose chief function is to remind men that "we have not here a lasting home." In contrast, the atheist is more likely to be rooted in the present and to build his home in this world rather than passively awaiting the coming of another. He is, in a word, *kairological* in orientation because he proclaims the present time worthy of his attention. It is true, of course, that the Christian should be kairologically-oriented; but the few "modern" Christian theists who are often go unnoticed because of the many who are not.

If, however, there are some theists who deeply believe in the meaning of present experience, there is at least one instance in which there exists a similarity rather than a difference between modern theists and modern atheists. It is ironic that a description of modern atheists who are "steeped in anxiety, passionate and utopian, but also generous, inspired by a dream of justice and progress, striving toward a divinized social order"[15] appears as an enviable portrait of modern theists.

What the modern world is witnessing is a new kind of atheism. Not only does it in many respects reveal a truer dedication to genuine humanist ideals than has hitherto been characteristic of theism but, in addition, it is totally unlike the atheism of the ancient world.[16] Is it then completely unreasonable to suggest that if genuine theism were shorn of its liturgies it would appear nothing short of modern atheism? Would it not also follow that if genuine atheism were to construct of its perspective a describable liturgy, it would appear to be indistinguishable from theism?

If such a theoretical *entente* is possible, would it not also follow that the distinction between modern theism and atheism has been based largely upon some historical intervention which altered the course of genuine theism and engendered the valuative construction of a countervailing power in the form of modern atheism? Indeed, some observers have pointed to the intervention not merely of official theism and pseudo-belief as a cause of such an occurrence, but more importantly of scholastic theism. This, it is suggested, may have contained the dragon seeds of atheistic humanism by minimizing the possibilities of the humanism inherent in Christian theandric theology.[17] It has also been argued that by absolutizing certain forms of religious experience Christian theism surrendered its status as relative and conditional. Insofar as traditional theism has maintained an absolutist posture, modern atheism by refusing to absolutize any instance of experience appears more Christian than theism. In the name of the divine, theists should at least equally refuse to absolutize contingent experience, since any such instance must necessarily become a false God.[18]

THE SEARCH FOR AN INNER RITUAL

We have suggested that the task of contrasting the roles of the theist and atheist in the modern world is complicated by the ambiguity inherent in the meanings of the terms "belief" and "unbelief," and indeed of "theism" and "atheism." The fact that these roles are necessarily expressive of forms of human life implies that each possesses a cultural base.[19] Thus, an attempt to explicate this cultural relationship might prove useful to our task.

It is clear that every culture has both internal and external ceremonies and rituals that express the character of men in a particular society. Furthermore, every system of expressive rituals conspires to unite the members of that society in a common enterprise. Hence, it does not seem unreasonable to search for rituals which both outwardly and inwardly characterize atheists and theists.

The question of how atheists do in fact differ from theists has already been raised. In the present context this question can be reconstructed in the more particularized form: "On what single ritual can one draw a distinction between atheist and theist?"

Obviously, the answer is to be found in their respective expressions of viewpoints about the issue of God's alleged existence or alleged non-existence. Here, too, the more fundamental question must be reframed in terms of what traditional theism has made of God. It must take account, for one thing, of the fact that the theistic-atheistic dispute rests not on whether or what God is, but on whether or what God is said to be. It is assertions-about-God that constitute both the great stumbling-block to theistic-atheistic dialogue and the cultural ritual characteristic of their relation.

Revealingly, theistic assertions about God's existence have

invariably been based on assertions about the character of that existence. Ever since Protagoras,[20] the task of philosophical theology has appeared to consist less in the effort to determine the fact of God's existence than in the attempt to expatiate upon his nature. Strangely, this assumes that very existence and tends to support itself by arguments based on the essence of that existence. Thus, traditional theistic arguments for the existence of God are grounded in the concept of the evident reasons for a Necessary Reality.

Not unremarkably, such proofs have conspired to widen the differences between the views of theists and atheists. Might not the atheist ask why, if God's existence is reasonably evident, so much energy has been expended in proving it? Would it not also seem equally strange, only because it is evident, to attempt to prove the existence of Nature?[21] The ideological obstacle symbolized in "proofs" that God exists not only have done little to ease theistic-atheistic differences, but, as some theists have pointed out, have become more of a hindrance to reaching God than the assertions that He does not exist.[22] Accepting or rejecting God is fundamentally distinguishable from accepting or rejecting the validity of propositions about God.

In this external ritual of constructing assertions about the nature of God's existence,[23] there lies an important distinction between theists and atheists. In one sense, the historical relation engendered by such a ritual can be understood as a negative dialectic in which atheism is merely a reaction to, and hence a function of, theism. Atheists, in turn, have made their case not only by destroying theistic arguments, but by demonstrating that theism cannot reasonably account for certain crucial contradictions between its own assertions and the experience of human life. Perhaps the most emotionally charged instance of this is to be found in the apparent contradiction between the existence of evil and the assertion that God is All-Good and All-Powerful. Nevertheless, by revising its notion of God's power from that of a cosmic magician intent on testing man to that of a Creative Lover, modern theism has to some extent blunted the force of this contradiction. As the notion of power has changed, its

application to God has become that of the Infinite Compassion-
ator and Companion who transforms by love rather than alters
by whim. This change has and will continue to mark a crucial
shift in the character of theism. Thus, though in the moral world
shared by both theist and atheist, evil is not only plausible but
inevitable, this insight is already an inner ritual which unites
both theist and atheist.

The question of the moral consequences of evil for human
life suggests other inner rituals which conjoin rather than separate. One such inner ritual, of course, is the view shared by
both theist and atheist on the justification of criticism against
tribalistic religion. Each can appreciate Freud's observation that
"religion" acts as a necessary illusion which preserves men from
individual fears only at the cost of uniting them in a common
"psychosis." Likewise, each can admit the justice of Marx's
criticism of tribalist religion as symbolic of an institutional betrayal of this earth and its present experience in the name of
a future experience and another world.

Nevertheless, by the very seriousness of their lives, both
the modern theist and the modern atheist share certain ultimate
concerns, a category that has also been used to describe authentic
religious interest.[24] On the basis of common ultimate concern,
it would follow that the theist (admittedly a man of religion)
and the atheist (presumably of irreligion) are united in their
inner commitment, and so can be said to share a common religious standpoint. If this conclusion is plausible, it would also
follow that one can speak of "a religion of atheism" as well as
of "a religion of theism."

There is another area of agreement between these two points
of view. This concerns the awareness by each that the God referred to by public tribalistic religion is a God of Exigency,
a God of Exodus, physically and emotionally depended on by
man and used as an intellectual crutch. If God becomes for
much if not most traditional theism a proximate answer to what
is not yet otherwise explainable or a final answer to the mysteries
of existence, he is no longer God but a methodological device.
It is precisely the awareness that man no longer needs such

a God of Exigency which constitutes a common inner ritual for theists and atheists.

Finally, if it is true that "the contemporary presence of God is his absence," and that both the theist and the atheist must "act *without* God," then both indeed "share the same existential situation."[25] For both, God's absence from experience is an expected absence. Both ritualistically understand that God is not found, but can at most only be sought.

In this case it might be argued that we have simply uncovered a ritualistic difference rather than a similarity, since the theist would presumably continue to look for God while the atheist would not. In that case, the critical issue arises not in the search itself but in the reasons which prompt it and in the attitudes with which it is undertaken. If it were undertaken without the conviction that it would terminate in a "finding," then the difference between theist and atheist would be less distinguishable. Yet, the very Christian notion of an infinite God denies the possibility of ever "finding" Him in a finite and particularized sense, and this is the only sense in which "finding" is humanly understood. The infinitude of God must imply that He will never be fully reached, even in the "eternal confrontation" which the theist accepts as a future event.

THE SEARCH FOR AN INNER FAITH

The point which requires greater clarification is the assertion that, because "the contemporary presence of God is his absence," the modern theist and atheist share the same existential situation of acting without God. Does this not suggest that there can be no way of acting in the modern secular world which would unmistakably distinguish the theist from his atheist counterpart who expressly argues that God is absent from the world?

The fact that each can act in the same existential situation implies a faith in action, just as the ability of each to think genuinely or live authentically implies a transcendent thrust to a faith in existing and thinking. No form of faith in acting in the world and, more fundamentally, no form of faith in the world can be its own warranty or demonstrate its own claims. Faith in a world which demonstrates the accuracy of that faith would neither be a proper faith, nor would it be addressed to a present and real world. Yet the faith of theist and atheist is surely found in their respective life-modes, just as their respective life-modes symbolize a faith without explaining it.

Why then should it be said that while atheism "antedates all theories,"[26] theism does not? Is theism more natural or indigenous a faith for man than atheism? If, as seems evident, both modern atheists and modern theists lead meaningful lives in the secular city, on what ground could one be considered to have a more authentic faith than the other? Were it true that the world is a paradise for unbelievers and a prison for believers the distinction between them would be easily established.[27] But atheists often suffer the burden of the world more than many so-called believers. It would consequently appear that if we are to understand the meaning of theistic-atheistic faith, we must first inquire into the meaning of faith. It is an unfortunate limitation of the English language that there exists in it no verbal form of the noun "faith." There is, of course, the usage "to have faith in"; but since this usually substitutes for the formula "to have confidence in," or "to be convinced by," it is not the equivalent of "to faith." The nearest equivalent for such a regrettably missing verb would more likely be the expression "to believe-in," which implies not merely "acceptance" but "caring-for."

To believe-in a person does not mean that one passively accepts his every word and action, although genuine acceptance may be said to be contingent on one's genuinely believing-in him. In other words, "to believe-in" is anterior to "to accept" because it provides the fundamental existential ground for accepting. On the other hand, acceptance may remain ungrounded, being, as the parable of the seed reminds us, sown in shallow soil. In this case, acceptance of another would be based on self-projection and illusion. To believe-in someone requires that I desire his fruition as a person and dedicate myself to this end: that

I care both about, and particularly for, him. Because this is concerned with a perfecting, it does not cut off all possibilities of criticism.

Faith, or believing-in, is not to be confused with "belief," which requires prior assertions or reasons; instead it connotes a free decision to which credentials, warrants, or proofs are irrelevant. Consider what this would mean, for instance, in understanding St. John's report of the royal official whose son was cured at Capharnaum. He learned of this cure on his way home, and from that moment he "believed and his whole household with him."[28] If this miracle was causative, either it ignited a belief rather than faith, or else it gave previous believing-in a new significance and direction as was the case of Anselm's well-known *Proslogion* argument which he constructed for his co-religionists at the Abbey of Bec. Reliance on miracles to explain the inception of faith, or believing-in, is a double-edged sword. If a miracle acts as a warrant, it deprives faith of its character of free decision, since by providing an antecedent reason it forces acceptance. On the other hand, if a miracle confirms faith or brings faith to fruition, it does not incept it.

One way, then, in which belief differs from faith is that faith, as a free decision, is unsupported by prior warrants, while belief is not. They also differ inasmuch as belief is pluralizable into numerable, finite, and therefore exhaustible beliefs, while faith is not.

Because the free decision of believing-in replies to the authenticity of what is loved, proofs for it are unreasonably asked for. St. Thomas carefully insists that faith cannot be proved,[29] and St. Paul seems no less insistent in his attempts to explore the character of faith by observing that it is concerned precisely with what cannot be seen.[30]

St. Paul's language is also interesting in other ways, since his expression "hoped for" does not appear to mean either "wished for" or "expected." Hope is quite different from expectation, since hope implies trust whereas expectation and wishing do not. It is on this foundation that its relation with believing-in is grounded.

Faith is not a settled, but an unsettling matter. It is not a resting-place for intellectual conviction, but an existential response to the openness and genuineness of what is loved.[31] It is precisely a response to the transcendence of the other, a thrust to an inner and renewable order of the beloved. It is always "standing-before" more than a mere "now."

The beloved's question about a loving act: "Why did you do this?" is usually answered by saying, "Because I love you." But what could be the answer to the question, "Why do you love me?" As a cognitive question, it can have no justification without implying that there is something other than the beloved which explains either the act of loving or that the beloved is loved. If the question were literally answerable, by definition the beloved would not of himself be loved. What is loved is not something possessed by the beloved, but the incarnative value or the beloved himself.

For the beloved this means that there is no mere or ungrounded acceptance on the part of the lover and, on his part, no mere assent. Thus faith, like love, is not an assent to something or someone, but an ascent-toward someone or something. Essentially because it is a reception, it is not simple acceptance. Grounded assent requires ascent; really to say "yes" to another means to rise up, and to go beyond "roles," "functions," and "appearances" into the deepest center of historical possibilities.

Once "faith" is transformed into a verbal act, its difference from "conviction" becomes clear. Believing-in is a transitive act which moves outward from the believer-in. It is intrinsically unlike the intransitive verb "to be convinced," which does not pass over from one person to another. "To be convinced" is not a "social" but a "private" reality, for in it I am deprived of another's presence and deprive another of mine. In it I remain uncommunicated and incommunicative, and trans-action is "exhausted" because further questioning and interest cease.

What is more, faith is essentially historical, whereas belief is not. Like love, faith may develop and grow; beliefs merely multiply. Believing-in someone brings me into a realm of his personal history. Rather than abandoning me merely in what a person has been, it thrusts me into what a person is becoming, that is, into his life. As a historical activity, believing-in someone involves me in the being-in-history of another, while implying my own being-in history.[32] An existential encroachment takes place on both sides.

Existence, specifically one's personal existence, lies deeper than thought or conviction.[33] This inexhaustible character of existence thus suggests its relation to the inexhaustibility of faith and history. The historical character, literally the profundity of faith, provides another reason why faith or believing-in cannot be 'proved.' Its nature is not to prove but to reveal.

If the entry into faith is also an entry into history, then an entry into history should also be an entry into faith. If for me "to believe-in" is also for me "to-be-in-history," then the movement of faith is likewise a movement of self-analysis. Self-analysis, history, and faith share the existential, transcendent thrust toward freedom. Historically, however, freedom is not found alone, but with its counterweights: individuality and personality.[34]Together, they can alter the meaning not only of one's own life, but of life itself.

What consequences follow for the interpretation of the faith of theism and atheism?

First, it should be recognized that the atheist who believes-in this world is, in this act, no different from the theist who also believes-in this world. Neither necessarily means that this world, as it is now, is sufficient or is incapable of transformation and renewal. To believe-in someone does not imply that he is incapable of becoming any better than he is now.

In the second place, the atheist who believes-in this world is not satisfied with it or himself. Indeed, it is the critical or judgmental nature of his viewpoint which makes salutary his caring-for and caring-about the world. Thus, the common denominator of genuine theistic and atheistic faith is a perpetual criticism of itself and of the world. More importantly, theistic faith is blind to the demands of faith itself when it ignores the fact that atheism commands present-day attention both in view of its own positive ideals and against the backdrop of the increasing irrelevancy of church-theism. Modern atheism can no longer be understood merely as an excuse for license because, for the most part, its ascendency signals a more urgent faith in the problems of men, and one that stands in marked contrast to the uninterest characteristic of the "faith" of "respectable" Christianity.

Thirdly, if for the theist and the atheist the world is lovable, there cannot be any justification in asking why it is lovable. To say, "It is lovable because it was lovingly created by God," is merely to relegate an unreasonable question to a less assessable level. To say, "It is lovable because its Creator is lovable, and He is lovable because He is Love," is simply a recognition of the unanswerability of why anything is lovable. If the world is loved only because it is the premonition of a more lovable world-to-come, this world dissolves its own lovability in another but equally unresolved lovability.

Furthermore, the irreducible nature of theistic or atheistic faith necessarily discounts any attempt to provide a warrant for either. This is but another way of recognizing that there cannot be any ultimate case for either, since proof or disproof cannot be advanced for what is inexhaustible.

Finally, in the freedom of both theistic or atheistic faith, it is the meaning of existence that is being created. What is crucially the same in the outlook, inner ritual, and faith of the symbolical posture of both atheism or theism is their dedication to the significance or experience and the world.

For the theist, God encroaches on inner life and subjects it to demands which alter its symbolic density; for the atheist, it is suffering and injustice which so encroach. This encroachment has its message, for the defiance of the atheist and his agony at the condition of contingent events fill his life with the pathos of the world, much like Jacob wrestling with the angel. Freedom makes the life of the atheist markedly different from the "unperturbed" life that experiences no suffering, the lack of which Tolstoy identified as the life of irreligion.[35] The life of suffering is, indeed, the religious life in its most profound sense, just as it is the life of ultimate concern in its most genuine sense. Insofar as the theist and the atheist live a "disturbed" existence, they live the same symbolical existence, because through this they achieve an understanding which alone, as Aeschylus once said, comes through suffering.[36]

The disturbance which experience works on any life is critical, in both senses of the term. As a committed person, the atheist cannot lead an undisturbed life, for he is shaken by the encroachment of contingency; leading an examined life, he cannot remain unperturbed, which is to say, unhistorical; being compassionate, he cannot not suffer. The unencroached-upon life is the unsuffering life; it is also the unexamined life, which in the language of Plato is not worth living because it is no life at all.

This encroachment is experienced by both theist and atheist, and often in the same way. If God encroaches upon the life of the modern theist in His absence, this negative encroachment should also be experienced by the atheist. It seems plausible, then, to conclude that the examined life, the suffering life, the life encroached-upon can be lived both theistically and atheistically.

TOWARD A NEW THEISM AND A NEW ATHEISM

It also would seem true that a life which "stands for man and humanity, for value and the dignity of personality, for freedom, for social justice, for the brotherhood of men and nations, for enlightenment, for the creation of a new life"[37] can be lived both theistically and atheistically. Yet, to conclude from this that the atheist is merely a surreptitious theist does not appear to satisfy the difference between them. How, for example, could the atheist agree at last that living according to his own moral ideals as a righteous man, he must have, as Augustine suggests all righteous men have, "Christ for his Head"?[38]

Should the modern theist feel that such traditional insights are invalid, he may be tempted to despair of Christianity and theism. Since he finds himself in such moral and intellectual sympathy with the modern atheist, he also would be tempted to conclude that as a theist, it is useless to speak to the modern world. Nevertheless, the abrogation of Christianity or the conversion of atheists will not solve this problem. Christianity is not a substitute for human reflection, but neither can it remain unrelated to it.[39] What is required of Christianity in the present and future is what has been required of it in the past, that is, an advance to new points of reference and new dimensions of experience.

The signs that Christians are entering upon a new and creative age are, if not undeniable, at least plausible.[40] Unless the fear of failure freezes development, there is every hope that Christian theists can move into a more realistic, that is, a more modern relation to the secular world. The reflective theist should be among the first to admit that no religious position can, in a world of change, remain the same; the atheist should be able to make a similar admission for his own position. In a world come of age, theism must itself come of age, and so, too, must atheism.

The rethinking of Christian theism should not be interpreted as a search for the legitimization of former patterns of thought; nor should the reformation and reformulation be undertaken only for the sake of modernizing Christianity, for this would involve an obvious inversion of principle. Modernization should come as a salutary effect rather than as an immediate and ex-exclusive goal. What is first needed is a sounder view of Christianity, and only secondarily one that is more modern. It is not merely new doctrinalizations of Christian theism that are needed, since these would be confined to propositions, which are exhaustible. The primary needs, then, are the continued Christianization of Christianity, the theification of humanism, and the humanization of theism.

What then of the truth of a new Christianity? Clearly truth can no longer be formulated as a "conformity of ideas to things." What matters most of all is the status of truth, and this is to be sought in fidelity to genuine life, rather than in conformity to exhaustible propositions. In short, truth is more akin to a life of faith or a believing-in than to acceptance of beliefs. If Christianity is as culturally fruitful as it has shown itself to be in the course of two millennia, and if its inner message is to continue to bear upon human life and practice, it must be born again in thought, however eternal its "truths" might at first sight appear.

This fruition must take place not only in respect to what those outside the Christian community may interpret as new forms, but more fundamentally, it must take place within the Christian community. It is insufficient to show a new face to the world, hence, the restructuring of the church-politic and of religious foundations is pointless unless these symbolize a transformation of the inner ritual of the Christian community. Hence, what is needed is a change not only *of* the church but most of all *in* the church, not a change of governance but a transfiguration of inner vision.

In changing, the church may find that it will be able to adjust tribal values to the needs of new generations of men. This shift may indeed affect views which, in the scattered course of events, have appeared to be central to its life, for example, the historical distinction between nature and supernature, the meaning of liturgy, and the substantive conception of God. A new formulation, for example, of the Christian perspective might at least provide a more authentic framework for the meaning of theandric theology, and allow theists to conceive God more nobly and man more divinely.

For the personal life of the Christian, moral action may become possible only insofar as it becomes pragmatically enshrined in the furtherance of human life and hope—not for the values of "another world" but for those of this-world-being-transformed. This would place the differences between theist and atheist action in the world in a different light. The future of theist action is unquestionably wedded to the future of concerns established most perceptively by the atheist. It does not seem unreasonable to suggest that neither theist nor atheist can act privately. There is required between them a "conspiracy of action"; they must breathe together, since neither alone can do so successfully.[41]

The ultimate concerns of both must converge like meridians approaching the poles of the world's unity. Hence, it is more important that the destinies of theist and atheist be considered in terms of what unites rather than of what separates them. The future of both when acting together should be different from the future of each acting alone, and their continued confrontation can have little but salutary effects upon both. There is no reason to assume that it is only theism which must alter as a result of such confrontation; it is equally likely that atheism must itself undergo transformation. Both together, should become more tough-minded, less hard-nosed, and less hard-headed.

Such continued confrontation should not be thought of as a device to diminish the attractions of atheism, and thus to act as a secret support for traditional theism. The result to be expected is a new and purified theism-atheism, each essentially bent on fulfilling the authenticity of the other.

The world, as Albert Camus has observed, needs Christians who *remain* Christians.[42] The attempt to become a Christian means essentially to become a new being, to have a new vision, and to draw a new circle for one's life. The only viable alternative to current atheism is not merely a renewed Christianity, important though this be; it is the vision of theism. Yet, an equally genuine alternative is still the possibility of an altered and more developed form of atheism itself.

◇

1. See E. L. Mascall, **The Secularization of Christianity** (New York: Holt, Rinehart and Winston, 1966).

2. Qualitatively defined figures on this are hard to come by, and those available usually tend to inflate active membership. Figures carried in the latest **Yearbook of American Churches**, ed. C. H. Jacquet, Jr. (New York: National Council of the Churches of Christ in the U.S.A., 1967) report 1965 membership at 124.6 million or 64.3% of U.S. population for

a 1.1% annual gain, as compared with a 2.4% gain for 1961. Church attendance is listed as 44% of adult population (a 5-point drop since 1958, but indicating a similar increase since 1950). The unreliability of such statistics has impressed many observers. Thus, editors of one periodical recently asked: "How many of the one-third outside the churches would be inside were the churches earnestly facing the issues confronting mankind today? And how many of the two-thirds would leave the churches if they performed this duty? . . . To what extent is the visible church the deadliest foe of the invisible church?" "Numerolatry," **Christian Century**, LXXXIV (1967), 67. See **Yearbook**, pp. 217-20. Cf. "Depletion in the Pew," **Christian Century**, LXXXIII (1966), p. 101.

3. See Ignace Lepp, **Atheism in Our Time**, trans. B. Murchland (New York: Macmillan, 1963), p. 190; cf. Michael Novak, **Belief and Unbelief** (New York: Macmillan, 1965), p. 182. See Leslie Dewart, **The Future of Belief** (New York: Herder and Herder, 1966), pp. 66-68. See also Martin E. Marty, **Varieties of Unbelief** (New York: Doubleday, 1966), pp. 4, 204; cf. Abel Jeannière, "Atheism Today," **Cross Currents**, XVI (1966), 2. Illuminating remarks on the point are contained in Cornelio Fabro, **God in Exile: Modern Atheism** (Glen Rock: Paulist-Newman, 1968), as well as in his "The Positive Character of Modern Atheism," **Concurrence**, I (1969), pp. 66-76.

4. See Paul van Buren, **The Secular Meaning of the Gospel** (New York: Macmillan, 1963); Robert L. Richard, **Secularization Theology** (New York: Herder and Herder, 1967). Cf. Leslie Dewart, **The Future of Belief**; also **The Future of Belief Debate**, ed. Gregory Baum (New York: Herder and Herder, 1967). See also Harvey Cox, **The Secular City** (New York: Macmillan, 1965); cf. **The Secular City Debate**, ed. Daniel Callahan (New York: Macmillan, 1966); Daniel Callahan, **Honesty in the Church** (New York: Scribner's, 1965).

5. Christopher Dawson, **Religion and the Rise of Western Culture** (New York: Sheed and Ward, 1950), p. 22.

6. J. V. Langmead Casserly, **The Christian in Philosophy** (New York: Scribner's, 1951), p. 261.

7. Benedetto Croce, **My Philosophy**, trans. E. F. Carrett (London: Allen and Unwin, 1951).

8. Thus, Bishop John A. T. Robinson, as is now well known, was termed "an atheist" by Alasdair MacIntyre in his "God and the Theologians," in **The Honest to God Debate**, ed. D. L. Edwards (Philadelphia: Westminster, 1963), pp. 215-28.

9. The attempt to **harmonize** "Christian" and "secular" life seems to assume that (a) each has its own identity; (b) there are substantial differences between these two modes of life; and (c) they must be resolved, like notes on a scale. But life-modes are not notes, and such a

"resolution" would perpetuate differences, not dispense with them. **Harmonizing** two kinds of life suggests that they must still both be lived simultaneously, although their conflicts must be diminished—a difficult qualification.

10. Michael Novak, "Christianity: Renewed or Slowly Abandoned?" **Daedalus,** XCVI (1967), pp. 262-63; Martin E. Marty, **Varieties of Unbelief, p.** 4.

11. Jeanière, "Atheism Today," p. 9.

12. See Gabriel Marcel, "Philosophical Atheism," **International Philosophical Quarterly, II** (1962), 501-14.

13. Jeannière, "Atheism Today," p. 2.

14. The question has been posed by Michael Novak, "Christianity: Renewed or Slowly Abandoned " p. 266; cf. his "The Christian and the Atheists," **Christianity and Crisis,** XXVI (1966), 51-55.

15. The words are those of Paul VI (**Ecclesiam Suam,** 108), quoted in Jeannière, "Atheism Today," p. 2.

16. Atheism (**asebeia**) was a charge levelled against Anaxagoras and Socrates (cf. **Apol.,** 26D; Xenophon, **Mem.,** I. 1.1; Diogenes Laertius, **Lives,** II. 40) for failure to reverence the public gods; but Plato turns atheism into a question of "unscientism" by making it synonymous with denying order in the cosmos (**Laws,** 886C-887C).

17. See Dewart, **The Future of Belief,** pp. 152-64, esp. p. 163.

18. A similar point has been made by Robert O. Johann in "Modern Atheism," a paper read at the Notre Dame Conference, **Christian Philosophy in an Age of Renewal,** September, 1966.

19. See Ernst Cassirer, **An Essay on Man** (New York: Doubleday, 1956), p. 233; cf. Florian Znaniecki, **Cultural Science** (Urbana: Univ. of Illinois Press, 1963), pp. 311-17.

20. See Werner Jaeger, **Humanism and Theology** (Milwaukee: Marquette Univ. Press, 1943), p. 38.

21. Cf. Aristotle, **Phys.,** 193a3.

22. Paul Tillich, **Theology of Culture** (New York: Oxford Univ. Press, 1964), p. 5.

23. Such proof mainly rests on the concepts of teleology and order (cf. **Phaedo,** 97B; **Meta.,** 985a18; Xenophon, **Mem.,** IV. 3; also, **Laws,** 894; **Phaedrus,** 245C; **Timaeus,** 27D; **Meta.,** 999b6, 1070a4, 1071b3; **Phys.,** 198a35).

24. See Tillich, **Theology of Culture, p.** 8.

25. Eugene Fontinell, "Reflections on Faith and Metaphysics," **Cross Currents,** XVI (1966), p. 39.

26. John Courtney Murray, **The Problem of God** (New Haven: Yale Univ. Press, 1964), p. 95; a point made strongly by Fontinell, "Reflections on Faith and Metaphysics," p. 30.

27. The language suggests a well known Hadith of the Prophet Muhammad, later expounded as the difference between **Muslim** ("believer") and **Kafir** ("unbeliever"): see Toshihiko Izutsu, **The Concept of Belief in Islamic Theology** (Tokyo: Institute of Cultural and Linguistic Studies, 1965); also see his **Ethico-Religious Concepts in the Qur'an** (Montreal: McGill Univ. Press, 1966).

28. **John,** 4:46-53. Cf. the language used by Jesus and the official's cross-examination of his servants.

29. Thomas Aquinas, **Summa Theologica** (New York: Benziger Brothers, 1947), I. 46. 2.

30. **Hebr.,** 11:1; cf. II **Cor.,** 5:7; **Rom.,** 8:24. See also Augustine, **De Civitate Dei,** ed. W. G. Most (Washington, D. C.: Catholic Univ. Press, 1949), XV, xviii. If faith is of the 'unseen,' then the 'visionary' in an act of transport could not be said to have faith.

31. The classical language of Anselm is "Credo ut intelligam," not "Intellego ut credam." In any case, the causal clause appears to provide a false emphasis.

32. See Martin E. Marty, **Varieties of Unbelief,** p. 183; cf. J. V. Langmead Casserly, **Toward a Theology of History** (New York: Holt, Rinehart and Winston, 1965), pp. 118-19.

33. See Soren Kierkegaard, **Philosophical Fragments,** trans. D. K. Swenson (Princeton: Princeton Univ. Press, 1936), p. 22.

34. See Charles N. Cochrane, **Christianity and Classical Culture** (New York: Oxford Univ. Press, 1944); cf. R. G. Collingwood, **Speculum Mentis** (Oxford: Clarendon Press, 1924), chap. VI.

35. Leo Tolstoy, **Anna Karenina,** trans. Constance Garnett (New York: Modern Library, 1950), Part 8, Sect. 8.

36. Michael Novak takes a different view of this: see his "The Christian and the Atheist," p. 54.

37. Nikolai Berdiaev, **The Fate of Man in the Modern World,** trans. D. A. Lowrie (New York: Morehouse, 1935), p. 119.

38. **Ps.,** xxxvi; **Serm.,** iii, 4.

39. See Albert Schweitzer, **Out of My Life and Thought** (New York: New American Library, 1953), p. 184.

40. Novak, "Christianity: Renewed or Slowly Abandoned?" pp. 252-53.

41. Marty, **Varieties of Unbelief,** p. 205.

42. Albert Camus, **Resistance, Rebellion, and Death,** trans. J. O'Brien (New York: Knopf, 1961), p. 70.

PART III

Humanism and the Problem of Theism

The Beauty of Earth[*]

◊

Michael Novak

I WOULD LIKE to reverse the contemporary argument for a "religionless Christianity" in order to argue for the cultivation of religion. Writers like Bonhoeffer criticize "religion" and argue, instead, for "faith." But to those who are genuinely secular the word "religion" includes what Bonhoeffer calls "faith." Thus, secular students find Bonhoeffer and Cox just as "religious" as any other writers. For many college student in America, talk about Christian faith has been hopelessly compromised by unpleasant experiences with organized religion. A "religionless Christianity" often seems to them just as irrelevant as a "religious" Christianity. On the other hand, many of the brightest students have had experiences which they find it difficult to speak of in the categories of pragmatism and science. With each passing year they are becoming more open to religious discourse, even while, for various reasons, rejecting the language of American Christianity and Judaism.

In this context, I would like to argue that certain human experiences are ordinarily prerequisite for an understanding of Christianity and, further, that the malaise in contemporary Christian theology is due to inattention to certain kinds of human experience. Consequently, I wish to argue for a greater openness to the lessons of nature and a greater responsiveness to actual human experience, apart from any reference to Christianity. Christians do not need more Christianity, but less; Christians need a greater openness to nature.

THE IMPORTANCE OF NATURE

Let me begin by citing four exceedingly important movements. (1) Probably the most significant development in the contemporary religious world is the growing attraction which Eastern and other world religions are beginning to exert upon the consciousness of Christian nations. (2) The hippie culture of California has become a prototype of a new spiritual experience for an increasing number of young people. (3) The growing use of psychedelic drugs has given birth to a new type of experience, which cries out for expression in religious language. (4) The growing emphasis placed upon myth and symbol by contemporary sociology, psychology, and anthropology seem to signify the end of the Protestant, rationalistic, pragmatic, and scholastic era. No doubt these four interrelated movements depend upon the affluence and electronic technology of the present period. But they mark, I believe, the beginning of a new age in the history of religion that may be characterized as the re-emergence of the category of "nature" in human consciousness. This may be seen by studying the work of a man who received the Nobel prize for illuminating the conscience of our time.

No writer is so widely read and profoundly cherished by young Americans as is Albert Camus. Yet one aspect of Camus' writing, which critics have consistently overlooked and which is indispensable for understanding the contemporary consciousness, is his turning away from the Christian man of northern Europe to the "Mediterranean man" of the noonday sun.[1] Many writers interpret the modern period as one of conflict between secularity and Christianity, between the German secular discovery of "historical consciousness" with its ideology of "the future" and the more static Christian political and philosophical concepts. Camus reads modern history in a different light: "The profound conflict of this century is perhaps not so much between the German ideologies of history and Christian political concepts, which in a certain way are accomplices, as between German dreams and Mediterranean traditions, ... in other words, between history and nature."[2] Camus links Germanic devotion to the future with Christianity. He regrets the loss of Hellenism and its respect for nature, its view of man as an organic fruit of nature and child of earth. "When nature ceases to be an object of contemplation and admiration, it can then be nothing more than material for an action that aims at transforming it."[3] Camus understood very well the lesson John Updike has drawn from the most future-oriented of all countries, the United States:

> We in America have from the beginning been cleaving and baring the earth, attacking, reforming the enormity of nature we were given, which we took to be hostile. We have explored, on behalf of all mankind, this paradox: the more matter is outwardly mastered, the more it overwhelms us in our hearts.[4]

In brief, Camus' diagnosis of our illness is precisely the opposite of those who ask Christianity to assume an even more one-sided orientation toward the future. For Camus, we have drunk too much history and have repressed nature.

Let us dwell on Camus' analysis a little longer—it is a point he made in his *Notebooks*,[5] in the *Myth of Sisyphus*,[6] and also in *The Rebel*.[7] Camus used the phrase "German ideology" to refer to "the violence of eternal adolescence," to "romanticism," and to a "nostalgia rendered more acute by knowledge and by books."[8] "Despite its pretensions," he says, "it begins in the absolute and attempts to mold reality";[9] it uses the future as a lever against the present. By contrast, "rebellion" is grounded in "Mediterranean traditions," in "virile strength" and "courage reinforced and enlightened by the experience of life"; "it relies primarily on the most concrete realities." In this contest between history and nature,

> German ideology has come into an inheritance. It consummates twenty centuries of abortive struggle against nature, first in the name of a historic god and then of a deified history. Christianity, no doubt, was only able to conquer its catholicity by assimilating as much as it could of Greek thought. But

when the Church dissipated its Mediterranean heritage, it placed the emphasis on history to the detriment of nature, caused the Gothic to triumph over the romance, and, destroying a limit in itself, has made increasing claims to temporal power and historical dynamism. When nature ceases to be an object of contemplation and admiration, it can then be nothing more than material for an action that aims at transforming it. These tendencies—and not the concepts of mediation, which would have comprised the real strength of Christianity—are triumphing in modern times, to the detriment of Christianity itself, by an inevitable turn of events. That God should, in fact, be expelled from this historical universe and German ideology be born where action is no longer a process of perfection but pure conquest, is an expression of tyranny.[10]

The source of the death of God, for Camus, lies neither in the use of the Hellenic category of "being" nor in any of the other places divined by theologians whose nourishment comes from northern European sources. God dies because man has been uprooted from nature, historicized, and rendered both a tyrant over and an alien in his own environment. Yet there is, Camus senses, "an irrepressible demand of human nature, of which the Mediterranean, where intelligence is intimately related to the blinding light of the sun, guards the secret."[11] In the common condition of misery, the eternal demand is heard again; nature once more takes up the fight against history. Naurally, it is not a question of despising anything, or of exalting one civilization at the expense of another, but of simply saying that it is a thought which the world today cannot do without for very much longer."[12]

Camus, of course, is not interested in rehabilitating the notion of God: he is interested only in making human life more possible for man. He finds it humiliating that for twenty centuries the West has had a Christian image of man.[13] "Who can say what we should be if those twenty centuries had clung to the ancient ideal with its beautiful fate?"[14] Here Camus has hold of something that is extremely important—the vitality and power of man's biological life. Man cannot restore his contemporary culture to sanity unless he becomes reconciled to his body.[15] In the phrase of Alan Watts, man is not an ego trapped in a bag of skin and alien to his environment; he is a part of nature, brought forth from the universe like fruit from a tree. The universe is a thou to him, inseparable from his own self; it is part of him, and he is in dialogue with it. As an apple tree "apples," so the universe "peoples"—if again we may use a phrase of Alan Watts.

Thus Camus saw with joy and urgency the need for a return to nature. He saw the need for a return to nudity and to simple delight in the beauty of the flesh.

For the first time in two thousand years the body has appeared naked on beaches. For twenty centuries men have striven to give decency to Greek insolence and naivete, to diminish the flesh and complicate dress. Today, despite that history, young men running on Mediterranean beaches repeat the gestures of the athletes of Delos. And living thus among bodies and through one's body, one becomes aware that it has a psychology of its own. The body's evolution, like that of the mind, has its history, its vicissitudes, its progress and its deficiency.... How can one fail to participate, then, in that dialogue of stone and flesh in tune with the sun and seasons?[16]

One senses in California today, as in Algeria so loved by Camus, the burgeoning renewed trust in the human body. One finds young people trying to put Humpty-Dumpty together again, as it were; they begin with the things closest to them and which their hands can touch, learning the meaning of community, dignity, sadness, joy.

I have the mad hope that, without knowing it perhaps, these barbarians lounging on beaches are actually modeling the image of a culture in which the greatness of man will at last find its true likeness. This race, wholly cast into its present, lives without myths, without solace. It has put all its possessions on this earth and therefore remains without defense against death. All the gifts of physical beauty have been lavished on it.... And yet, yes, one can find measure as well as excess in the violent and keen face of this race.... Between this sky and these faces turned toward it, nothing on which to hang a mythology, a literature, an ethic, or a religion, but stones, flesh stars, and those truths the hand can touch.[17]

There is something of penetrating beauty in this natural return to paganism, this wholehearted sense of nature in its measure and its limitations.

At a time when doctrinaire attitudes would separate us from the world, it is well for young men in a young land to proclaim their attachment to those few essential and perishable possessions that give meaning to our lives: the sun, the sea and women in the sunlight. They are the riches of the living culture, everything else being the dead civilization that we repudiate. If it is true that true culture is inseparable from a certain barbarianism, nothing that is barbaric can be alien to us.[18]

Moreover, Camus sees in this modest sense of nature the solid base of a revolutionary ethic. He well realized that, within a few miles of the beaches of Algeria on which his maroon athletes lounged, there were villages where people, scabbed with various diseases, starved to death. Camus wished to find a way of wedding political consciousness to respect for nature, and he found it in his concept of rebellion. The Greek myth of Nemesis guided his thought in this, as had the *Myth of Sisyphus* in an earlier period.

The revolutionary mind, if it wants to remain alive, must therefore return again to the sources of rebellion and draw its inspiration from the only system of thought which is faithful to its origins: thought that recognizes limits. . . .

Rebellion, at the same time that it suggests a nature common to all men, brings to light the measure and the limit which are the very principle of this nature.[19]

He wrote further:

> Analysis of rebellion leads at least to the suspicion that, contrary to the postulates of contemporary thought, a human nature does exist, as the Greeks believed. Why rebel if there is nothing permanent in oneself worth preserving? . . . The slave asserts himself when he comes to the conclusion that a command has infringed on something in him which is common ground where all men—even the man who insults and oppresses him—have a natural community . . . from this point of view human solidarity is metaphysical.[20]

For Camus, in short, the rebel rejects and disputes history in the name of nature.[21] Camus does not deny that man is responsible for history; he only wishes to make plain that man is part of nature. Man may possibly be "evolution become conscious of itself," but Camus wishes us to be certain that we do not become conscious in an alienated, rootless, or unnatural way. Nature lives in us and we in it. Nature is historical, as history is natural. To wave a banner either in the name of history against nature, or in the name of nature against history is to misunderstand our own identity.

> For some time the entire effort of our philosophers has aimed solely at replacing the notion of human nature with that of situation, and replacing ancient harmony with the disorderly advance of chance or reason's pitiless progress . . . , nature is still there, however. She contrasts her calm skies and her reason with the madness of men. Until the atom too catches fire and history ends in the triumph of reason and the agony of the species. But the Greeks never said that the limit could not be over-stepped. They said it existed and

whoever dared to exceed it was mercilessly struck down. Nothing in present history can contradict them.[22]

IN DEFENSE OF RELIGION

What is the bearing of the new paganism of Camus upon the problem of God? It suggests that the problem of God is not to be solved by seeking a "religionless Christianity," but by a move in quite the opposite direction. We might say that Christianity has been weakened because it has had too high a component of "Christianity," while its component of "religion" has been exhausted. Christianity may be a good seed; but it cannot thrive in thin, sandy, or rocky soil. Because it is religion which makes the human heart fertile, we need more religion and less Christianity.

"The Greek myths," I have recently heard a student say, "speak much more powerfully to me than Christian myths." Another student wrote in his term paper: "Christian stories never impressed so vividly as stories of the American Indian gods: tales of thunder and the Presence in the mighty rivers. It was in *those* stories that I first understood the meaning of "God," which I later lost in Christian education." Herman Hesse's *Siddhartha* startles many students into awareness, and the wisdom of the East begins to speak directly to their hearts.[23] Why is this?

I believe that Camus' theory is correct. German ideology, with its emphasis upon man's future projects, rests upon too cerebral, egotistical, and tyrannical a view of man. The organic, biological, and imaginative life of Americans and other future-oriented peoples has been starved. "God" has died not because the Hellenic concept of being was used to speak of Him, but because the word "being" has lost its roots in human biology, experience, and imagination The great, profound Om which Siddhartha labored long to find deep in the pit of his stomach says much more adequately what "being" used to say. We do not need to dehellenize the word "God" but to turn to nature and myth as did the Greeks in order to give human depth to our faith.

There is, of course, an ambiguity in the word "religion." When Bonhoeffer attacked "religion," he attacked that widespread kind of inwardness, separateness, and artificiality which led religious people out of the center of life.[24] Religion did this because it had lost its roots in nature, that is, in sea, wind, the nudity of beautiful human beings, sunlight on beautiful women, courage, and political consciousness. It should be noted that just as Bonhoeffer was working out his vision of a religionless Christianity, Camus was working out his vision of secular sanctity. The basic momentum in both arguments is to turn men toward the center of life—toward the kiss of lovers, the coolness of the evening air, the demand today for quiet courage in rebellion against the manipulators of the future.

"Religion" has atrophied and God has died because Americans try in the name of "religion" to cover up reality. They dread public use of four-letter words, insist upon cleanliness and neatness, consider human genitals dirty, fear controversy, will not admit drinking and gambling into public life, refuse to imagine that their leaders could ever lie, use power tyrannically, or kill innocent people. Christianity without raw nature, Christianity without reality, is the *Logos* who never became flesh. Genuine and honest religion is the flesh which the Word assumes, the soil in which the seed is sown.

Thus the tack taken by those who follow uncritically in the path of Bonhoeffer is, I believe, mistaken and sterile. If there is no God, the figure of Jesus is without interest, and so long as we do not turn to nature, there can be no God. But how does turning to nature lead one to God?

THE GOD WITHIN

A series of insights is needed if an American is to discover God in his own experience. For example, an American student will commonly imagine that "turning to nature" means turning to objects "out there" in the environment. The ordinary American student has been taught to think of himself as a center of consciousness, imprisoned subjectively in a sheeting of thin flesh, and confronted with an environment full of objects out there to be observed objectively and mastered. In brief, the American has been taught to view the universe as made up of two kinds of stuff, conscious and unconscious, of which the first is an alien, an intruder, an outsider. To many it is a surprise to recognize that "the objective observer" is in fact a myth. It is equally amazing to them that they are free to look at themselves quite differently as living organically in their environment as an apple lives on a tree. Nature courses through them and shares its consciousness with them. They are free to feel "at one" with nature, to which they may speak as to themselves. They may imagine that their relationship to the ocean, to trees, to buildings, to chairs, and to desks may be presented in the imaginative form "thou" rather than "it." Consciousness, intelligibility, presence—we fumble for the telling word—prevades all things. The famous Hindu expression *"Tat tvam asi*: That art Thou" articulates this identity of the soul and God, an identity whose presence extends to every moment and to every place.

I would argue that it is important for Westerners to begin to recover ancient experiences of man's relation to the world and to one another. It is not true that metaphysics is at an end; it is only beginning. The functional patterns of scientific thinking have their place in serving the purposes of prediction and control, enabling man to extend the power of his aims and purposes over his environment. But the logic of science is the logic of tyranny; the scientific model for action is the manipulation of object. As Francis Bacon saw, scientific knowledge is power. Applied to metaphysical questions, scientific thinking destroys metaphysics.

Nevertheless, the expansion of scientific information and its extension through technology is bringing about a major correction in the assumptions of recent generations. Questions about nature and about man's nature are regaining their primacy in the most technologically advanced nations. As men begin to take responsibility for building the urban centers of the future, they are forced to ask: "What sort of cities do we desire? What forms best realize human potential? Who are we?" In recent years anthropological and sociological societies have discovered that, while their methods may in some sense be value-free, their employment on real human beings has empirical, social effects that involve investigators in serious value commitments. Among engineers who dream not only of the constructs which will be operational in a few years, but of those not yet realized even in design, the fundamental question no longer is: "Can we do X?" It is obvious that, given enough time and enough resources, X certainly can be done. The fundamental questions are: "Should we do X, and by what values should we decide which X's to do?"

In brief, what Aristotle called architectonic questions of politics and ethics are beginning to dominate human consciousness. The mysteries of the human self, the multiplicity of future possibilities, and an almost universal identity crisis are reasserting their primacy. The fundamental question for the children of an affluent society, trained to technical skills, is: Who are we? What do we wish to do with ourselves, and with our power?

A second series of insights emerges when students try to answer the question, Who am I? If they keep a diary, or attempt to write out who they think they are and what they think are their values, they speedily discover that what they commit to paper one day seems woefully inadequate the next. The self is elusive; its values and sense of identity refuse to be condensed in words. In answering the Socratic question they begin to understand the point of the Socratic method: knowledge is not power, it is knowledge of ignorance. Moreover, the self is inextricably and organically linked to its environment and its societies. The question "Who am I?" launches a dialectic that leads to discoveries about one's economic, social, political, mythical, and biological history. The Hindu insight, That art Thou, *(Tat tvam asi)* is verified in greater richness than one had at first anticipated.

Thirdly, it is commonly impossible for young Americans to deal with the Socratic question or with the question of God unless they have shared the experience of communion with at least one other person. For them, this experience is more rare than one might expect. There has perhaps never been a generation for whom the sense of loneliness is so acute. Their parents love them after a fashion, but the family is no longer, nor can it be, the nest it used to be. Moreover, young people have been taught that other people are their competitors, objects whose friendship and influence they must try to win. Achievement is rewarded; popularity and acceptability are established as criteria for human relations. The Beatles comment accurately: "She's leaving home / After living alone for so many years." It is not unusual for college students, suddenly aware of one another, to fall into each other's arms, to hug one another tightly, and to cry both from fear and joy. Many young people from "good middle-class homes" have never known the sense of community with another human being.

Moreover, Christian society in America has publicly treated the human genitals as organs of embarrassment and shame, the *pudenda*. Consequently, the genital organs and terms are surrounded by taboos and the actions of love-making are thought to be "obscene." Nevertheless, the mutual revelation of two people to one another gives rise to the most poignant sense of the sacred in our society. In sexual openness, one "transcends" the stultifying mores of society; in intimacy and tenderness, one "transcends" the acquisitive, impersonal human interchange of our society. For many persons it is only, or chiefly, in sexual love that one encounters the category of an end in itself that is the category of the sacred: everything else in our society appears to be a means. The commercialization of sexuality and the common ecclesiastical view of sex threaten to degrade even sexual love into a means. Yet for many of the young no human experience is more full of awe, joy, and holiness than sexual intercourse. For many, it is from this experience that religious language becomes meaningful once again. The honesty, community, and absolute respect for the other which good lovers are led to share takes them beyond the categories of the pragmatic, the rationalistic, the isolated self.

Christian society tolerates violence and murders by the dozen in movies and in evening television, but outlaws manifestations of sexual love.[25] It has come to prefer repression of vital and sacred instincts: it has conceived of God as the transcendent, all-seeing Eye who detects every violation of sexual taboos. The God of American Christianity has been the idol of inhibition, repression, and shame. The death of this God should have been predictable.

Conventional American society, in short, has been hostile to every basic human experience from which language about God commonly springs. If conventional American society is "religious," then by all means we need a "religionless Christianity."[26] Yet I have been trying to suggest that American society is not genuinely religious; it is self-contained, repressive, uncritical, and idolatrous. The question which remains to be answered is why the experiences of nature, the self, community, and sexual love lead many young Americans to a religious language. Why do these experiences constantly break through the ordinary patterns of life and establish the sacred in the midst of man's strength?

Perhaps the best way to understand the emergence of religious categories is to grasp the character of the technological, pragmatic life in advanced countries like the United States. From the perspective of studies in Marx and Freud, Herbert Marcuse in *One-Dimensional Man* has come to describe such life as effectively totalitarian. Though people think that they are free, their freedom is restricted to the limits established by the pragmatic consensus. Technical society awakens false needs and false consciousness by which, more than at earlier stages of man's development,[27] it is virtually impossible not to be inwardly determined. M. Garaudy, the famed Marxist interpreter of Christianity continually assaults Christianity for its "inwardness" and "subjectivity."[28] Unfortunately, on this point Christian critics appear to concede too much to M. Garaudy. It is the strength of Christianity and the weakness of Marxism that the criteria of humanistic life are centered in the human person and the critical community rather than in the impersonal processes of technical, pragmatic life. On the other hand, the inwardness of existentialism and of Christianity is by no means contained within the private sphere. Sartre and Camus possess an acute social and political consciousness; there is an existentialist politics.[29]

The heart of existentialist politics, in fact, lies in its rejection of the presuppositions of the present technical consensus, which it judges to be inhuman and irrational. It is neither a mistake in government nor the fault of any one administration that the United States and Russia spend so many billions of dollars for desructive armaments. The irrationality of the Cold War springs from the dominance of pragmatic and technical considerations over a radical humanistic critique of the system under which the secular city is being built. Consequently, it appears to be a mistake for Harvey Cox[30] and Johann B. Metz[31] to surrender the strength of subjectivity and inwardness because of Marxist objections.

To be sure, the private inwardness of interior life that is oblivious to the power of institutions and economic structures and irresponsible in social and political affairs is pale and sickly. A great many sins of this sort have been committed by Christians. The cure for sickly inwardness, however, is neither pragmatism, nor a zest for technique, nor devotion to the future of man, but a conversion to social and political responsibility.

But why should a man be concerned about other men? Why should he become involved? The history of our time seems to indicate that political life is murderous and that society is impervious to intelligence and courage. The great leap of faith is faith in man. Despite appearances, one must trust in the power of critical intelligence, courage, and compassion. Despite odds, one must go on struggling for a more brotherly city. Solace between individuals is not enough; community structures must be changed. A reconstruction of the economic, social, and political order is called for if men are to develop into men.

Thus openness to nature, to the Socratic question, to the experience of community, and to sexual love become both models for what it is to be a man, and sources of faith in man. It is only when persons awaken from their sleep and recognize that the assumptions of a technical, pragmatic society have blinded them to their inner possibilities that hope for a political revolution can be generated. The awareness of the mystery of the self and of community becomes the criterion by which social, economic, and political realities are judged: do they stultify or do they stimulate this awareness?

To become aware of the mystery of the self and of communion with others is to gain a sense of "participation" and of "unity." In this sense of being part of something one loses not one's own identity, but one's alienation and isolation. In being honest, one has the sense of being honest against oneself and yet somehow in the name of oneself. It is not like being under the glare of an All-seeing Eye, but as "participating" in a light greater than one's own emotions, interests, or rationalizations. In loving another as other, one has the sense of responding outside the categories of subject and object, of interest, or need, or stimulus and response. In moments of courage, one has the sense of surrendering the interests of the self, not exactly for an abstraction or even a value, but for a self more important than the interested self.

From such experiences of honesty, community, and courage, religious language is bound to spring. Human life is not self-contained. He who has belief in man has already made the giant leap of faith, compared to which the leap to religious language is only a step. The sense of man as an end in himself suggests that the radical structure of the universe in which we live is neither hostile nor even impersonal, for those who treat men as ends in themselves seem to live most fittingly. One cannot help wondering why this is so, though one rejects the repressive, transcendent "God" of false religiousness, the wonder which is the ever-fecund source of true religion springs up like clear water in the heart. No one sees God. All that we encounter is the sense of human experience leading beyond pragmatic and technical categories and out of the area of means and ends. It is at this point that there arises the sense of the sacred and the darkness of which the mystics wrote.

IS JESUS ENOUGH?

What are some of the fruits of turning to nature? Thomas J. J. Altizer has told us eloquently that the God of history is dead. Who is the God of history? He is the Trancendent One, Providence, the Repressor, the Father. Altizer takes seriously the crisp affirmation: "God was in Jesus." The transcendent God "emptied Himself," negated Himself, becoming so immanent in history that the only legitimate way of speaking of Him is through affirmations about Jesus.[32] Though I believe that Altizer is making several most important points, I think it is necessary to go beyond his position in two ways.

In the first place, Jesus is not, of himself, especially attractive. A man among other men, he suffers too many liabilities. Too many innocents have died on account of him and for centuries too many horrors have been committed in his name, not only upon Jews and Arabs, for example, but upon the sexual and psychological life of countless Christians as well. Moreover, his own character and deeds are ambivalent; not all men are attracted to him, not all admire him in every respect.

In the second place, it seems to me that a common Protestant understanding of the transcendence of faith is faulty. On this understanding, a man cannot come either to experience or to knowledge of God except through the historical, "inbreaking" grace of Jesus. Apart from Jesus, any knowledge of God at what man arrives through his own experience and understanding is idolatrous. Yet we are told in the prologue of St. John's gospel that in the beginning was the Word, and that all things were made through him. The vision behind this prologue seems to suggest that every person, thing, and event in history has been made in the image of the Word. We should expect, then, that every culture, every person, every moment of history reveals the creative presence of the Word. Thus, the grace of the Word not only breaks into history through the historical Jesus, but all things have been made in him, through him, and with him. All things are graced. In the words of Yeats, "Everything we look upon is blest." Thus, I think we must say that even the historical

Jesus can be used idolatrously, that is, in a manner that over-looks the omnipresence and efficacy of Jesus in so far as he is the Word by whom, through whom, and with whom were made all the things that were made. Nature is a word mirroring and echoing the Word. As in Edward Albee's *Tiny Alice*,[33] it is a castle within a castle within a castle; it is reverberating air shaped by a Word.

Thus Teilhard de Chardin is able to step with swift strides from evolutionary nature and the Omega Point to Jesus as the Word. Is not the Alpha also the Omega, and does not abyss cry out to abyss in glory? Like Dostoevsky and Berdyaev, Teilhard de Chardin drew his nourishment from Greek Christianity, which saw a dynamic universe flowing forth from the *Pantokrator,* the *Logos,* the Risen Lord.[34] What has come to be despised in Scholasticism as "Hellenization" is, in fact, "Latinization." Rather than the Greek, it is the Latin categories, based on commerce and jurisprudence rather than upon potent and dynam-ic nature, that have led to the death of the transcendent God.

In the nature known to physical science and to ordinary human experience, there are, if Christianity be true, elements leading the reflective man to honesty rather than to dishonesty, to creativity rather than to destruction, to courage to be rather than to anomie, to community rather than to atomic isolation. The universe in which we live often seems impersonal, indifferent, hostile, and even cruel. Yet our experience within it often fills us with reconciliation, with a sense of unity and peace, with a profound stirring of ecstasy and the desire to create. The transcendent is immanent in the world as yeast in dough, as powers of growth in a mustard seed, and as shaping word in air. It is through nature as it is that God is to be found. Such a conviction is profoundly Oriental, profoundly Greek, and pro-foundly Christian: who says the Buddha's *"Om"* says *"Word."*[35]

What Christianity adds to Greek and to Oriental religions is a responsibility not only to reflect the world, but to change it. As creation is unfinished, each man, in the image of the creative Word, must utter a creative word. But by the first cycle of modern science, by the printing press, and by Germanic eschatology man was separated from his environment and history was separated from nature. Modern science has entered a new cycle in which the printing press has been replaced by electronic media, and it is now time to turn from Germanic eschatology to Mediterranean nature. Camus refused to surrender the present moment to the future. Visions share time, now, with the world of total present experience of the senses, of imagination, of emotion, of intelligence and will. Man is coming to life again. Taste and see that life is sweet! When man regains his roots in nature, the God immanent in nature once again courses through his consciousness; the dead God rises; and the arrowhead breaks through into a new and creative period.

◇

1. See " 'Greece in Rags' and the Young Barbarians" in Emmett Parker, **Albert Camus: The Artist in the Arena** (Madison: Univ. of Wisconsin Press, 1966), pp. 25-45.

2. Albert Camus, **The Rebel** (New York: Random House, 1956), p. 299.

3. **Ibid.**

4. John Updike, **Pigeon Feathers and Other Stories** (New York: Alfred A. Knopf, 1962), p. 248.

5. For related remarks, see for example: Albert Camus, **Notebooks 1935-1942** (New York: Random House, 1965), pp. 86-87; and Albert Camus, **Notebooks 1942-1951** (New York: Alfred A. Knopf, 1966), pp. 128, 136, 267.

6. Alfred Camus, **Myth of Sisyphus** (New York: Random House, 1960), pp. 134-137, 144, 298.

7. Camus, **The Rebel**, pp. 26-35, 79, 279-306.

8. **Ibid.**, pp. 298-99.

9. **Ibid.**, p. 298.

10. **Ibid.**, pp. 298-99.

11. **Ibid.**, pp. 299-300.

12. **Ibid.**, p. 300.

13. Camus, **Notebooks 1942-1951**, p. 8.

14. **Ibid.**

15. Norman O. Brown, **Love's Body** (New York: Random House, 1966).

16. Camus, **Myth of Sisyphus**, p. 106.

17. **Ibid.**, p. 111.

18. "Presentation de la revue **Rivages,**" **Rivages,** I (1939), 1, as quoted by Emmett Parker, **Albert Camus: The Artist in the Arena,** pp. 40-41.

19. Camus, **The Rebel,** p. 294.

20. **Ibid.,** pp. 16-17.

21. **Ibid.,** p. 289.

22. Camus, **Myth of Sisyphus,** pp. 136-37.

23. See for example Alan Watts, **The Way of Zen** (New York: Random House, 1957).

24. Dietrich Bonhoeffer, **Letters and Papers From Prison** (New York: Macmillan, 1962), pp. 162-66.

25. Lenny Bruce, **How to Talk Dirty and Influence People: An Autobiography** (Chicago: Playboy Press, 1967), pp. 191-92.

26. Dietrich Bonhoeffer, **The Way to Freedom: Letters, Lectures and Notes 1935-1939** (New York: Harper and Row, 1967), pp. 236-39.

27. Herbert Marcuse, **One-Dimensional Man** (Boston: Beacon, 1966).

28. See for example Roger Garaudy, "Christian-Marxist Dialogue," **Journal of Ecumenical Studies,** IV (1967), 207-22.

29. See my **Secular Saint: Toward an Ethic for the New Left,** DeYoung Lectures given at Illinois State University, **Journal of Illinois State University** (Fall, 1967).

30. Harvey Cox, **The Secular City** (New York: Macmillan, 1965).

31. Johann B. Metz, "The Controversy About the Future of Man: An Answer to Roger Garaudy," **Journal of Ecumenical Studies,** IV (1967), pp. 223-34.

32. Thomas J. J. Altizer, **The Gospel of Christian Atheism** (Philadelphia: Westminster, 1966).

33. Edward Albee, **Tiny Alice** (New York: Atheneum, 1965).

34. Teilhard de Chardin, **Phenomenon of Man** (New York: Harper, 1965).

35. Nancy Wilson Ross, **Three Ways of Asian Wisdom** (New York: Simon & Schuster, 1966), p. 24.

The Death of God in Contemporary Culture

◊

Gabriel Vahanian

IN THE SAME way that Graeco-Roman civilization survived the collapse of its pantheon by providing Christianity with both a metaphysic and the sense of order so explicit in the liturgical and hierarchical canons of the church, it may be said the Christian culture will contribute to our pluralistic, post-Christian world as to a civilization it has fostered but no longer controls. It is true that the new civilization not only is technologically oriented, but seems quite intent on by-passing all religious commitments that can still be found in the various Christian and non-Christian cultures of the world. Nevertheless, this technological civilization postulates certain principles whose ethos, though cut off from its Christian conscience, still so unmisakably reflects and challenges it that technology cannot be "exported" without also "exporting" this conscience.

The following factors concerning the impact of the technological revolution now governing the future of civilization are of even greater significance.

CIVILIZATION AND TECHNOLOGY

While sweeping away the religious heritage of mankind, technology does not necessarily destroy the "religious" dimension of existence, but opens it to new structures. As Bergson has pointed out, it was the industrialism of western civilization

[273]

that triggered the mysticism of a Ramakrishna or a Vivekananda.[1] In our milieu, popular religion is replete with self-help devices attuned more to the technological orientation of our age than to the faith they are meant to confess.

Modern technology radically differs from anything that preceded or even anticipated it. It necessitates a conception of existence which not only cancels the idea of a human nature, but invalidates the notion of man as history. Significantly, it substitutes the notion of "world" so construed as to both embody and annul man's transcendence and, in the last analysis, to make man himself superfluous to the very world over which he has acquired mastery.

From this it follows that technology cannot in and of itself provide human existence with either the theory or the praxis to eliminate the question of God, provided "God" does not mean some supernatural being. Admittedly, the technological revolution will bring about physiological and psychological alterations in man's constitution. These, however, will only bear out the fact that modern man will not revert to nature worship and that he will not "worship" history much longer under any one of its utopian forms, from the classless society to the millenium.

BIBLICAL ICONOCLASM

Nothing can obscure our understanding of the biblical world more than trying to view it from the standpoint either of theistic pre-suppositions or of religious speculations. The fundamental significance of the biblical view of the world lies neither in theism nor in religion, but in its iconoclastic character. No doubt this iconoclasm is of a peculiar kind, though in the last analysis its specific nature is included within the various more common definitions given by any dictionary. Biblical iconoclasm is obviously directed against the worship of idols as well as against the idolatry of which oneself or one's society is in effect the object. But it is equally, if not more significantly, directed against absolutism in all its aspects, and in particular against the absolutism of religion and of unbelief. Genesis or the Book of Revelation could be mentioned in support of this contention. Furthermore, it is only in this light that, for example, the doctrine of the trinity can be truly evaluated. When this is done it rather unexpectedly provides us with an adequate argument both against the kind of absolute theism which has fallen into disrepute and against the opposite temptation of atheistic relativism.

In other words, this iconoclasm is at work not only concerning the biblical view of man, but in making possible the biblical understanding of God. To abandon either aspect of this twofold exigency, would mean (like Dostoievski's Shigalov who, starting from the postulate of unlimited freedom, could only arrive at unlimited despotism) starting from unlimited religion only to arrive at unlimited atheism. Indeed, if the tragedy of theism is that in the end it makes either God or the world superfluous,[2] religion itself cannot survive without finally alienating man from both God and the world or from himself.

Yet the drama of religion does not consist in the commonplace description of its impotence to overcome man's alienation. It consists in the fact that this failure does not annul, but merely objectivizes the psychological, economic, and general environmental factors from which the religious analysis of man's alienation is not inconsistently derived. Ultimately God and the world are sundered and the stage is set for one Grand Inquisitor or another. As Dostoevski's legend poignantly shows, it makes no difference whether the inquisitor be a theist or an atheist, for theism can be as idolatrous as atheism. All ratiocinations to the contrary not withstanding, as the doctrine of the trinity suggests, absolute theism can only lead to absolute idolatry. Indeed, there is not a trace of iconoclasm in the Grand Inquisitor's pseudo-humanitarian religious programme. Its metaphysic will stand only so long as man cannot or will not say "no" to being fallaciously dispossessed of his humanity by a fraudulent ideology, either of the social environment or of the natural milieu, in the name of some pseudo-God. Perhaps idolatry diminishes God; it certainly diminishes man.

Biblical thought is iconoclastic to the extent that by virtue of a "mythological" view of the world—to borrow a celebrated formula—it dares to speak in divine terms about man and in human terms about God. For the Bible, speaking of God is an iconoclastic way of speaking about man and his conceptions of himself, for man as a subject is not reducible to that to which he is empirically reduced as an object. Correspondingly, speaking of man is an iconoclastic way of speaking about God and man's conceptions of God, for God is not as we imagine him to be.

The Bible supports this view by means of the "myths" of creation and incarnation, which respectively govern the Old and New Testaments. In the Old Testament, creation signifies the context or, rather, the way in which the glory (i.e., the reality) of God is embodied, though without resulting in the divinization of the world. By the same token, creation also signifies the context within which the experience of human reality attains precisely the infinite qualitative difference between God and man or the reason why the creator is infinite. His infinitude does not consist in his being either that which man lacks or the necessary complement of this world's finitude. Rather, he is infinite in the sense that the possibilities for the world to be the arena of God's reality or the possibilities for man to embody God's image are infinite, that is, not predetermined or predicated on a God-hypothesis. Conversely, man is finite only insofar as finitude is that aspect of infinitude which can be experienced.

From this, it begins to appear that the question is no longer whether God is necessary or not. Nor do I think that by quoting Barth in support of this I am twisting the meaning of his comments on the first article of the Creed: "The wording itself," of the first article, "... does not speak (in analogy with the expression of the second and the third articles) of a *creatio coeli et terrae,* and therefore of a *mundus a Deo creatus,* but—and that is something different—of the *creator coeli et terrae.*" Consequently, Barth adds, it is "of these two worlds," that man "is the citizen encompassed in truth with a special mystery or the wanderer between these two worlds which indeed in God's sight are only *one* world, the created world."[3] Finitude itself is thus expressive of that aspect of infinitude which can be experienced as well as of the fact that human reality is ultimately neither reducible nor replaceable.

The iconoclasm of the "myth" of incarnation is or, rather, should be equally obvious: God is not as we imagine him, though at the same time he is only insofar as we can imagine him. To borrow Kirillov's Voltairean remark. God *is* only insofar as we can invent him. Like the story of creation, incarnation makes it plain that God is only to the extent that we can let him come in. But, unlike Dostoievsky's Kirillov, what the New Testament also contends is that Christ is the only way that God can be "invented," that is, brought into the objective reality of human existence, without objectifying him. This conforms to what the New Testament states: without Jesus there is no God.

However, the New Testament makes it equally plain that Jesus, as such, is no evidence of the deity. The dilemma which seems to appear at this point is immediately resolved upon realization that the New Testament confronts us with this question: "With Jesus, how dare we imagine God in such a way that our very conceptions of him (*ipso facto*) turn us into idolators?" With Jesus, which is to say when the human reality is experienced most concretely, how can we turn God into an idol? Such is the principal meaning of creation and incarnation if they are understood as iconoclastic statements, rather than creation being a description of the Christian view of the world and incarnation being a description of the Christian view of God.

CHRISTIAN SUBJECTIVISM AND THEORIES OF RADICAL IMMANENTISM

Recent developments of Christian thought generally reveal a deliberate attempt to re-think tradition by radically re-examining, if not rejecting, its latest avatars from neo-thomism to dialectic theology. Ever since the Second Vatican Council, even those for whom this would have been inconceivable are beginning to awake to the idea that Thomism must go. To be sure, Protestants demonstrated this possibility by the fact in the sixteenth century. That theological systems come and go is so accepted by them that they are inclined to apprehend in this light, and thereby somewhat minimize, the protracted obsolescence of Thomism. Similarly, they do not find it abnormal that Protestant thought is distancing itself from the whole movement of dialectic theology, as if this merely indicated that Protestant theology was not about to embark upon the course of a new scholasticism like the one that followed upon the Reformation. In fairness to him, it must be added that Barth had actually warned against such an outcome; indeed, theology is more often impeded by its zealots than by its detractors.

Dialectical Theology and Radical Immanentism

The question of whether dialectic theology explicitly discouraged and even disowned beforehand any scholasticism becomes secondary when one ceases to assess its significance by contrasting it with modernism or liberal Protestantism, that is, by considering its development in the light of its source (*terminus a quo*). Dialectic theology cannot conceal its weakness when considered, as it must be, in the light of its goal (*terminus ad quem*). In that light it becomes all too apparent that dialectic theology merely sought to bury its head in the sand of radical immanentism—the wound through which our age leaks. This mood is so prevailing that even in the context of theological discourse it has, finally and over the dead body of dialectic theology, necessitated substituting methodological atheism for the traditional God-hypothesis.

It is not that the end of dialectic theology diminishes either its stature or our debt. But this debt can no longer exonerate it from its inherent and congenital incapacity to come to grips with the precise factor which blocks modern man from the horizon of the Christian faith, the death of God. This cultural phenomenon could not be unprimed by any dialectic; it allows no other view of the world than one from which God can only be superfluous *(de trop)*. Consciously or unconsciously dialectic theology thus both belongs to and closes the theological evolution that typifies and is necessitated by the ecclesiastical world view of the Christian era and its supernaturalistic method. The death of God is the secret of dialectic theology.

Because of dialectic theology Christianity is left without any alibi for its responsibility in the obsolescence of God, in the discreditation of the church, and in the rise of secularism. This remains true even though it was by this theology that Christian thought was somehow being spared from secularism, so that it now can meaningfully come to grips with the cultural and religious implications of the death of God. The history of dialectic theology demonstrates the extent to which Christianity had capitulated to and endorsed its own secularization by divorcing itself from the world. More fundamentally, by dishabilitating itself, Christianity does not make way for a world which, having supposedly come of age, will carry on the cultural vocation that once enabled the proclamation of the gospel to create a certain kind of life style. Rather, it makes way for a world in which it may well be unable to resume any aspect of the cultural vocation Christianity has fulfilled until now, and which is being neutralized by the rise of secularism and the various ideologies of radical immanentism. In other words, dialectic or otherwise, theology has in our time failed both the church and the world.

Appearances to the contrary not withstanding, it is with respect to the church that Barth's failure becomes most flagrant, just as it is with respect to the world that Gogarten's failure becomes equally manifest. These assertions are made in spite of the fact that Barth has deliberately construed his dogmatics as a church dogmatics, and that in Gogarten's theology it is the world rather than the church that is the more explicit intention of the harmony of faith and the secular.

Before proceeding further I should perhaps state that I am not attempting to adjudicate the weaknesses of one approach by the merits of the other. This would only demonstrate that what is a primary category for Barth becomes secondary for Gogarten and *vice versa,* and thus illegitimately exclude the possibility that the difference is perhaps only one of terminology. More significantly, it would overlook the fact that Barth's minimal understanding of the world vitiates his concern about the church, while Gogarten's minimal concern about the church does not actually tolerate his understanding of the world. What is involved here is the question whether or not ecclesiology can continue to spell out for our time the structures of the cultural dimension of theo—logy. That both Barth and Gogarten are concerned with this problem need not be contested. This acknowledgement, however, is especially necessary because it also reveals at what point either method ultimately flounders.

World: The Secular Dimension of the Church

To say that ecclesiology is the cultural dimension of theo—logy means that the world is the secular dimension of the church. The church, as the embodiment of God's claim upon man and the whole creation, must refer not to itself but to the world as the means through whose structures this claim is communicated. In this sense alone can the church be said to be the means of grace.

In other words, what Paul says about the relation between Christ and the church or, quoting Genesis 2:24, what he says about the relation between a man and a woman applies to the relation between the church and the world.

No man ever hates his own flesh, but nourishes and cherishes it, as Christ does the church, because we are members of his body. For this reason a man shall leave his father and mother and be joined to his wife, and the two shall become one. This is a great mystery, and I take it to mean Christ and church.[4]

As is well known, the word "mystery" in this last sentence is rendered in Latin by *sacramentum,* a word which in the New Testament, as Vacant's *Dictionnaire de théologie catholique*[5] itself recognizes, is still far from anticipating the various ritual acts of the church. Brunner writes that even "in the ecclesiastical sense of the word, a "sacrament" does not denote a sacred symbol, but means the communication of grace by means of the church."[6] I should like to add that this is true of a church which has "become one" with the world: the church lies in the world, the world is made manifest in the church (*ecclesia in mundo latet, mundus in ecclesia patet*). Thus, in Paul's view a sacrament is what expresses membership in the Body of Christ, that is to say a style of life through which the world is claimed as "the Lord's," Κμριφκος (from which the English word "church" is derived). To paraphrase Jesus' rejoinder that the temple is what "has made the gold sacred" and the altar what "makes the gift sacred,"[7] the church is what validates the world. This is to say that the church embodies the sacramental dimension of the world.

Barth and Ecclesiasticism

It is particularly important to note this in view of Barth's parochial definition of theology as well as the church. Once Barth defines theology as the self-critical task of the church, in order to make meaningful any discussion of the nature of the church, he is forced to introduce and even to predicate everything upon a concept of revelation. In the light of this concept, the world is rendered "useless" and, like man in Barth's interpretation of the virgin birth, "deemed improper for God's design." It is not that Barth explicitly endorses a pessimistic view of the world; his intention is exactly the opposite. But surely the dichotomy between church and world is not overcome if grace is understood as rendering nature useless, and if the charismatic goodness of the creation (*justitia originis*) must give way to a general scheme, as Bonhoeffer called it, of a "revelational positivism." By so doing, Barth merely carries further and stresses the general spiritualistic tendency of Protestantism. This tendency has consisted in denying the world as sacramental sign (*sacramentum*) of the church (*res sacramenti*), and in transforming the church into the sphere of faith.

Instead, as Ebeling points out, faith should be understood in such a way that its only proper sphere is the world itseslf. The church does not abrogate the world but assumes it, just as grace does not abolish nature but makes it natural. The defect of Protestant spiritualism is that it turns the sacraments into mere symbols by shifting the locus of the medieval work of the deed itself (*opus operatum*) from the sacrament to faith or to revelation. Protestantism continues rather than corrects what already vitiated medieval sacramentarianism, namely its tendency to negate the structures of the world as the very means of grace in favor of those of a counter-world, the church. One might even call it a counter-creation inasmuch as, like Ivan Karamozov, one must hand back one's ticket to the former either because it is unacceptable or because it is rendered useless. It is not surprising that the Anabaptists should have made the sacraments as well as the church itself dependent upon faith. While Luther and Calvin vehemently denounced such a tendency, subsequent Protestantism diluted their teachings, much as Augustine's were accomodated earlier to the needs of a Pelagianizing church.

If I seem to insist on the church as the sacramental reality (*res sacramenti*) of the world, this is for two reasons. (1) It is the church which testifies to the secularity of faith understood as eschatological existence. Such an aim can be achieved only if the world is not rendered superfluous but restored to its true worldliness, that is to say to its sacramental function. Only in this way can the church avoid introducing itself as some sort of a sacred but superfluous (*tertium quid*) factor in the picture. It would also prevent the church from sanctioning historicism as well as sacralism. Obviously, this is a function which today cannot be performed if the church's self-understanding still calls for a supernaturalistic dichotomous order of this world and the next. 2) The sacrament is what testifies to the worldliness of the church, that is, to the fact that the world is not superfluous to the church. What Robert Funk says of language and history can be applied to the relation between the church and the world.[8] The church is the means by which man exists in the world; but only where world is validated is there church. The new Jerusalem, which comes "down from God out of heaven," is "prepared as a bride adorned for her husband."[9]

In other words, the communion of saints (*communio sanctorum*) also includes the holy (*sancta*), that is, the claim that the whole world is "the Lord's," Κμριφκος, the church. During his interrogation by the Prefect Rusticus, Justin Martyr is reported to have answered the latter's question, "Where do ye meet together?" by saying: "Where each wills and can. Do you really think that we all meet in the same place? Not so: for the God of the Christians is not confined by place, but being unseen fills heaven and earth, and is worshipped and glorified by the faithful everywhere."[10]

The church is not a place; we should thank Barth for reminding us that it is an event. But it does not happen in spite of the world; it happens through the structures of the world, here and now (*hic et nunc*), and can embody the city of God (civitas dei) only through its empirical evidence, the earthly city (*civitas terrena*). By contrast, Barth's conception of the church is supernaturalistic.

Gogarten and Secularism

For the same reasons one might raise similar objections to Gogarten's most timely reinterpretation of the Christian faith and obligation to secularity. In this connection, it may be worth remembering that, because sacralism and the Christian faith could only exclude one another, the Middle Ages had sought a solution by shifting the locus of the sacral from nature to the church. By moving it from the church to the word, to revelation, Barth himself was simply reiterating the spiritualistic tendency of Protestantism. What is important to note is that, in keeping with biblical thought, this general movement away from sacralism was only meant to vindicate holiness to God alone. The desacralization of nature was thus the necessary channel through which to validate the secularity of faith.

My contention, against Gogarten, would be that while this desacralization was accompanied by a process of secularization, the latter must not be confused with the former, let alone be advocated as the ultimate implication of the Christian faith's call for secularity. Secularization, as the history of Western civilization has made all too obvious, can only refer to the expropriation of the Christian tradition, to the dishabilitation of faith. Desacralization need not lead to secularism, to wit either the medieval or Calvin's conception of the world as well as of society. By contrast, when secularization becomes the key motif of the Christian's obligation to secularity, then the only result is secularism, that is, immanentism or, to borrow Gogarten's term, subjectivism. Gogarten's own analysis, indeed, demonstrates that what has taken place in the last twenty centuries of western culture is the mere substitution of subjectivism for the sacralism of the pre-Christian world. The so-called secularization of the world can only describe the process by which faith is obliterated and the world is, not come of age, but surrendered to the idolatry of radical immanentism. It scarcely needs to be added that I would therefore consider the "secularization of Christianity" as the best adjuvant to the consolidation of that inevitable concomitant of either subjectivism or immanentism, namely ethnolatry. As Pascal said: "Why do you kill me? What! do you not live on the other side of the water? If you lived on this side, my friend, I should be an assassin, and it would be unjust to slay you in this manner. But since you live on the other side, I am a hero, and it is just.... A strange justice that is bound by a river! Truth on this side of the Pyrenees, error on the other side."[11] In *The City of God,* Augustine had written: "And this is the characteristic of the earthly city, that it worships God or gods who may aid it in reigning victoriously and peacefully on earth not through love of doing good, but through lust of rule. The good use the world that they may enjoy God; the wicked, on the contrary, that they may enjoy the world would fain use God—those of them, at least, who have attained to the belief that He is and takes an interest in human affairs."[12]

A new subjectivism thus results from a secularized sacralism, or from the twofold process of secularization as Gogarten understands it. Inasmuch as subjectivism implies, on the one hand, the obliteration of the church as the sacramental reality of the world and, on the other hand, the obliteration of the world as the empirical authentication of the church, secularization entails a further alienation of man from the world, from himself, from God. The world is thereby turned in upon itself and changes into a world of artifacts, of objects. Far from healing the subject-object dichotomy, secularization serves only to sanctify it either by reducing it to subjectivism or its converse, objectivism, as is demonstrated in the so-called "objectalism" of the "new world."

Thus, while both Barth and Gogarten are correct in rejecting contemporary subjectivism, their respective alternatives merely reinforce it either through ecclesiasticism or through secularism, the twin error which no distinction can release from the charge of idolatry. Ecclesiasticism is, so to speak, the Christian version of secularism. Both Barth and Gogarten thus demonstrate the extent to which the Christian faith has forfeited its iconoclastic vocation—a forfeiture which is corroborated by the death of God. In this light, dialectic theology marks the end of the beginnings of Christianity.

CONTEMPORARY SECULARISM AS POST-CHRISTIAN PAGANISM

As the history of religion clearly manifests, the death of God (or of the gods) can only refer to a cultural phenomenon. This becomes even clearer as soon as, in order to explain what such a phrase may mean, one speaks of how things now stand in contrast to what they used to be. Any radical break in the rhythm of man's consciousness of the world that alienates him from the gods is a cultural phenomenon expressive of the substitution of one world-view for another. To object that this only means that a certain concept of God has now become obsolete entirely misses the point, for there has never been a concept of God which did not hark back to a life style concretizing even the most speculative notion of the deity. Whatever God is, man is created in his image: there is no God-in-general any more than one is man-in-general. Concrete existence, in other words, is the fabric through which God is to be "conceptualized." What is more, from a Christian point of view faith is not merely a private but a public matter. Hence, with the disappearance of what articulates the Christian faith into artistic, social, and political, as well as theological terms, the Christian era becomes another exhibition of the religious museum of mankind. Throughout the ages, the death of the gods has marked the end of a tradition.

Having said this, it must be observed, however, that tradition also is what makes revolution possible, as Claude Mauriac has argued in another context. If one admits that the Christian tradition itself has brought about the death of God, then such a cultural phenomenon must be seen not only as the result of the neutralization of the Christian tradition, but also as a possible expression of its iconoclastic obligation. Given that biblical iconoclasm is directed against any attempt to take God for granted, what better ally can be found than the methodological atheism which today the death of God imposes on us all by definitely canceling the supernaturalist frame of reference to which Christian thought has been confined and restricted? Admittedly, the death of God makes us the orphans of a certain cultural embodiment of the Christian faith, but it allows us to come into our inheritance—the world where there is no world but this one in which to live by faith, in which here and now life is "the word of eternal life,"[13] for in which, as Psalm 139 implies, not even heaven, let alone hell, can separate man from God.

The note of crypto-triumphalism that some hostile ears might like to hear at this point is eliminated by the candid admission that what has occurred from let us say, stage A (Christian culture) to stage B (our inchoate post-Christian civilization) is not merely a transition, but rather a mutation of such magnitude that the word "God" itself corresponds to nothing which modern man can experience. This is true even though, as Ebeling remarks, "at this point the atheistic secularism of the modern age, for all its profound difference, is strangely close to mysticism."[14] Indeed, between A and B there is both continuity and discontinuity. That is why the transition from stage A to stage B cannot be construed in terms of a mere maturation, say, from adolescence into manhood. It must also express a radical mutation if between A and B the discontinuity is to receive as much emphasis as the continuity.

Another way of characterizing this mutation consists in drawing attention, as does Bultmann, to the substitution of a scientific view of the world for the mythological worldview of the New Testament, or in speaking of a levelling-down from the radical monotheism of the Judaeo-Christian tradition to the no less radical immanentism of the present situation. In the Christian era the world was viewed from a supernatural standpoint, whereas our post-Christian world is weaned on the secularization of the Christian faith.

This, of course, by no means implies that one worldview is better than the other, or that man today is less religious than was the case in the Middle Ages or at any other time. What is meant is simply the fact that, as W. H. Auden put it in *For the Time Being*:

> Instead of building temples, we build laboratories;
> Instead of offering sacrifices, we perform experiments;
> Instead of reciting prayers, we note pointer-readings;
> Our lives are no longer erratic but efficient.[15]

It is not that the scientific revolution and technological orientation of today's intellectual and moral climate is to be blamed for the obsoleteness of Christianity, for science and technology must be distinguished from scientism and technologism. There is, however, something ironic in the fact that our addiction to the benefits derived from science, instead of emancipating us from the cares of the world, makes us even more subservient to the instruments needed to continue asserting man's conquest over nature. It is more than ironic that what distinguishes present-day technology from its antecedents is its separation from the humanities, from man. Though, as Bertrand Russell said, what science cannot discover mankind cannot know, it is no less true that what man cannot know science cannot discover.

Thus, the transition from radical monotheism to radical immanentism is not only indicative of the cleavage between the Judaeo-Christian tradition and the frame of reference by which our culture gropes after its image and seeks to understand and to express itself. It is also indicative of the secularization of that tradition, of its expropriation and its dishabilitation, of the paganization of Christianity. A new paganism has emerged which, for being Christian, is all the more hostile to the preservation of the Christian faith. It is as if after approximately twenty centuries of Christian influence upon the mind and heart of western man and his culture, the best results that could be achieved was the substitution of a culturally Christian paganism for the hellenistic paganism of the world into which Christianity was born.

This is what Kierkegaard saw in stating the death of Christendom and Nietzsche in pronouncing the death of God. If any difference is to be made between them, it is that Kierkegaard denounced the church and Nietzsche theology. More precisely, it is that according to the former our experience of the human reality can, and according to the latter must, make God himself superfluous to its clarification. Therefore, whether he is or not, Sartre will subsequently argue that God is irrelevant to the decisions man must make in order to be what he wills himself to be. Instead of the traditional assertion that everything is grace because God is, modern man claims that the goodness of the world can only preclude the reality of God. Everything is grace because God is dead. As Camus stated it in an obvious reference to the Christian contention that there is no salvation outside the church: the world is beautiful and outside it there is no salvation.

CHRISTIAN CULTURE AFTER THE DEATH OF GOD

In the preceding, I have been a critic of both traditional Christianity and the secularism of the modern temper. Against the former I would contend that the death of God makes atheism a valid alternative to the Christian faith and denies theism any kind of privilege. Against the latter I would say that either it is not iconoclastic enough and its atheism is as passé as is traditional theism, or it has domesticated God and religion. In this case, religion is made the vehicle of a national idea while the former is reduced to the status of a cosmic force. This is merely a stop gap of a different order from that of the God up there or out there; it denotes nothing more than perhaps a return of the idea of a divine nature in the form of a divine cosmos. In other words, the real believer is the one who can confess his unbelief, and the real iconoclast is the one who rebels against idolizing his ownself. Religion, whether that of the church or that of society, is no guarantee against idolatry. As the Bible maintains, God cannot be domesticated—because he is imageless. This is precisely what is asserted by the biblical myth according to which man is created in the image of God.

Creation and World

An entire civilization was molded by the notion that God created man in his image. As Paul explicitly states, this signifies that man is not merely a faint image but the image and glory of God.[16] It is as if it were in and through man that God's glory becomes manifest, as if God has no other glory than this image which is man. Indeed, the book of Genesis even goes so far as to suggest that this image must be understood in terms of a "physical" resemblance.[17] Today "physical" is somewhat too strong a term because it is generally associated with the notion of an independent human nature. In biblical thought, where there is no such concept of "physis," it denotes the notion that the human reality is the sacramental manifestation of God's glory.

As this is not the place to go into a detailed, technical exegesis of the biblical myth, it will suffice to underline its most significant aspects. First of all, to speak of the world in terms of creation means not only that it is not per se divine, but that in itself the world has no meaning or is, as it were, neutral. I say this fully realizing that, according to the supernaturalistic thinking in which Christianity has been transmitted, this world is a reflection of the world to come. It is, therefore, pretty much determined by a certain pre-established harmony, and the best it can do is to adumbrate the supernatural order that governs its destiny. Even for supernaturalism, however, the natural makes no sense until it is assumed by the supernatural.

This does not mean that the world can have no meaning; quite the contrary. The doctrine of creation militates against both the divinization of the world and its reification. The world is neither divine nor is it a gadget; it is neither to be identified with worldliness nor to be regarded merely as a world-of-artifacts. The world is what happens when God speaks; it is the arena of his glory and the image of his reality. As the sacrament of that promise by which the creator binds himself to his creature, it is the means of his grace. Theology meant no less when it defined the church as the means of grace. As Karl Rahner observes, surely the medieval emphasis on the "ecclesiastical character" of grace could not imply that one cannot "attain salvation without the grace of Christ," unless, grace being "always related to the incarnation," the church itself is the *res sacramenti* of the world.[18]

Church and Man

The church thus is not some sort of supernatural entity descended for the benefit of but a few privileged ones and remaining in splendid isolation. It is the biblical way of asserting the world and of celebrating life and the secular. It is the iconoclastic way of saying that there is no God other than he whose gracious claim upon man is mediated through the world. Instead of serving as a principle of spiritual segregation, the church is the objective dimension of that kingdom of God *(regnum dei)* which, being always in this world but never of this world, can never be objectified. In this light, today's secularism is as much a perversion of the world as the supernaturalism of our church-going masses is, in effect, a denial of the church. As Jesus said, the sabbath was made for man, not man for the sabbath.

But what is man? As Bultmann points out, to say that man is created in the image of God is to establish man's sovereignty over all other creatures. However, man is a creature who stands against the world, rather than just being a part of its nature or its process. He stands in need of that very world in order to be independent of it. It is, therefore not merely a question of whether man is interpreted in the light of the world or the world in the light of man. Instead, because the world is meaningless, that is, because it does not in and of itself postulate the reality of God, it undermines man's autonomy, his *hybris,* his idolatry, as Paul contends on the Areopagus. In this regard Niebuhr's remark is quite appropriate: because man is created in the image of God, he cannot be satisified with a god made in his image, for this would in the first place contradict his own capacity for self-transcendence.

In the words of Rilke, the world is nowhere but within that human reality where the world is the world to come,[19] and where man is not determined by the past but constantly open to the future. Existence is the improvisation of one's destiny, which destiny is neither bound to the past nor subjected to the future.

The Future

If subservience to the past distorts and mummifies tradition, similarly the present can be stultified for the sake of some hypothetical future. The former view relies on the primacy of nature, the latter on that of history. There is no reason to opt for either if world is understood as what lies beyond the caprices of both nature and history and embodies the infinite qualitative difference between the creator and the creature. Both creation and last judgment signify this in unmistakable terms. Not only is there nothing which has taken place that predetermines the human reality but, however one experiences it, its values or lack of value in no way modifies the "verdict": God's judgment is not retributive. If certain theologies have implied that it was, they were confusing eschatology and history on the one hand, and on the other, reading creation as a theodicy and man's generations as the process by which man degenerates. Instead, in keeping with Augustine's view as Etienne Gilson reminds us, man's generations should be considered as the context of his regeneration. In the Roman Catholic tradition this view is still upheld theoretically by the fact that from baptism to extreme unction what is celebrated is authentic life from birth to death. Otherwise creation becomes a curse and eschatology the pretext for totalitarian subjugation to some utopian ideology, whether in its Christian ersatz, or in one of its secularized, versions.

· In other words, existence is a task; it is an act of faith and not merely an empirical datum. In this light faith becomes constitutive of the human experience, whose structures it does not contradict but manifests and asserts. As Calvin would say, the image of God means that the structures of the human reality are neither autonomous nor heteronomous, but theonomous. It is not that God becomes necessary for the experience of the human reality; he would, indeed, be superfluous were it not for the fact that this reality itself is not superfluous to him. As Barth contends, only when man is a creature does he resemble the creator. This resemblance is not physical but eschatological, it is not a datum of nature but an act of faith in the light of which God remains wholly other than his creation, even while creation is the manifestation of his presence. God is not a noun, but a verb which governs and articulates the experience of the human reality. That is why the image in which man is created is that of an imageless God. God, Kierkegaard said, has nothing obvious about him. He is elusive, invisible. "I am who I am," said the voice that Moses heard. "O God," Augustine writes in his *Confessions*

> you who are highest and nearest, most hidden and most present, have not parts greater and smaller; you are wholly everywhere yet nowhere limited within space, nor are you of any bodily

form. And yet you have made man in your own image, and man is in space from head to foot.[20]

Clearly, if the asymmetry of Augustine suggests anything, it is that man does not reflect the glory of God by imitating God. The story of the fall is there to remind us of that. The myth of man's being created in the image of God excludes the notion that it is the business of man to become God. The Greek word for image is "icon." To say that man is created in God's "icon" certainly cannot mean anything if the "icon" should stand for that of which it is the witness. Indeed, for man to be an "icon," he must of necessity be iconoclastic, that is, he must act and be in such a way that nothing can tarnish the image of God. The pecularity of the biblical view of man thus consists not of speculations about his religious nature, but of the notion that the human adventure has meaning to the extent that it is determined by a choice between iconoclasm and idolatry. There is no empirical way of proving which is which, or else God would be an idol.

God

What then is God? By merely suggesting that as a verb God is that by which the human experience or the world itself for that matter is articulated, I have no doubt scarcely sketched any concept of God. By contrast, in a supernaturalistic universe where nature was still more or less hostile to man as a person it was normal to project God into a realm up there and to conceive him as a supreme Being. Nevertheless, this transcendent reality is "objectified" in the Christ-event; in other words, in the Christian view God is that verb which becomes flesh. In the New Testament, accordingly, God is not known except through Christ. That is to say, to know God is to know him through his works, through the world. Looking for him elsewhere "falls short of the mark,"[21] although one cannot find him in the world by divinizing it or in Jesus by deifying him. From this standpoint alone is it possible to concur with Jaspers when he writes: "That God is tangible in the here and now—in the man Jesus—is a main thought of Christianity."[22]

It is not surprising, then that the story of creation is a way of talking about God in terms of the world and of man. As Paul states in his epistle to the Romans: "What can be known about God is plain. . . . Ever since the creation of the world his invisible nature, namely, his eternal power and deity, has been clearly perceived in the things that have been made."[23] The story of the incarnation harks back to that of the creation and corroborates it by saying that God can only be known or invented through the "things of this world," though this need not imply the necessity to transform God himself into a thing. To this extent one can say that the Christ-event signifies God's objective reality without objectifying him, and his accessibility to man without making him a projection of man. In Christ, as the authentic experience of the human reality, it is not God who is edged out of the world, but our own idols—the gods that die.

◇

1. H. Bergson, **Les Deux Sources de la morale et de la religion** (Paris: Presses Universitaires de France, 1942), p. 289.

2. Acts 24:22.

3. Karl Barth, **Credo** (New York: Scribner, 1936), pp. 28, 30.

4. Ephesians 5:29-32.

5. A. Michel, "Sacraments," **Dictionnaire de théologie catholique,** ed. A. Vacant (Paris: Librairie Letouzey et Ané, 1939), Vol. XIV, c. 494-98.

6. H. E. Brunner, **The Divine Imperative** (Philadelphia: Westminster, 1947), p. 649.

7. Matthew 23:16-22.

8. Robert Funk, **Language, Hermeneutic, and Word of God** (New York: Harper and Row, 1966), p. 40.

9. Revelation 21:22.

10. Roland H. Bainton, ed., **Early Christianity** (Princeton: Von Nostrand, 1960), p. 97.

11. B. Pascal, **Pensées** (New York: Dutton & Co., 1931), pp. 293-94.

12. St. Augustine, **The City of God,** trans. Marcus Dods (New York:

Modern Library, 1950), XV/7, p. 485.

13. John 6:46-49.

14. G. Ebeling, **God and Word** (Philadelphia: Fortress Press, 1967), p. 9.

15. W. H. Auden, **For the Time Being** (New York: Random House, 1944), pp. 93-94.

16. 1 Cor. 11:7.

17. Rudolf Bultmann, **Primitive Christianity in its Contemporary Setting** (New York: Meridian, 1956).

18. Karl Rahner, **The Church and the Sacraments** (New York: Herder and Herder, 1966), p. 22.

19. Cited by E. Heller, **The Disinherited Mind** (Cambridge: Bowes and Bowes, 1952), ch. V, p. 134-40.

20. Augustine, **Confessions,** trans. F. J. Sheed (New York: Sheed & Ward, 1943), p. 10.

21. Karl Jaspers, **Truth and Symbol** (New Haven, Conn: College & Univ., 1962), p. 75.

22. **Ibid.,** p. 46.

23. Romans 1:19-20.

God After the Death of God

◊

Richard L. Rubenstein

WHAT KIND OF God can we believe in after the death of God?

It is not surprising that the death-of-God movement has been one of the best publicized and the least understood movements in modern theology. A number of contradictory religious philosophies have all been designated as death-of-God theologies. Some religious thinkers, such as Prof. Thomas J. J. Altizer, maintain that God literally died in our times. Others believe that the death of God is something that happened to us, not God.

THE GOD OF HISTORY

I believe that the death of God is a cultural event experienced by men and women who are no longer able to believe in the biblical God who acts in history. To believe in the God of history requires the conviction that history is an unfolding drama and that its decisive events are expressions of a divine plan. Such a faith requires an ultimate optimism which seems impossible in our times. Belief in the God of history means interpreting such events as the destruction of six million Jews, the degradation of the black man, and the strife which permeates our times as exemplifications of God's way of leading mankind to its final redemption. Many thoughtful people find

[297]

this perspective too great a strain on their credulity. Their experience of the death-of-God rests upon their loss of faith in this God of history.

Faith in the God of history is also rendered improbable by his promise of future redemption. The God of history is a redeemer God. His promise is that the sorrows of the present will be justified ultimately by the establishment of the "kingdom of heaven." This belief entails the conviction that history has a meaning, a purpose, a goal. This conviction has been so pervasive in the Judaeo-Christian west that hope for the coming of God's "kingdom" is no longer dependent upon the existence of God. The Judaeo-Christian vision contrasts with the religious sensibility of the orient. In oriental religion men hope that the wheel of wordly pain and suffering will ultimately be brought to a stop.

The oriental view is more consistent with the facts of human biology than is the western. The human organism is a system of contradictory needs. We are gregarious animals, yet our bodily cravings often compel us to respond to the call of instinct, even when this implies our social hurt. Though we cannot endure without the love and recognition of our fellowmen, even the most loving of human encounters is inextricably beset by ambivalence and conflict. Aggression is inate in every human being. We are not always capable of controlling our own destructiveness. Our animal inheritance compels us to choose between the equally undesirable alternatives of directing aggression outward toward others or inward toward the self. We are the prisoners of an inheritance we can never entirely master.

Every human action is an attempt to gratify some need. This is as true of such pervasive phenomena as breathing as it is of such spiritual activities as prayer. If all needs were perfectly satisfied, the bodily organism as we know it would hardly persevere. Redemption promises an end to the tragedies and the ironic vicissitudes of the human adventure. In reality, only death ends the limitations and the pain of the human condition. Redemption may ultimately involve the annihilation

of the self. It may thus bear a greater resemblance to the
Buddhist Nirvana than to the western conception of the triumph
of God's "Kingdom."

Faced with apparently insuperable difficulties involved in
believing in the God of history, traditional theologians have
sought to defend their belief as best they can. One of he most
influential attempts in the twentieth century was that of Karl
Barth's crisis theology. Barth sought to defend faith in the
God of history by separating this belief from any basis in
human reason. We would agree with Barth's conviction that the
God of history cannot be comprehended by human reason,
we would, however, question whether there can be any other
basis for believing in such a God.

One current attempt to maintain belief in the God of history is that offered by adherents of the theology of hope. They
maintain that God who must not be regarded as "he who is"
but as "the God who will be," the God who promises redemption
to mankind in the future. As we have noted, it is possible
that the "redemption" of mankind may be totally devoid of
empirical content, rather than some great culmination of the
historical process. Nor can the theology of hope entirely escape
the suspicion that faith has been focused on the future because
it is the only remaining domain available to contemporary man
for credulity, fantasy, and wish-fulfillment.

HOLY NOTHINGNESS AS THE GROUND OF ALL

We cannot construct a meaningful conception of God while
fleeing from an honest confrontation with the world as we know
it. I believe there is a conception of God which does not falsify
reality and which remains meaningful after the death of the
God of history. It is a very old understanding of God with deep
roots in both western and oriental mysticism. In this conception
God is spoken of as the "Holy Nothingness." God, thus designated,
is regarded as the ground and source of all existence. To speak
of God as the "Nothingness" is not to suggest that he is a void;

on the contrary, he is a *plenum* so rich that all that exists derives from his very essence. God as the "Nothing" is not absence of being, but a superfluity of being.

The use of the term *Nothingness* rests in part upon a very ancient observation that all definition of finite entities involves negation. The infinite God, the ground of all finite beings, cannot be defined; in no sense is he a thing or a being bearing any resemblance to the finite beings of the empirical world. The infinite God is not a thing; he is no-thing. At times the mystics spoke of God in similar terms as the *Urgrund,* the primordial ground, the dark unnameable abyss out of which the empirical world has come.

At first glance, these ideas may seem to be little more than word play. Nevertheless, men in all of the major religious traditions have expressed themselves in almost identical images when they attempt to communicate their conceptions of God. Notably, those who believe that God is the source or ground of being usually believe human personality to be coterminous with the life of the human body. Death may be entrance into eternal life, the perfect life of God; it may also end pain, craving, and suffering; but it involves the dissolution of individual identity. Thus, in speaking of God, we also formulate an explicit judgment concerning the nature and the limitations of the human predicament.

Perhaps the best available metaphor for the conception of God as the Holy Nothingness is that God is the ocean and we the waves. Each wave has its moment when it is discernible and distinguishable as a somewhat separate entity. Nevertheless, no wave is entirely distinct from the ocean, which is its substantial ground. Furthermore, because the waves are surface manifestations of the ocean, our knowledge of the ocean is largely dependent on the way it manifests itself in the waves.

The waves are caught in contradictory tendencies. They are the resultants of forces which allow them their moment of identifiable existence. At the same time, they are wholly within the grasp of greater tendencies which would merge them into the oceanic ground from which they have momentarily distinguished themselves without ever really becoming separate from it. Similarly, all living beings seek to maintain their individual identities, yet there is absolutely nothing in them which does not derive from their originating ground. This is especially evident in the most intimate of all human activities, sexual love. Nothing could be more private or personally involving. Nevertheless, at no time is the individual more in the grip of universal forces than in the act of love. Only to the extent that the individual is capable of letting these overwhelming forces flow through him of their own accord will the act of love be complete and without flaw. Only he who has the capacity to lose himself totally in love can be fulfilled.

The same truth is evident in our bodies and in our life cycle. Because our bodies are the most deeply personal aspects of our beings, identity begins as body-identity and the earliest development of the ego is as body-ego. Basically, our fundamental projects are related to the care and nurture of our bodies. Yet nothing is more universal and impersonal than the shape, demands, and sexual character of our bodies. We did not choose to be born; we did not choose whether to be male or female; finally, we did not choose the timetable of life from our earliest cellular existence through physical maturity and finally death. We simply repeat in our own unique way a destiny common to billions of other human beings. We all possess a certain measure of freedom to work out our adaptation to the world. Nevertheless, both the individual and the race are the resultant of vast, non-personal forces which transcend yet permeate them in every activity and project they pursue.

In the Middle Ages, there was an important controversy in the fields of logic and metaphysics concerning the nature of universals. One group of thinkers regarded the universal as the name given to a class of objects which resembled each other. Another group insisted that the universal has a reality of its own which is manifest in each of its individual exemplifications. The controversy was one of the most complicated and abiding in the history of philosophy. Since the time of Luther, the nominalist tendency to regard individuals as real and the universal as merely a name has largely predominated. The social and cultural effects of the triumph of nominalism are reflected in the growth of individualism and the stress on private rather than corporate experience. In the political order, nominalism was paralleled by the rise of the middle class and its preference for free, unregulated, individualistic competition and commerce.

The opposite, realist, doctrine insisted on the reality of universals. Though realism has largely gone out of fashion, its insight into the extent to which our personal and social lives are pervaded by universal, non-personal forces suggests that it contains important truths. In addition to the facts of biology, there has been a return to supra-personal corporate experience in the twentieth century. Within the privacy of the home even the family participates in the contemporary renewal of universal forms of corporate experience. Through the communications media, to an unprecedented degree, we share identical sensory experiences and even thought-contents. Marshall McLuhan has suggested that one effect of the communications revolution has been to bring about the return of tribalized man, whose experiences are more universal, corporate, involving, and sensuous than those of the inner-directed, isolated individualist described by David Reisman in *The Lonely Crowd*.[1] The ego of contemporary tribalized man, like that of archaic tribal man, tends to share a common content with that of his peers. In an age of electric technology, we are no longer isolated individualists, but exemplifications of an all-embracing totality which ultimately is God.

HEGEL AND THE WORLD AS THE EXPRESSION OF DIVINE UNITY

Though one cannot press the metaphor of the ocean and waves too far, it is both very useful and very old. The ancient Summerians saw all things, even the gods, as arising out of the divine oceanic substratum of all reality which they called "Nammu." Nammu was the archaic sea-goddess in Summerian mythology. She was not goddess of the sea, but the goddess who was the sea. Hegel used a similar metaphor at the conclusion of *The Phenomenology of the Spirit* when, after describing the full scope of human activity and human passion as it developed in the course of history, he concluded that all of the apparent diversity of the human drama was the expression of one, underlying, ever-changing and yet ever-constant, divine spirit. At the end of the *Phenomenology* he adapted a line of the poet Schiller to summarize this paradox of divine unity and diversity:

"The chalice of this realm of spirits
Foams forth to God his own infinitude."[2]

When, in admittedly inadequate language, I suggest that God is the Holy Nothingness, what I attempt to assert is that the divine ground of being is beyond all finite categories. It may be the source and precondition of the empirical world, but it is not that world. There is an inescapable tension between God's essential unity and his unfolding process of self-manifestation in the multiplicity of the empirical world. Hegel caught something of the tension between, on the one hand, God as ground and abyss and, on the other hand, the natural and historical world as epiphenomenal manifestation of the divine reality. This is reflected in the Preface to the *Phenomenology:*

> *Per se* the divine life is no doubt undisturbed identity and oneness with itself, which finds no serious obstacle in otherness and estrangement. But this *per se* is abstract generality. . . . The truth is whole. The whole, however, is merely the essential nature reaching its completeness through the process of its own development. . . .[3]
>
> Spirit is alone reality. It is the inner being of the world, that which essentially is, and is *per se;* it assumes objective, determinate form and enters into relations with itself—it is externality (otherness) and exists for self; yet, in this determinateness, and in its otherness, it is still one with

itself—it is self-contained and self-complete, in itself and for itself at once. . . .[4]

Hegel used a very complicated philosophical language to express himself, yet the idea of the fundamental identity of God as unchanging unity and of the world as his way of expressing himself in diversity is clear. I prefer the metaphor of the ocean and the waves to Hegel's more abstract terminology, but the fundamental conception underlying both images is much the same.

Hegel calls the divine ground *Geist* or Spirit; Paul Tillich preferred to use the term "ground of being;" I have suggested Holy Nothingness. All three designations reflect a preference for metaphors rooted in maternity rather than paternity. Words like "ground," "source," and "abyss" have maternal overtones. This is also true of the image of God as the oceanic substratum. In the symbolism of both religion and dreams, ocean often equals womb. In the development of the species, the womb is a substitute ocean providing terrestial animals with a replica of their original habitat with which they can recapitulate the development of the race in the course of their own ontogenesis.

Terms like "ground" and "source" stand in contrast to the terms used for the biblical God of history. The biblical God is a father-God; he is a creator, a judge, a maker. When he creates, he does so with substances external to his own nature. The father-God is a transcendent God; he remains essentially outside of and judges the creative process he has initiated. God as ground and source creates as does a mother, out of her own substance. God as ground of being participates in all the joys and sorrows of the creative drama which is the deepest expression of the divine life. God's life and that of the cosmos are ultimately reflections of a single unfolding reality.

Although I have cited Hegel and Tillich, I could have quoted a long line of eastern and western mystics who have had similar conceptions of God. J. N. Findlay, one of the best of the contemporary commentators on Hegel, has observed that Hegel's conception of God as the unitary spirit underlying the multiplicity of nature and history "has an obvious parentage in the glorious mysticism of mediaeval and renaissance Germany."[5] He finds echoes of Hegel in Meister Eckhart, Angelus Silesius, and Jakob Boheme. Findlay comments:

> In all these systems there is that approximation of the finite to the infinite Spirit. . . . There is also that profound, theologically heretical stress on the necessity to the infinite Spirit of a world of Nature and created Spirit, which by enabling him to exercise his creative energies and redemptive love, also enable him to know and be himself. Hegel quotes with approval the following statement of Meister Eckhart: "The eye with which God sees me, is the eye with which I see Him, my eye and his eye are one. In the meting out of justice I am weighed in God and He in me. If God were not, I should not be, and if I were not, He too would not be." . . .[6]

This conception of God also implies a judgment on the overly-individualistic experience of the self which has predominated in the western world. The tight, repressed, western individualist can never really let down his guard, even before those he loves most passionately. He can never trust himself to let himself go. Elsewhere, I have dwelt at greater length on our profound need for a less rigid, less individualistic self which draws its deepest strength from its capacity to lose itself.

In spite of the resemblance between the term Nothingness as a designation of the divine substratum and Hegel's use of the term Spirit to point to the same reality, there is an absolutely crucial difference between them. Hegel saw the self-unfolding of Spirit as a process leading to a final goal. He suggested as goal that Spirit would finally come to know itself as Spirit. For Hegel the ultimate goal of all existence would be the fully realized self-knowledge of God. God will come to know himself fully as God only when he finally recognizes every event in natural evolution and human history as the very road he has had to travel both to become and know himself. Everything that has happened would then be seen as a moment in God's life.

Had God not gone through the infinite pain of human history his self-knowledge would have been empty, a void. In order to be God, he had to suffer the tortuous path which we call history. Without it, God would not have had a self, so to speak, to know. The image is not unlike that of human self-knowledge. The new born infant has no possibility of self-knowledge or self-recognition. Such insight is only possible when the self has a history of events, conflicts, mistakes, and victories. True self-knowledge involves recognition and acceptance of the fact that the unique path the individual has walked was indispensible to the person he or she has become. For Hegel the goal of the historical drama will come when God recognizes that all the diversity of existence is but his own unique life-story.[7]

BIBLICAL AND COSMOLOGICAL IMAGES OF GOD

There is a strong element of biblical teleology in Hegel, which is shared by many contemporary thinkers. Pierre Teilhard de Chardin, for example, saw the totality of the cosmic process as an unfolding of the divine reality. He saw this process as having a goal which he called the Omega-point. Taking the incarnation of God and man in the Christ as his starting point, Teilhard looked forward to the moment when the cosmic Christ would be "All-in-everything." Then all of matter and spirit would express fully and completely the perfect unity already made manifest according to the Christian tradition in the incarnate Christ.[8]

Biblical religion expresses itself in redemptive hope. To the extent that Hegel, Teilhard, and Karl Marx saw history as a process with a goal, they were influenced by the aspirations of biblical man. Nevertheless, this note of cosmic optimism is hardly warranted by anything evident in the cosmic process or to which that process points. On the contrary, there may very well be reason for suggesting that the cosmic process has neither goal nor meaning. If creation can best be understood as the self-unfolding of God's life, the process itself may ultimately be a vast cosmic detour originating in God's Nothingness and terminating in God's Nothingness. There seems to be little convincing evidence of a goal or of the notion that man has any special cosmic significance beyond the significance he creates for himself.

Sigmund Freud rejected faith in any special goal or meaning to human existence. He saw organic existence as primordially inclined to seek a return to the inanimate condition out of which it had arisen. According to Freud, both the animate and the inanimate realms are ultimately linked by the common tendency of all things in the universe to return to the simplest equilibrium of the total cosmic system within itself. This meant that the universe would ultimately "run down." Freud observed that the goal of all life is death. This doctrine of Freud in *Beyond the Pleasure Principle*[9] is unrelieved by even a shred of biblical hope. Nevertheless, an Norman O. Brown and others have noted, the Freudian doctrine has deep affinities with the great mystical system in which the goal of all existence is to return to the divine ground out of which it has arisen.[10]

I have many times repeated my conviction that omnipotent Nothingness is Lord of all creation.[11] This affirmation of mystical faith seems to offer a most economical way of unifying mystical, dialectical, psychoanalytic, and archaic insights concerning God as the ground, content, and final destiny of all things. This affirmation acknowledges the ultimacy of God, but in a way that also suggests that human existence cannot be based on any hope which transcends the terms and limitations of the body and its timetable. He who speaks of God as the "Holy Nothingness" abandons all ultimate hope. If we have any hope at all, according to this vision, it is that we shall have little cause to regret the life we have lived and are living.

A somewhat similar vision of the human condition can be expressed in cosmological images. For those who maintain that the universe originated with a cosmic "bang," there are two general hypotheses as to its ultimate destiny. Some suggest that all of the exploding matter of the cosmos has been rushing away from itself and will continue to do so forever. Others reason that, if space is curved, the matter of the cosmos will eventually implode and finally return to its cosmic starting point. I am by no means competent to judge the evidence, but the second hypothesis seems more consistent with an appropriate theological vision after the death of God. It is certainly possible that this vast cosmic implosion might be followed by another cosmic explosion and that the universe might be a vast exploding-imploding domain taking about eighty-four billion years to complete its circle. This vision would resemble that of the archaic pagans who believed that time is more of a circle, ultimately returning to its starting point, than a straight line proceeding to a future fulfillment.

LIFE vs REDEMPTION

In a recent issue of *The Christian Century,* Dr. Ronald Goetz has commented on the conception of God I have suggested here. He maintained that to regard God as the Holy Nothingness is to regard him as death. He based this observation on my suggestion that ultimately we have nothing to hope for but a return to the Nothingness of God.[12] Admittedly, a radical rejection of ultimate hope presents many difficulties to men and women brought up in a culture rooted in biblical faith. Nevertheless, the rejection of ultimate hope, difficult though it is, may be part of the psychic surgery we must inflict upon ourselves if we are to enjoy the potentialities of this life to their fullest. Illusion is comforting only on a very superficial level. On a deeper level, we really know in a total, certain, and non-reasoning way that death entails the final disappearance of the self, the return to Nothingness. Every attempt to persuade ourselves that this is not so flies in the face of deep and certain knowledge that never leaves us. The price of redemptive hope is an undue and painful inner conflict which retards achieving what is possible in life.

God is not death; he is the source of both life and death. Death is the final price we pay for life and love, but death is not all there is. Life has its supreme moments of joy and fulfillment. Nevertheless, we must accept life's joys without illusion. Were there no death of the individual, there would be no biological necessity of love in the order of things. Every act of love truly consummated is in some sense a joyful dying to the self. Simply to see God as love is to be unduly one-sided, for love and death are inseparable. Above all, we must not refuse to pay the full price of admission to authentic human existence. To acknowledge the finality of death requires a certain clarity and courage. God creates out of his own substance; he nurtures, but he also annihilates. The creative process is a totality. It is impossible to affirm the loving and the creative aspects of God's activity without also affirming that creation and destruction are part of an indivisible process. Each wave in the ocean of God's Nothingness has its moment, but it must inevitably give way to other waves. We are not, like Job, destined to receive back everything twofold.

William Hamilton, the distinguished Protestant theologian, has taught me many things. Perhaps I am most indebted to him for the insight that the world of the death of God need not be a gloomily morbid domain. One need not live forever in order that life be worth living. Creation, however impermanent and ultimately imperilled it be, is real and full of promise. Those who insist on the inseparability of the creative and the destructive in God's activity thereby affirm their readiness to pay in full measure with their own disappearance for the gift of life.

If redemption is a pathetic dream, how shall we understand mankind's hope for a messianic redeemer? I have been compelled to suggest that if there is a Messiah, he can only be the Angel of Death. Understandably, this somewhat paradoxical idea has been the subject of some confusion. To refer to the Angel of Death as the Messiah is another way of saying what we have attempted to say here: that the dilemmas and ironies of personal existence can only be terminated completely by death, that life necessarily involves the limitations and the ambiguities of unredeemed existence. Death is the price we pay for life, love, and joy; so to is our unredeemed existence.

This does not mean that we should seek speedily to be redeemed. On the contrary, we must forsake the quest for redemption and accept life with its limitations and ironies. It is better that the Messiah tarry, for His kingdom is not of this world. All we have is this world. Let us celebrate its joys and endure its wounds in undeceived lucidity. There is a certain insatiability in those who seek more than the life of the body. Only those who have not fully lived seek for more than life.

◇

1. David Reisman, **The Lonely Crowd** (New Haven, Conn.: Yale Univ. Press, 1950). For an easy introduction to McLuhan's seminal conceptions, see his **The Medium is the Message** (New York: Bantam Books, 1967).

2. G. W. F. Hegel, **The Phenomenology of Mind**, trans. J. B. Baillie (London: George Allen and Unwin, Ltd., 1949), p. 808.

3. **Ibid.**, p. 81.

4. **Ibid.**, p. 86.

5. J. N. Findlay, **Hegel: A Reexamination** (London: George Allen and Unwin, Ltd., 1958), pp. 48 ff.

6. **Ibid.**

7. **Ibid.**, pp. 34-47

8. Pierre Teilhard de Chardin, **The Divine Milieu** (New York: Harper and Row, 1965). For a sympathetic presentation of Teilhard's religious philosophy, see Henri de Lubac, **Teilhard de Chardin: The Man and His Meaning**, trans. René Hague (New York: Mentor-Omega Books, 1967).

9. Sigmund Freud, **Beyond the Pleasure Principle**, trans. J. Strachey (London: Hogarth Press, 1950).

10. Norman O. Brown, **Life Against Death** (New York: Vintage Books, 1959).

11. Richard L. Rubenstein, **After Auschwitz** (Indianapolis: Bobbs-Merrill, 1966).

12. Ronald Goetz, "God: Love or Death?," **The Christian Century** LXXXIV (1967), pp. 1487-90.

The Religious Meaning of Secularity[*]

◊

Louis Dupré

DURING THE LAST five centuries Western man has brought
ever more spheres of existence under his control. Simultaneous
with this conquest he has come to consider himslf as the creator
of his own values. His awareness of creative autonomy has
extended from the artistic and the technological, to the scientific,
and presently even to the moral sphere.

HUMAN AUTONOMY AND THE DISAPPEARANCE
OF THE SACRED

Modern man knows that truth consists not in conforming
the mind to a fully given and ontologically true object, but in
bringing the objective world into conformity with the mind.
The objective world is given only to the extent that man brings
it actively to givenness. The scientist no longer is puzzled by
the parallelism between the laws of nature and those of the
mind, because he knows that laws are laws only for the mind.
Economic goods are no longer considered a gift of divine largesse,
but man's own responses to self-created needs. What artists
dimly felt in the past, they now bluntly assert: the work of art
is not an imitation of nature and subject to an extrinsic code;

[311]

it creates its own norms and reality. What is more, in his moral behavior, man is assuming full responsibility. Thus, as a free being, he has no use for a divinely imposed, unchangeable code of conduct. Finally, he is now discovering that even religion is a human activity, and that its symbols are expressions of the human mind structured according to immanent schemas.

It is this unprecedented awareness of his creative power, which is causing today's religious crisis. In the past, religion was the integrating factor of human existence and related all values to a transcendent principle. In a universe which dominated man more than he dominated it, the general feeling of dependence made such a reference indispensable. However, once man discovered that all power to control the world is within himself, the need to relate each value to a transcendent principle ceased to exist. This emancipation of human values from their religious basis is the essence of secularization. Bonhoeffer summed it up in the statement that everything gets along without God just as before and what we call God is being edged out of life altogether.[1]

For most contemporaries, including most believers, no particular sphere of existence can still be called sacred. They no longer directly experience the holy either in the world or in the mind. The outer world has become totally humanized, while the inner mind knows no experiences which could unambiguously be called religious.

It was different in primitive cultures where the border line between the sacred and the profane was rather vague and where man moved freely from the non-sacred to a sacred that he was able to experience spontaneously and without effort. Modern man on the contrary, no longer as a rule finds his sacred symbols in the world; for him sacred space and sacred time have vanished. A Belgian psychologist, Antoine Vergote, concludes:

> The world has become a-religious, or a-theistic in the privative sense of the term. It is no longer haunted by God's omnipresence: it has found a self-consistency in accepting its relativity and its reality is the proper domain of man.

Taking the expression in its etymological sense, we may say that the world has become "humanized"; it is no longer directly perceived in a perspective of eternity.[2]

We might add that the sacred is removed not only from man's perception of the outside world, but from his entire field of direct experience. He no longer "undergoes" the sacred, and if he does so at a rare occasion he feels uneasy and distrustful.

Nevertheless, the transcendent remains a matter of constant concern in human existence. It may not be a concern about the God of traditional religion, and it is no longer rooted in a simple, unambiguous experience. But the concern is as real as ever, and it is a mistake to ignore it. However, modern man's experience of the sacred is seldom direct. If he happens to be religious, the experience which he interprets as sacred presents itself in a questioning rather than in an assertive way and seems to invite free decision rather than passive submission. Instead of passively experiencing the sacred as did his forebears, modern man freely interprets some ambivalent experiences in a religious sense. One such experience is the mystery of the universe in its totality, (which partly accounts for the great success of Teilhard de Chardin's work among religious minded people). Another is the recognition of human existence as contingent. Neither of these experiences are religious in the strict sense of that word. They allow for a number of interpretations, including atheistic ones, but we observe that wherever religion is present in modern man it seems to be rooted as in its mother-soil in one or both of these experiences.

SECULARITY AS ANTI-REDUCTIONISM

Can we attribute any religious meaning to the absence of all direct experience of religion in the present world? It is the thesis of this study that secularity, insofar as it actively opposes any direct experience of the transcendent, protects religion against its worst enemies: subjectivism and objectivism. Against the subjectivist interpretation which reduces religion to a mere experience, secular man perhaps exaggeratedly denies that religion is an experience at all. Against objectivism which reduces religion to what can be experienced as object, secularism excludes the sacred entirely from the world of objects. Secularity, therefore, can be more than a humanistic assertion of man's autonomous creativity; it can be an assertion of God's transcendence against all subjective and objective reductionism.

"Subjectivist reductionism"[3] today has found a foundation in psychology. Assuming that psychology can fully account for the entire realm of consciousness, many reduce religion to what can be experienced in the religious act. A second reduction usually follows this first one, if religion in no way transcends experience, then it is not what it claims to be and must be accounted for by the non-religious. Examples of such a reduction of the religious to a deeper, non-religious level abound. Thus, to interpret Luther's lifework exclusively as the expression of a compulsive personality structure, or St. Teresa's writings as the result of hysterical tendencies, is pure psychologism.[4]

Equally destructive, although perhaps more obvious, is the approach which, in the name of the positive sciences, insists on subjecting the intended "object" of the religious act to the laws of scientific objectivity. Although it is generally agreed that such an approach would be absurd in the field of aesthetics, and in spite of the obvious similarity, even religious people continue to submit the transcendent term of the religious act to the restrictions of the objectivation process. Positivism and naturalism restrict truth to objectivity and assume that only those facts that are verifiable by an objective process can be true.

Religion obviously has no facts which can be understood in a purely objective way. A religious fact is an interpreted one, that is, a fact which exists only within a certain perspective. Whatever factuality there is outside this perspective cannot be called religious; pure objectivity simply does not exist in religion. The religious consciousness entirely assumes the factual matter into its own intentionality. Purely objective "facts" never justify the transition to a transcendent reality, for facts are

always immanent in this world. Religion is never purely objective and its "object" is not an object in the ordinary sense.
The object of religion, although it refuses to be reduced to the
religious experience, cannot be detached from the religious
experience itself.

The same problem exists on the level of expression. As long
as truth is restricted to object language, religious language
can make no truth claims. All consistent neo-positivists accept
this conclusion and take religious statements to express subjective beliefs or attitudes, but not truths. These negative conclusions imply that one should never attempt to "objectify"
the sacred since such an approach subjects it to conditions
which it is unable to fulfill. Unfortunately, this is precisely
what is done in most discourse about God. The traditional
theist apparently shares the position of the positivist inasmuch
as he is unable to conceive any form of discourse that is not
about objects. The term of the religious act can never be objectified in the full sense of being opposed to the religious subject. What differentiates religious language from ordinary language is that its object is as closely connected with the subjective
experience as are aesthetic and ethical objects while, at the
same time, being intended as totally transcending this experience. Though the religious man may seem to speak the
language of the scientist or the philosopher, he is in fact expressing something that cannot be understood in the ordinary,
objective usage of this language.

Whatever else secularization may have done to religion, it
has obliged it to face the fact that God is not to be found in
the world of objects and that we cannot even speak of him in
objective language. A Dutch theologian has pointed this out
very clearly:

There is a positive content in the expression "God is
dead." It implies a justified rebellion against the so-called
objectivization of God within the Church's Christianity. . . .
God and faith belong together. God has been detached from

faith, however, and subsequently objectified and hung some-where "up there."[5]

SECULAR THEOLOGY IS NEGATIVE THEOLOGY

Secular theology has understood the religious importance of the negation of the secular movement. In giving this nega-tivity a religious meaning it places itself in the profoundly religious tradition known as negative theology. All religion is negative in the sense that it must constantly negate its own assertions in order to maintain the transcendent truly tran-scendent. However, without a new affirmation of the transcen-dent this negation becomes destructive of religion itself. Secular theology directs this negation against religion itself, rather than against its "worldly" elements. Instead of purifying the religious form, it claims that the religious content is now known to be purely immanent and that its "transcendent" form is thereby reduced to an empty shell.

There have been radically secular reinterpretations of re-ligion before, most notably that by Feuerbach, but they had never been presented in the name of religion. Secular theology, however, though opposed to organized religion, still wants to retain its religious roots. Thus, according to a position which is strangely remindful of the later writings of Soren Kierkegaard, the most consistent way of being a Christian is to work toward the abolition of the Christian religion. In the future, Christi-anity must be a particular attitude toward the universe, rather than an organized religion. Religion represents an earlier stage of development in which, instead of controlling his own universe, man still takes his orders from above. The new man will find the divine within this world, not above it.[6] If the entire meaning of secularity is expressed in this negative, secular theology, then it tolls the death bell for religion in the name of Christi-anity.

However, secular theology itself can remain religious only so long as its negation is counteracted by a new affirmation of the transcendent. For if the relation to the transcendent is abandoned, the secular loses its religious depth and becomes indistinguishable from a shallow, atheistic humanism. Far from being the most consistent form of Christianity, such a view omits its most essential element, namely, that in Christ man meets the transcendent in a unique way. To detach Christianity from this religious meaning is to make it altogether meaningless. If Christ does not speak with divine authority, his word is not essentially different from that of any other moralist; it could be replaced advantageously by that of a philosopher who uses direct, "secular" language.

Secular theologians feud to have a singularly undialectical vision of religion. They mostly ignore that by its very nature the religious negation is dialectical and, hence, calls for a new affirmation of the transcendent. The secular loses its religious meaning altogether if it is viewed as final. One simply creates a religious vacuum by eliminating God in favor of the immanent, and it is too simplistic to expect that this vacuum will be filled by a stronger affirmation of secular values. The insufficiency of the secular which leads man to religious values is not quantitative but qualitative.[7] Our ancestors may have been naive in substituting God for medicine and technical training; but it is much more naive to substitute medicine and technical training for God.

To consider the sacred a poor substitute for secular values in more primitive times is to misunderstand its nature altogether. Some secular theologians underestimate the ambiguous but very real experience of contingency. As man has become more aware of his autonomy he also feels more strongly the contingency of his human condition. This feeling does not vanish in the face of cultural and moral progress. On the contrary, movements of cultural protest are increasingly being directed against the complacent self-sufficiency of modern life which some secular theologians preach as an ideal of the future. Modern man has not eliminated the transcendent dimension from his existence, but he has become aware of the relativity of the forms in which this dimension is expressed.

Though many still attribute the present religious crisis to the fact that outdated symbols have lost their meaning, the difficulty goes much deeper. It results from the new insight that all forms of knowledge and of action, including those dealing with man's relation to the transcendent, are human and therefore relative. To see the relativity of what one had believed to be absolute is a painful but essential part of growing up. In religion it is a necessary moment of the dialectic of faith. If, as Kierkegaard claims, the religious attitude consists in taking the absolute absolutely and the relative relatively, then secularity marks a decisive step toward the religion of the mature man.

RELIGION AFTER SECULARIZATION

In the meantime we are left with the difficult task of rethinking the basic religious categories in the light of this new insight. How can man retain his belief in the absolute nature of revealed religion after having discovered that he himself, though relative and continually developing, is the principle of all human values? More specifically: What becomes of religious truth when man views himself as the principle of truth, or of rite and cult when the human mind itself is found to be the principle of all symbols and myths? What is the future of religious law when man has learned that freedom is its own law?

The first of these questions determines the Christian's future attitude toward revelation and its authoritative interpretation in the Church. Because truth expresses man's view of his relation to the universe, it is man-made and changes as this relation itself develops. If revealed truth is to be truth at all, it must possess the same qualities: it must be a truly human creation rather than a meteoric bloc hurled at man from another world, and it must be sufficiently dynamic to assimilate the changes in man's relation to the universe.

This can be compatible with the notion of a divine and

lasting authority only if this authority respects man's creative role in both the conception and expression of revealed truth. That is, divine authority must not freeze man's relation to his universe—and this includes the transcendent—into an unchangeable permanence. Even the most authoritative expression of religion, the words of the God-man must not be detached from the human psychology of him who spoke them. They must not be stifled by religious attitudes that allow no further development. Did Christ himself not say that those who have faith in him would do greater things than he had done (Jn 14, 12). The authority of the Bible and of its authentic interpretation are not connected with a rigid immobility of meanings and expressions, incompatible with the dynamic nature of truth. Their authority lies in adequately expressing principles or facts indispensable for establishing authentic and dynamic relation with God. Such an authority excludes neither the cultural limitations of its carrier nor the incompleteness inherent in any description of a developing relationship.

The practical problem here is that of distinguishing the accidental expression from the essential, permanent intentionality. The notion of demythologizing hardly seems to do justice to the complexity of this problem, for the symbolic or "mythical" form is so intimately connected with content that it cannot be eliminated without affecting the content itself. This is precisely what the religious man has in mind when he claims that not only the content but the expression of the Scripture is revealed. Perhaps the solution lies in the peculiar nature of religious truth. The transcendent nature of its content differentiates religious expression from ordinary language. Religious man is constantly aware that he can never fully express what he wants to communicate. Religious language is always strained or paradoxical, because of the basic shortcoming of its symbols in expressing a transcendent reality. Even when religious discourse seems to recur to ordinary language, the relation between form and content remains loose. Thus religious language attains a unique flexibility which enables it to develop its meanings while retaining its original symbols. By their ability to develop within a tradition, religious symbols can grow beyond their original meanings without cutting their ties with the life-giving source of revelation.

It is obvious, however, that these meanings must develop within limits set by revelation, lest the original symbols become an empty facade behind which any meaning may develop. Augustine's symbolic interpretations of the numbers occurring in certain passages of the Gospel can claim no more than an arbitrary connection with the original message. Modern man prefers entirely new symbols to such an artificial exegesis of the letter of the revelation. On the other hand, the development toward new meaning is much more than a transition from the implicit to the explicit, as the old theory on the evolution of dogma held. The novelty is genuine. To retain religious authority all innovation must remain in full continuity with the tradition. All truth in revealed religion must be traditional.

The same tension between autonomy and theonomy is being felt in cult and sacrament. Here, too, man has become aware that the sacred assumes its symbolic expression from man's attitude toward the universe. The rites of baptism and the sacred meal give an ultimate meaning to gestures that have been repeated since the beginning of history, but, in order to do so, these ritual actions must be separated from ordinary life. This is particularly the case when the sacred ritual is revealed. The danger of ritual separation is that the gestures lose their original life content and gradually assume a magic objectivity that severs them entirely from ordinary existence. Once the subject becomes fully aware of his own hierogenic function, he feels a strong need to bring the cult back to every day life in which it originated and to restore its earthly meanings.

Here, the balance between tradition and creativity is even more difficult to find than it was in the reinterpretation of the Revelation. It is a common mistake today to think that only the basic gesture must be preserved. But the revelation has already taken this gesture out of everyday life and drawn it into a sacred drama from which it cannot be detached. Those who advocate an entirely new liturgy have not understood the ultimate connection between sacred word and sacred action. Renewal is necessary in this age of creative awareness. However, unless the participants are able to experience (which is considerably more than just to know theoretically) the continuity between what they are doing and what was done in the mythical past of revelation, the revealed meaning of the sacred drama is lost.

Finally, the new awareness of *moral* autonomy creates a problem for an outlook which views morality as obedience to God-given law. Kant already knew how difficult it is to strike a balance between the consciousnss of autonomous freedom and a theory of divine law. Today the opposite to a divine law morality becomes manifest within Christianity in the form of situation ethics.

Is the notion of divine law really necessary to preserve the religious nature of morality? If divine law means the obligatory and divinely sanctioned quality of moral norms, the answer is yes. If it means an immutable moral code, descended from heaven, the answer is no. To be religious the moral law does not have to consist of a set of unchangeable precepts invented by God and delivered ready-made to man. It is the law of man, gradually invented by man and developing with his own dynamic nature. Its religious character lies not in the denial of autonomy but in the acceptance of the createdness of this free, autonomous nature. This createdness implies that the norms by which this nature rules its own development, while remaining intrinsically human, are also sacred and divinely sanctioned.

◊

1. Dietrich Bonhoeffer, **Letters and Papers From Prison,** ed. Eberhard Bethge, trans. Reginald H. Fuller (London: SCM Press, 1967), p. 194.

2. Antoine Vergote, **Psychologie Religieuse** (Brussels: C. Dessart, 1956), pp. 85-86.

3. The expression is from Emil Fackenheim.

4. This, of course, by no means implies that every psychological study of the religious person or his experience is psychologistic. Freud, for example, probes beyond the mere experience when he says that religion for him is a relation of some sort. William James very clearly distinguishes psychologism from psychology in **The Varieties of Religious Experience** (New York: Collier, 1961). Nor does all subjective reductionism interpret religion as being rooted in the non-religious. Quite the opposite, anticipating the Death-of-God theologians, Feuerbach saw atheism as the most consistent religious attitude.

5. Robert Adolfs, "Is God Dead," in **The Meaning of the Death of God,** ed. B. Murchland (New York: Random House, 1967), p. 88.

6. Thomas Altizer writes in **The Gospel of Christian Atheism** (Philadelphia: Westminster, 1966), p. 108: "From this perspective it would even be possible to understand Christendom's religious reversal of the movement of the Spirit into flesh as a necessary consequence of the Incarnation, preparing the way for a more comprehensive historical realization of the death of God by its progressive banishment of the dead body of God to an ever more transcendent and inacessible realm. . . . For so long as consciousness remains bound to religion, it must exist in an alienated form, closer to the inner reality of Spirit by its very belief in an alien Other. This traditional form of faith is the product of a divided consciousness: it can only know redemption as a reconciliation with an Other lying beyond itself, and must experience the actuality of the present as a world merely awaiting its transfiguration. Yet, Christianity has now at least implicitly evolved to an absolute form wherein it can realize the final epiphany of Spirit as immediately present and actualized for us."

7. As Roger Hazelton writes: "One can scarcely draw meaningful contrast between God and the world if the world is to be thought of as catching up wholly within itself the values formerly ascribed to God. . . . The alternatives 'God' and 'world' are simply unreal as possibilities for choice or as options for belief. A refusal to turn to God for the sort of help which the world can give, moreover, is not confined to those who are persuaded that God is not available or approachable. Such refusal is fully consonant with the liveliest faith in the divine presence and power." Roger Hazelton, "The Future of God," in **The Meaning of the Death of God,** ed. B. Murchland (New York: Random House, 1967), pp. 132-133.

INDEX OF NAMES